Richard Wolfe

KIWI

A Curious Case of National Identity

Oratia

COVER IMAGES
TOP LEFT: New Zealand Insurance Company window decal.
TOP RIGHT: Kiwi image used by NZ Department of Health, 1940s.
BOTTOM RIGHT: The kiwi is at the centre of the roundel on New Zealand Defence Force uniforms.

Unless otherwise credited, all images property of the author. Thanks to Joseph Stanton for additional photography.

Published by Oratia Books, Oratia Media Ltd, 783 West Coast Road, Oratia, Auckland 0604, New Zealand (www.oratia.co.nz).

Copyright © 2024 Richard Wolfe
Copyright © 2024 Oratia Books (published work)
The copyright holders assert their moral rights in the work.

This book is copyright. Except for the purposes of fair reviewing, no part of this publication may be reproduced or transmitted in any form or by any means, whether electronic, digital or mechanical, including photocopying, recording, any digital or computerised format, or any information storage and retrieval system, including by any means via the Internet, without permission in writing from the publisher. Infringers of copyright render themselves liable to prosecution.

ISBN 978-1-99-004264-5

Editor: Carolyn Lagahetau
Designer: Sarah Elworthy

The publisher acknowledges the generous support of Creative New Zealand for this publication.

First published 2024

Printed in China

Contents

	Introduction	5
1	A land of birds: From Gondwana to Zealandia	10
2	The hidden bird of Tāne	14
3	'A perfectly new genus': Discovered by science	26
4	Settlement from Europe: The kiwi under threat	44
5	Early symbols of identity: Kiwi in Fernland	54
6	'Rara Avis': A bird of the people	66
7	Kiwi at the Front: The patriotic *Apteryx*	80
8	Consolidation: The rise of kiwi symbolism in the 1920s and 1930s	92
9	Back to the Front: The kiwi during the Second World War	118
10	Aftermath: The post-Second World War kiwi	134
11	Mid-century: The 1950s kiwi	144
12	Cultural matters: Kiwi to the fore	160
13	The high-flying kiwi(fruit)	178
14	In survival mode: Conserving the kiwi	186
	Notes	196
	Bibliography	204
	Index	206

Introduction

In the early 1900s a small, flightless nocturnal bird began to assume symbolic status in New Zealand. Thanks, in large part, to an Australian brand of boot polish, it became associated with this country's soldiers stationed in Europe during the First World War. The connection with the bird caught on and was carried back to the Antipodes, and before long New Zealanders at large were being identified and referred to as 'Kiwis'. The fact that the actual kiwi was the most unusual and, arguably, most original of birds — in fact, a bird like none other — probably encouraged rather than hindered this connection.

But while it was closely associated with the ordinary New Zealander, the kiwi did not acquire any official status. The symbols selected for the nation's coat of arms and national flag were the silver fern and Southern Cross. By way of compensation, the kiwi gained increasing popularity as a representation of the people, as demonstrated by the frequency of its use as a commercial trademark. Among its many duties, and despite it being an unlikely sporting symbol, the bird began backing New Zealand at international events. Although generally a shy and withdrawn bird, it could be extremely aggressive when necessary, which was a very handy

asset on the sports field. By the 1980s this approach was being encouraged from the sidelines with the cry: 'Give 'em a taste of kiwi!'

But even as the kiwi was gaining traction as a popular symbol, there was another development with the potential to cause confusion. Around 1920 a small, brown and hairy fruit was introduced to New Zealand from China, and once successfully transplanted and developed here it proved to have potential as a valuable export. To increase its chance of success overseas it underwent an image makeover and a name change from Chinese gooseberry to kiwifruit. As such it was seen as yet another example of a national characteristic already associated with its avian namesake: kiwi ingenuity.

The rebranded fruit would become known internationally as a 'kiwi'. If New Zealanders had a clear sense of who they were, it would not now be so apparent to persons from abroad. There was confusion — and perhaps bemusement — at the idea of people sharing their name with a small, brown, hairy fruit.

The rise of the recognition and popularity of the kiwi — both the bird and the fruit — has not been without challenges. Ironically, the kiwifruit has had to compete in the world marketplace with fruit grown from cuttings that were developed in New Zealand and then exported overseas. But the original kiwi faces a much more serious test: that of its very survival. For millions of years, prior to the arrival of humans, it existed in a predator-free environment. In the last 800 or so years it has been hunted, and threatened by bush clearances and introduced animals. Despite conservation measures, there is always the possibility that it may follow its larger ratite cousin, the moa, down the road to extinction. There may be some humour

OPPOSITE, TOP: Originally known in New Zealand as the Chinese gooseberry, this small, brown hairy fruit is better known around the world as the kiwifruit.

182887661, Studiocasper

BOTTOM: A North Island brown kiwi *Apteryx mantelli* in its natural habitat.

1167545747, Lakeview Images

PAGE 4: In the 1970s, Air New Zealand passengers could stir their drinks with these complimentary plastic swizzle sticks.

to be found in the association between the New Zealander and a small, brown fuzzy-haired fruit, but there can be none in the potential demise of the bird that gave it — and us — its name. This country already has a grim record when it comes to the loss of its native species, and we must ensure that the kiwi does not join that list.

From the late 1800s, New Zealanders were referred to variously as Maorilanders, EnZedders, Fernlanders and Diggers, among others. This apparent confusion began to be sorted out, thanks to the Australian boot polish, and in time the kiwi outstripped all other claimants such as the tūī and fern, to be an unofficial national symbol. As such it has grown accustomed to being overlooked for more significant duties, such as the search in 1985 for a new symbol to promote this country overseas. The kiwi was passed over in favour of the miha: the young, curled fronds of rarauhe (bracken fern). This was described by its detractors as looking more like a snail. Anyway, the miha didn't catch on, dying a quick death — and the kiwi lives on.

The kiwi may have anticipated an official role at the nation's 1990 sesquicentennial, marking 150 years since the signing of the Treaty of Waitangi. Once again, the kiwi missed out, but in this case for the inspired choice of another bird, the kōtuku (white heron), which represented the fact that all New Zealanders have, like the migratory bird, come from elsewhere.

The kiwi has also insinuated itself into the New Zealand consciousness. During the early days of settlement from Europe, there was the suggestion of something inventive going on here. The distance from Europe and the lack of access to technology were said to have encouraged, out of necessity, a 'can do' approach. Such a quality was hardly new to these islands; the original settlers from east Polynesia were also confronted with an unfamiliar environment to which they needed to adapt, and in the process developed their unique and distinctive traditions of stone and wood carving and weaving, among others. By around the mid-twentieth century, this alleged ability of the New Zealander to be able to make or fix anything with available resources, which typically involved a length of No. 8 fencing wire, came to be known as 'kiwi ingenuity'.

The 1980s were a time of massive global changes, both economically and socially, and in New Zealand there was a tendency to look back on our recent past. Much had changed; the influx of multinational companies threatened local enterprises, while television and other media meant that this country was no longer isolated from the outside world. In this period of nostalgic reflection, this country's popular culture became recognised as 'kiwiana' and, before long, the term had entered the national vocabulary.

As is documented in this book, for as long as humans have settled in this country, the kiwi has been at risk. However, extinction is not necessarily a problem for national symbols, official or otherwise, as suggested by the British lion and Scottish unicorn. The kiwi might also take heart from the bald eagle, adopted as North America's national emblem in 1782 because of its power, strength, determination and resilience, and also as a representation of freedom. In 1967 the bald eagle was officially declared an endangered species in southern parts of the United States, but since then populations have recovered and in 2007 the bird was taken off the endangered list.

When New Zealand's earliest towns and cities were established, there was an understandable preponderance of King and Queen streets, and also a generous number named Princes, Princess, Victoria or Albert. Since then, native trees have also been a regular source of inspiration for town planners, in particular Tōtara, Kōwhai, Rātā and Rimu. Birds have proved popular, too; Tūī in particular, followed by Huia and Kiwi. To date, Auckland has a Kiwi Esplanade, a Kiwi Place, two Kiwi Roads and two Kiwi Streets. But, curiously, New Zealand does not yet appear to have a close named after the bird (as they do in Australia and England). Perhaps one day the authorities responsible for naming such things will decide there is something endearing about our having a Kiwi Close.

1
—
A land of birds: From Gondwana to Zealandia

In the beginning there was Pangaea, the original landmass on Earth. About 200 million years ago it began to break up, spawning two supercontinents: the northerly Laurasia and the southerly Gondwana. The latter, also called Gondwanaland and named after geological formations in central India, incorporated present-day South America, Africa, Arabia, Madagascar, India, Australia, Antarctica — and New Zealand.

Powered by continental drift, about 180 million years ago Gondwana began to split apart. Africa was first to leave, followed some 40 million years later by India. Then, 80 million years ago, the landmass that was to become New Zealand broke away, splitting from Australia and Antarctica as the Tasman Sea opened up. New Zealand was carried away on a mostly submerged landmass now recognised as the Earth's eighth continent, and known since the mid-1990s as Zealandia. The full separation between New Zealand and Australia took over 20 million years, with the Tasman Sea reaching its present width of 2000 km around 60 million years ago.

The name Gondwana was adopted by geologists in the early 1870s,[1] but the first many New Zealanders may have heard of it was in a 1908 report by the Geological Survey Department.[2] In 1990 the landmass that would break away and become New Zealand was colourfully named 'Moa's Ark' by English botanist, writer and broadcaster David Bellamy, and it carried a cargo of flora and fauna that would evolve into a distinctive biodiversity. As the separation took place the ocean rose and fell, causing an intervening string of islands to emerge and disappear. These provided stepping stone opportunities for species of flora and fauna to migrate from one island to another. Because the separation from Gondwana took place long before modern mammals had begun to evolve, about 37–24 million years ago, there were none in the surrounding seas or on the land that would become New Zealand.

Until relatively recently it was believed that New Zealand, unlike Australia, had never been home to dinosaurs. One explanation for the apparent absence was that island stepping stones would not have been conducive to the passage of such large lumbering beasts. But in 1975 amateur palaeontologist Joan Wiffen discovered the first dinosaur fossil in New Zealand. Embedded in rock in the Mangahouanga Valley in northern Hawkes Bay was an eight-centimetre tailbone from a medium-sized, two-legged carnivorous theropod.[3] Further finds confirmed that dinosaurs were definitely here, and probably came from Australia, prior to the formation of the Tasman. But even if the species had established themselves on Zealandia, their days would be numbered. Sixty-six million years ago a giant meteorite slammed into the Gulf of Mexico, sparking a mass extinction that wiped out most dinosaurs and the majority of the planet's plant and animal species.

One survivor of that calamitous event was an animal unique to New Zealand. It may look like a lizard but scientists classify it as the sole member of an ancient reptile order, Sphenodontia. It flourished alongside the dinosaurs until all but one species — our tuatara — died out.

Descended from dinosaurs

Birds are now believed to be the only animals around today that are direct descendants of dinosaurs, having evolved from a group of small meat-eating theropods, beginning perhaps 150 million years ago. Obviously, birds were well equipped to make the island-

Zealandia separated from the larger landmass, Gondwanaland, about 80 million years ago.

hopping journey from Gondwana to ancestral New Zealand, and once they reached this isolated island archipelago, they diversified. As a result, until recently this country was home to 91 species of land birds, many of which were found nowhere else.

Prior to human settlement, New Zealand's stock of mammals consisted entirely of three species of bat and several dozen species of marine mammals. As if to counter this lack of diversity, the country became to be known as a land of birds. Even after the arrival of Europeans in the mid-nineteenth century, the country was described as 'almost exclusively a bird's land' and, perhaps even more accurately, 'a land of birds and bird bones'.[4]

The richness of its birdlife was a feature of early New Zealand, but even more remarkable was the fact that many of its species were flightless. It is assumed they needed to be able to fly in order to get to New Zealand in the first instance, but having arrived here they subsequently lost the ability to take to the air. The reason was simple: there was no longer any need. There was plenty of food on the ground and — at that stage — no terrestrial mammalian predators to bother them. Equally, flying consumes a lot more energy than walking, while staying on the ground also had the advantage of avoiding such aerial predators as owls and eagles. Owls became nocturnal to avoid other birds of prey active during daytime. Also, most of the owls' prey was active at night, which improved their hunting opportunities.

As well as being the last habitable landmass on Earth to be settled by humans, New Zealand claims to be home to more species of flightless birds — both living and extinct — than any other country. Prior to the arrival of humans and the animals they brought with them, we had about 32 species of flightless birds, but today that menagerie has been reduced to just 16. The survivors include some extremely unusual types, such as the kākāpō. With an owl-like face, a penguin's posture and a walk like a duck, it has been labelled one of the strangest and rarest birds on Earth.[5] But much better known than the kākāpō is another of New Zealand's unusual birds that — in spite of or perhaps because of all its peculiarities — has achieved the (unofficial status of national symbol: the kiwi.

There are currently five species of kiwi, and it was once believed that they evolved from a flightless ancestor that walked onto ancient Zealandia prior to it drifting away from Gondwana. But recently, scientists have used DNA to discover that kiwi are most closely related to the extinct elephant birds of Madagascar, on the other side of the world. Therefore, it would appear that the ancestors of both kiwi and elephant birds were able to fly long distances and so travel to and settle in new areas.[6] Since then the kiwi has lost the ability to fly, but with its strong legs and talons it was well equipped to deal with at least some of the challenges that followed the human settlement of New Zealand.

APTERYX HAASTII, POTTS. ADULT ♂. JUV. ♀

2

The hidden bird of Tāne

Some 60 million years ago, as ancestral New Zealand was taking shape, the kiwi along with other flightless birds was adjusting to the rich resources of the forest floor in their new home. They no doubt relished their freedom from any mammalian predators, but it was a situation that could not last. New Zealand was the last large habitable land to be settled by humans, who began arriving in the thirteenth century.

According to Māori myth, the discovery of New Zealand (Aotearoa) is attributed to Kupe, a fisherman and rangatira (chief) from Hawaiki, the original homeland of the Polynesians prior to their dispersal across the Pacific. There are variations on this story, handed down by oral tradition, and according to one it began when Kupe's fishing grounds were being interfered with by an octopus. It belonged to another tohunga, Muturangi, who refused Kupe's request to control it. Determined to kill the beast, Kupe pursued it across the Pacific and, in the process, discovered New Zealand. After a great sea battle at the mouth of Te Moana o Raukawa (Cook Strait), Kupe finally managed to kill Muturangi's octopus.

During his circumnavigation of the North Island, Kupe named many of the locations he passed. On his return home to Hawaiki he

Kiwi

TOP: Kupe, the legendary Polynesian explorer who, according to oral history, was the first person to discover Aotearoa New Zealand.
NZ Post, Dave Burke

ABOVE: Te Wheke-a-Muturangi, the monstrous octopus which Kupe fought and overcame during his exploration of Aotearoa New Zealand.
NZ Post, Dave Burke

PAGE 14: A pair of great spotted kiwi, *Apteryx haastii*.
Keulemans, John Gerrard, hand coloured lithograph. PUBL-0035-1-008, Alexander Turnbull Library, Wellington

described New Zealand as a place with no people, but he did spot a number of birds and heard their calls. Kōkako, pīwakawaka (fantail) and weka are mentioned in one version of the story. Kupe was, of course, much less likely to have caught sight of the nocturnal kiwi.

The arrival of humans

An early European perspective on the date of the country's first settlement from east Polynesia was provided by surveyor and ethnologist S. Percy Smith (1840–1922), who familiarised himself with Māori language and custom. He recorded tribal history and mythology and, by counting back through the generations related in Māori oral histories, calculated that a migratory 'Great Fleet' of seven canoes reached these shores in 1350 AD. The concept of a Great Fleet has since been discounted, but was still accepted in 1940 when the subject of the halfpenny stamp in New Zealand's Centennial issue was 'The Arrival of Maoris in New Zealand 1350', depicting the exhausted first settlers struggling ashore. More recently, a 2010 study headed by Janet M. Wilmshurst of New Zealand's Landcare Research noted that carbon dated samples provided evidence that human colonisation took place around 1230–1280 AD.[1]

The adaptation of the first colonisers from east Polynesia to their new environment resulted in the emergence of a distinctive Māori culture, one in which the kiwi would play a significant role. Appropriately for a nocturnal creature, it was known as 'te manu huna a Tāne', the hidden bird of Tāne, god of the forest and birds. With the disappearance of the moa, the kiwi, along with the weka and kākāpō, was one of the flightless birds of most importance to Māori. Ethnographer Elsdon Best (1856–1931) noted the recording of the various names in te reo Māori for different species of kiwi: *Apteryx owenii* (Little spotted kiwi) was kiwi-hoihoi and kiwi-pukupuku; *Apteryx mantelli* (North Island brown kiwi) was kiwi-nui, kiwi-parure and kiwi-kura; and *Apteryx haastii* (great spotted kiwi) was roa and kiwi-karuwai. In addition, pio, rire and rirerire were recorded as names for the young of the kiwi, while the cry of the male kiwi was 'Hoire!' and that of the female was 'Ho! Ho! Ho!' There were, of course, regional differences; in the Bay of Plenty the cry of the female kiwi was 'Poai!', and that of the male 'Koire!' and 'Hoire!'[2]

Catching the kiwi

This country's once extensive forests teemed with bird life, which provided Māori with a rich source of food. The principal forest birds caught for this purpose were the wood pigeon (kererū, kūkūpa, kūkū), parrot (kākā), parson bird (tūī, kōkō), parakeet (kākāriki), bellbird (korimako), wood hen (weka) — and kiwi.[3] Some 60 years on from when that list was compiled, a number of those birds are now on the endangered list. The orange-fronted parakeet (kākāriki karaka) is listed as nationally critical; the great spotted kiwi, South Island kākā, Stewart Island weka and Chatham Island tūī are nationally vulnerable; the yellow-crowned parakeet (kākāriki) is at risk and declining; while the Poor Knights and Three Kings bellbirds are nationally uncommon. On a brighter note, and although still facing a risk of extinction, the little spotted kiwi population is small but increasing.[4]

    The kurī (dog) was the only domestic mammal of the pre-European Māori. It was described by Captain Cook as being very small and ugly, and by a later visitor, Frenchman Julien Crozet, as 'a sort of domesticated fox'. The kurī is believed to have been fed largely, or perhaps entirely, on fish.[5] It was capable of hunting ground birds as well as lizards, frogs and insects, and was used by Māori to hunt kiwi. It began when the fowler gave a hoarse whistle — 'Hoire! Hoire!' — known as korowhiti. A kurī, restrained by means of a light rod or cord attached to a plaited fibre collar, was then led to within a short distance of a kiwi that had answered the call, and then let go to seize the bird. In addition, fowlers could keep track of kurī by means of rattles made of hardwood

Kiwi's great sacrifice

In te ao Māori, natural phenomena were both controlled and personified by a pantheon of gods, and explained by what has been described as 'tales of ingenious invention'. These early examples of kiwi ingenuity include the following imaginative explanation for that bird's inability to fly.[6]

One day Tāne (also known as Tāne-mahuta), noticed that the trees in his realm were starting to wither, a result of being attacked by bugs on the ground. He spoke to his brother, Tāne-hokahoka, and they called all the birds together and asked if any would come down and live on the forest floor and deal with the pestiferous insects. But not one bird volunteered, so Tāne-hokahoka turned to Tūī, who explained that he didn't want to leave the sunny roof of the forest for the cold dark earth beneath, and that he was afraid of the dark. Pūkeko felt the same, and didn't want to get his feet wet. Tāne-hokahoka then turned to Pīpīwharauroa (shining cuckoo), who looked up and saw the sun filtering through forest and said he was busy building a nest.

Disappointed by the negative responses, Tāne-hokahoka then asked Kiwi if he would come down from the forest roof. He also pointed out that if Kiwi did agree to do so he would need to grow thick, strong legs so that he could break open logs on the ground to extract the bugs. He would also lose his beautiful coloured feathers and wings, so would never be able to return to the forest roof or see the light of day. Even so, Kiwi agreed, whereupon Tāne-hokahoka addressed the other birds. He told Tūī that because he was too scared to come down from the forest roof, he would now wear two white feathers at his throat as the mark of a coward, while Pūkeko, who did not want to get his feet wet, would now pay the price and forever live in the swamp. As for Pīpīwharauroa, who was too busy building a nest, he would never build another nest and instead lay eggs in other birds' nests. Tāne-hokahoka then turned to Kiwi and acknowledged his great sacrifice, and told him he would become the most well known and most loved bird of them all.[7]

This legend explains how the kiwi became a permanent resident of the forest floor, where it was now vulnerable to a new threat, the kurī which, along with the kiore (rat), had been introduced by early arrivals from east Polynesia. Kiore lived on berries, lizards, frogs and insects, and while they also ate the eggs and chicks of birds and contributed to the extinction of a number of species, did not pose a threat to kiwi. They became, in turn, a food source for Māori, caught in pit traps baited with berries.[8]

or bone attached to the animal's neck. Elsdon Best recorded how an inquisitive kiwi, attracted to the fowler's call, could then mistake the glimmer of a non-blazing bark torch for a glow worm and attempt to grab it, whereupon the cord was slackened to allow the kurī to seize the bird. Best also notes that by this means a pair of fowlers could often 'take more birds than they could carry home'.[9] But not all such kiwi hunts were successful; early colonist Joel Polack (1807–82) wrote that kurī often came off second best, attacked by the bird's 'powerful talons'.[10]

Much care was exercised when kiwi were plucked, to keep their feathers in good condition for use in cloak making. Māori also ate kiwi, preserving them in the birds' fat and steaming them in a hāngi (earth oven).[11] As for the taste of kiwi flesh, one early commentator described it as 'worthless and tough', whereas another, missionary Richard Taylor, considered it neither tough nor worthless, but much inferior to that of the pigeon and tūī.[12]

While early Māori could use the rich resources of the forest for food, the indigenous New Zealand flax (harakeke) provided for their clothing needs. The earliest garments were probably simple capes and waist mats, made by working flax and other suitable fibre materials, and ranging in size from small shoulder capes to full-length mantles. At the time of European contact, the most prestigious garment was the kahu kurī or dog-skin cloak, which was worn only by men of the highest social status. But the highly valued pure breed kurī became extinct soon after early European contact, probably through cross-breeding. Mongrel offspring were so common that the dog was no longer in demand for

Plants of New Zealand flax, *Phormium tenax*, whose woven fibres are used for the foundation of Māori garments.

Tomas Sobek

its skin, and so the making of kahu kurī was discontinued. Following the departure of the kurī, it was the kiwi that provided material for the most prestigious cloaks, usually reserved for chiefs. The birds' feathers were woven into flax cloaks, and the skins were sewn together to make feather cloaks or kahu kiwi.

Kahu huruhuru (feathered cloaks) are treasured by Māori for their beauty and the skill involved in their production, while birds are seen as messengers from the spiritual realm. The most prestigious of such garments were the kahu kiwi, utilising the feathers of the kiwi, which were used as much for adornment as for practical purposes. The cloak consisted of a kaupapa (woven foundation) of muka (New Zealand flax fibre), to which was attached a dense covering of feathers. The same cloak could incorporate feathers of varying shades of brown, sourced from different kiwi, and the whole garment could be edged with an intricately patterned woven tāniko or border.

Kahu kiwi were used as prestigious gifts; one such cloak in the collection of the Museum of New Zealand Te Papa Tongarewa was presented in 2006 by the descendants of Richard John Seddon, Prime Minister of New Zealand (1893–1906), and his wife Louisa Jane. The kahu kiwi became the most desirable garment towards the end of the nineteenth century, and one was placed around the shoulders of aviator Jean Batten after her record-breaking flight from England to New Zealand in 1936. It subsequently entered the collection of the Auckland Museum Tāmaki Paenga Hira through the bequest of film producer Rudall Hayward.[13]

The arrival of Europeans

The earliest — and most memorable — written first-hand account of the richness of the bird life that once existed in this country is surely that by Joseph Banks. Of the dawn chorus heard from *Endeavour*, anchored in Queen Charlotte Sound on 17 January 1770, Cook's botanist wrote: 'This morn I was awakd by the singing of the birds ashore from whence we are distant not a quarter of a mile, the numbers of them were certainly very great who seemd to strain their throats with emulation perhaps; their voices were certainly the most melodious wild musick I have ever heard, almost imitating small

Hōri Kīngi Te Ānaua was a leader of the Ngāti Ruaka people of Te Āti Haunui a Pāpārangi and signed the Treaty of Waitangi at Wanganui in 1840. Te Ānaua is wearing a finely woven kahu kiwi or kiwi feather cloak, which is considered a highly valued taonga or heirloom.

Auckland Art Gallery Toi o Tāmaki, gift of Mr H.E. Partridge, 1915

Portrait of a Māori man wearing a find kahu kurī (dogskin cloak).

PUBL-0037-15, Alexander Turnbull Library, Wellington

The Kiwi of Tāmaki Makaurau

In addition to providing for prestigious garments, the kiwi lent its name to a paramount chief of Te Waiohua confederation of iwi, Kiwi Tāmaki. According to one tradition, Kiwi in turn gave his name to Tāmaki Makaurau (Auckland). Kiwi Tāmaki's seat of power was at the massive pā of Maungakiekie (One Tree Hill), which at one time was probably the largest earth fort in the world. Kiwi Tāmaki died in about 1741.

The 182-metre volcanic peak of Maungakiekie, once the colossal fortified pā of Kiwi Tāmaki.

Darrin MacKenzie

A group of kiwi, along with moa and weka, surrounded by cabbage trees, flax, toe toe, nīkau and lancewood.

A-247-037, Alexander Turnbull Library

bells but with the most tuneable silver sound imaginable to which maybe the distance was no small addition …'[14]

As will be discussed elsewhere, the kiwi's introduction to European science took place in 1811 and in the following decades there were increasing reports of the birds by travellers in the country. One of the better known and more active of the writers was London-born Joel Polack, who arrived in New Zealand in 1831 and would shortly establish a general store at Kororāreka (Russell). He wrote two books of his time and observations in this country, described as representing 'valuable documentaries of [its] strange precolonial history'.[15] One book, published in London in 1838, included a detailed description of New Zealand's 'feathered tribes'. He acknowledged their morning 'concerts' but claimed: 'The musical voices of few of them equal, in delicacy of tone, the English songsters of the woods.' The kiwi — identified by Polack as the 'kiwi-kiwi' — would not have qualified as a songster, and further noted that it was so-named 'from the note of its voice'. He provided a colourful description of the bird, 'the most curious specimen of ornithology in New Zealand', being 'about the size of a large duck', covered with a 'hairy feather' similar to that of the cassowary, and possessing a beak similar to that of the curlew. Polack noted that English ornithologist John Gould, who had become curator and preserver [taxidermist] to the new Zoological Society's museum in London in 1827, had 'admirably figured' the male and female kiwi in his 'splendid work on Australian birds'. But as the kiwi is not included in Gould's 1837–38 publication *A Synopsis of the Birds of Australia and the Adjacent Islands*, we cannot be sure of the source of Polack's information. Nevertheless it was Polack who reported that the bird's flesh was 'worthless and tough'.[16]

Two years after the publication of Polack's book, the New Zealand Company began the organised settlement of the country. Its guide for intending colonists, published in 1840, noted that the native birds here were 'very numerous, and the music of the woods is dwelt upon with rapture by travellers', while also repeating Banks's account. At that stage the 'feathered tribe', especially of the South Island, was 'imperfectly known to naturalists', although pigeons were singled out as 'peculiarly beautiful in plumage and exquisitely delicious to the taste'. Of the 33 birds described in Polack's book, the longest account was given to 'the most remarkable and curious bird in New Zealand', the kiwi. It was described as being about the size of a three-months' old turkey, and with short legs that were 'remarkably strong for the size of the bird'. It would run 'very fast' and could only be caught by dogs, 'which they sometimes kick and bruise severely'. Their skins were highly prized by Māori for use as garments, while their flesh was 'black, sinewy, tough and tasteless'. As for distribution, all this publication was able to advise was that kiwi 'abounded' near Hikurangi, on the East Cape, but few were to be found north of there.[17]

Disappearing birds

The kiwi's nocturnal nature and the fact that its flesh was less appealing than that of other birds may have worked in its favour. In 1911, in one of his many newspaper articles, journalist and naturalist James Drummond referred to the 'remarkable' catches of birds made by Māori in the 'early days of settlement', when the slaughter was — apparently — 'on an almost appalling scale'. In particular, he noted that at the Tūhoe village of Ruatāhuna it was said that between 10,000 and 12,000 kākā were caught in a favourable season, and it was presumed that nearly as many pigeons were taken as well. Also caught were smaller birds including parakeets, tūī and bellbirds, although on this occasion the kiwi was not mentioned.[18]

During their exploration of the Nelson region in 1846, future prime minister William Fox, surveyor Thomas Brunner and artist, soldier and VC winner Charles Heaphy came across the remains of several bark huts, which had been built by local Māori during their regular hunts for the kiwi and kākāpō.[19] Heaphy noted that previously the kākāpō 'was to be met with abundantly' in that district and other parts of the island, and Māori attributed its extinction to wild dogs. Heaphy, however, suspected a more likely cause was the European rat, which had 'spread over the whole of the country' and was destroying the eggs and young in the lowly situated nests of both the kākāpō and kiwi.[20]

Elsdon Best recounted many of the reports by early European visitors and settlers, suggesting the richness of this country's birdlife was indicated by their early-morning performances. Following Banks (and Cook), in 1814–15 John Liddiard Nicholas was enraptured by 'the swelling notes of the woodland choristers'. Polack remarked on their 'wild melody', and in 1861 Julius von Haast wrote of the 'charms' of the dawn chorus. In the 1830s Polack had observed that some species of birds — most likely the kākāpō and kiwi — were disappearing, and a decade or so later the Rev. Richard Taylor noticed that numbers of those two birds, along with the weka, had decreased 'according to native evidence'. The situation would hardly be helped by the recommendation of Dr A.S. Thomson in 1859, that collectors should secure specimens of those birds that were decreasing before they entirely disappeared.[21]

Inevitably, the original New Zealanders had an impact on its birdlife. Most dramatically, the moa was hunted to extinction, and while the flesh of the kiwi may have been less tasty its feathers remained in demand for cloak-making. But the impact of hunting on the bird's population was probably fairly slight compared to the consequences of the next wave of settlement. European settlers and farmers brought new predators and practices, in particular large-scale forest clearances, that would have serious implications for the kiwi.

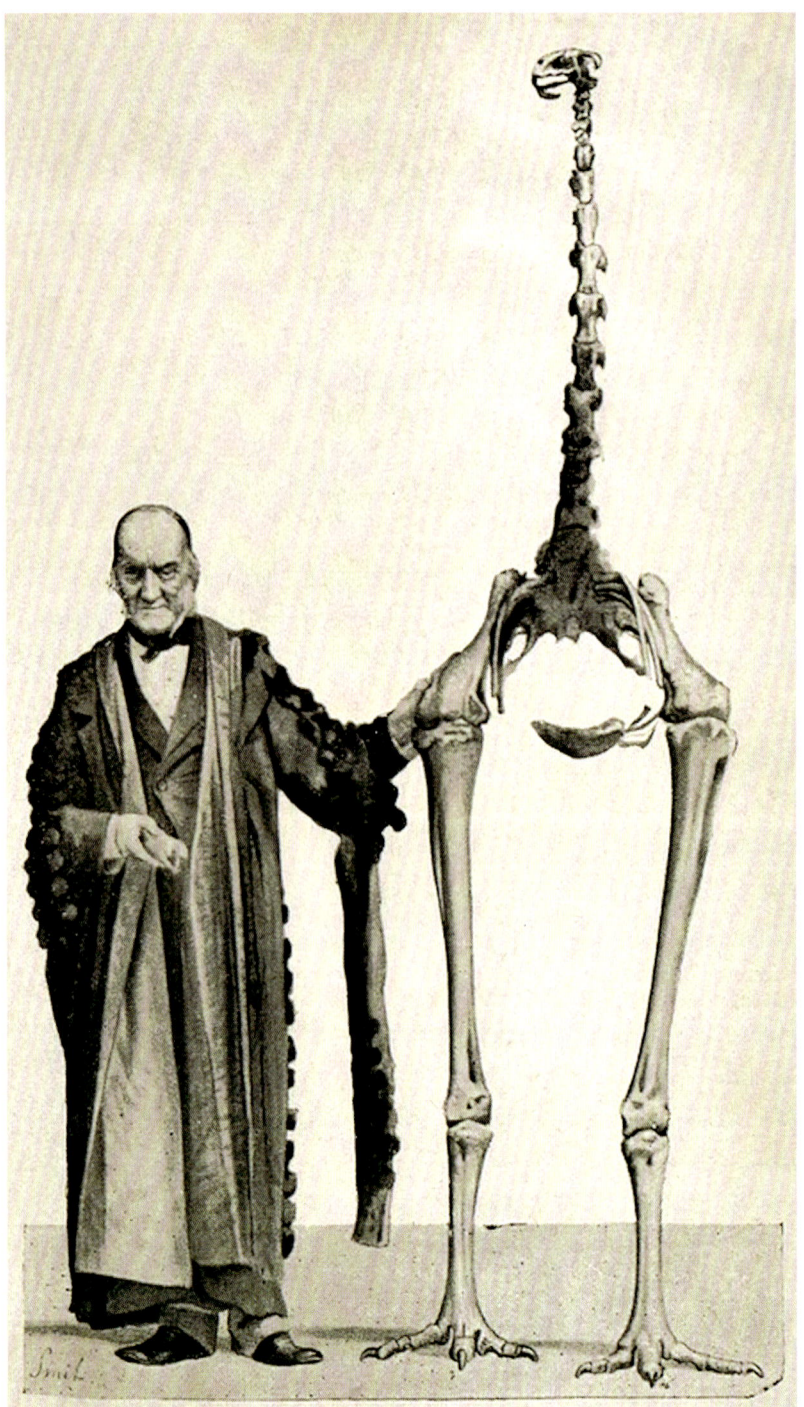

PROFESSOR OWEN AND THE SKELETON OF *DINORNIS MAXIMUS*.
Taken about 1877.

Richard Owen holds in his right hand the fragment of moa bone he received for identification in 1839. He stands beside the full assembled skeleton of a large moa.

From Richard Owen, Memoirs on the extinct wingless birds of New Zealand. *Vol. 2, 1879, London*

3

'A perfectly new genus': Discovered by science

If early visitors to New Zealand had heard about the existence of the kiwi, it was not until the second decade of the nineteenth century that the bird became known to European science. That contact was made possible by the *Providence*, a 649-ton convict ship, which arrived in Port Jackson, Sydney from Falmouth, England in 1811 with 174 'passengers'. It carried both male and female convicts; previously on-board prostitution had been such a problem that females were sent in separate ships, but for some reason this *Providence* was an exception. While it was in Sydney the captain, Andrew Barclay, obtained a kiwi skin, probably purchased from a sealer who had recently returned from southern New Zealand. The *Providence* subsequently left Sydney for China with a cargo of seal pelts for the Chinese market, and from there sailed for England, probably arriving in early 1812. The kiwi skin then entered the collection of Mr W. Evans, who drew it to the attention of George Shaw at the British Museum in Bloomsbury, London.[1]

Since 1791 Shaw (1751–1813) had been a keeper of the natural history department of the British Museum. For more than 20 years he produced, in instalments, the encyclopaedic *Vivarium Naturae*, or *The Naturalist's Miscellany*, a massive, illustrated work that consisted of 24 volumes comprising 281 plates of birds, 256 of insects, 164 fish, 84 shells, 58 reptiles or amphibians, 32 mammals or marsupials and, among others, 14 crustacea.[2]

The timing of the arrival of the *Providence* in England indeed proved providential in terms of the kiwi's introduction to European science. Based on the skin, Shaw was able to include a description and two plates of the creature he named *Apteryx australis*, 'southern wingless bird', in the twenty-fourth and final volume published in 1813. The timing was exquisite, for Shaw died that same year, on 22 July. Not yet known as the kiwi, the bird was included towards the end of the volume and illustrated by two plates, numbered 1057 and 1058 of the 1064 in the complete *Vivarium*.

With only the skin to go on, Shaw provided a detailed description of the *Apteryx australis*. In his view it represented a 'perfectly new genus' and did not bear any obvious resemblance to any of the 'established ornithological orders'. In Shaw's view it most closely resembled the Struthious (ostrich-like and flightless) and Gallinaceous (fowl- or chicken-like) birds. While its size was 'nearly that of a goose', he suggested the general appearance approached that of the penguin, while the plumage bore a strong 'alliance' to that of the brown or New Holland (Australian) cassowary. Shaw's suggestion that the bird was penguin-like was reinforced by one of the accompanying plates, the first-ever published illustration of the bird, showing a very anatomically inaccurate and vertical rendering. Given that Shaw only had a skin to refer to, such a misinterpretation was to be expected. The other plate depicted the bill, wing, leg and a feather of the bird 'in their natural size'.

As for the bird's features, Shaw recorded the bill as being 'long, slender, nearly strait [sic]', while the wings were 'rudiments only, consisting of a single joint or finger, about an inch in length, and terminated by a small claw or spur'. There was no tail, and the bird was of a 'pale ferruginous' (resembling iron-rust) in colour. Regarding the apparent lack of wings, he wondered whether 'any art of deception has been practised', but could not discover 'the least appearance'. He completed his description by noting that this 'curious bird' was a native of New Zealand. It had been brought to England by 'Captain Barcley [sic] of the *Providence*', and came to his attention thanks to the 'kind interposition' of his 'friend W. Evans Esq.'[3]

After Shaw's death his collections were sold at auction, and much of it, including the kiwi skin, had the distinction of being acquired by a future prime minister of the United Kingdom, Edward George Geoffrey Smith-Stanley, 14th Earl of Derby. Known as Lord Stanley, he was premier on three occasions, from 1852 to 1868. In 1851 his entire collection, along with the kiwi skin, was bequeathed to the City of Liverpool and formed the basis of the Liverpool Museum, now the World Museum Liverpool. In 2019, Adjunct Professor Paul Schofield and Fellow Vanesa De Pietri of The University of Canterbury Te Whare Wānanga o Waitaha visited the World Museum and obtained permission to take a small sample of skin for DNA analysis, 'to determine once and for all where European science's first kiwi was collected'. Following scientific testing there was little doubt that the kiwi came from Rakiura (later referred to as Stewart's Island) and, on the basis of where ships were sealing at that time, it was most likely from Rakiura's South Cape (Whiore).[4]

A French connection

The late eighteenth century saw the beginning of an age of French navigation, when a series of navigators and naturalists were dispatched to the Pacific. It began with Louis Antoine de Bougainville, who managed the first French circumnavigation of the world in 1766–69, and was followed to the Pacific by others including Jean-François de Surville, Marion du Fresne, Lapérouse, Antoine Bruni d'Entrecasteaux, Dumont d'Urville and René Lesson. Lesson was medical officer and naturalist in charge of zoology on the frigate *La Coquille* (later renamed *L'Astrolabe*), which undertook a global voyage in 1822–24. He would have a lasting association with New Zealand natural history, and the kiwi in particular.[5]

La Coquille spent a fortnight in New Zealand, calling at the Bay of Islands in April 1824. Lesson explored the region, collecting botanical and mineralogical specimens, and found the ornithology 'strongly interesting'. Among the birds observed were the tūī, bellbird and pigeon, and he described the kākā, grey warbler and fantail. And, as described by Michael Lee, Lesson 'realised he had a major ornithological discovery on his hands' when shown the feathered skin of a bird intended for use in the weaving of a chiefly cloak. He was told that it was from a flightless forest bird known as the 'kivi kivi'. Unaware of Shaw's discovery (which did not come to his attention until 1829), Lesson believed the bird to be a new and smaller species of the emu he had seen in New South Wales a few weeks previously. On the basis of having seen 'only a half-destroyed and shapeless skin', he described it as half the size of the Australian species, and with greyish plumage. He also noted that it was 'very common' in the forests of New Zealand and that the 'inhabitants' — who chase it with dogs — 'esteem the flesh'. Lesson named his discovery 'emu-kivikivi' *Dromiceius novae-zelandiae*, which appears to be the first record of the North Island brown kiwi.[6] Thus the *La Coquille* expedition introduced the indigenous name 'kiwi' to ornithology, it now being the common name applied to birds of the family Apterygidae.

Missionary times

By now an increasing number of adventurers, explorers and even missionaries were visiting New Zealand and providing observations on its distinctive flora and fauna. Samuel Marsden, assistant chaplain in the colony of New South Wales, was determined to introduce Christianity across the Tasman and in 1814 sent his brig *Active*, carrying animals and three missionaries and their families. Among them was John Liddiard Nicholas, who had recently arrived in Australia from England.

While his fellow passengers had more spiritual aims, Nicholas made note of New Zealand's natural history, and published his account on his return to England in 1817. He recorded that the feathers used in garments worn by rangatira were similar to those of the emu in New Holland (Australia), and so presumed the existence of a species of cassowary in New Zealand.[7] He was, of course, mistaken, for although he didn't spot it the existence of the kiwi was now known, and European science would shortly discover that New Zealand had in fact once been home to much larger flightless birds.

In 1834 another missionary, Rev. William Yate, left New Zealand after six-and-a-half years of work among the Māori people in the Bay

ABOVE: A hand-coloured engraving titled *Kivi-Kivi (Apterix)*, taken from a drawing of a kiwi by French artist Acarie-Baron (active 1800–1830s), which was probably based on a taxidermied specimen.

A-092-010-a, Alexander Turnbull Library, Wellington

RIGHT: A penguin-like reconstruction of a southern brown kiwi, based only on a specimen skin. In 1813 this image and a description of the bird were included by George Shaw, zoology keeper at the British Museum, in his series of encyclopedias.

Alamy, Florilegius

of Islands. On the voyage back to England he began writing an account of the work of his employer, the Church Missionary Society, which also included a detailed description of New Zealand's 'most remarkable and curious' kiwi. According to Yate it was a composite of several other birds, being about the size of a three-month-old turkey, and having feathers like those of an emu and a beak like a curlew's. Yate noted that its eyes were 'always blinking' and black hairs like cat's whiskers sprouted from its nostrils. While it had neither wings nor tail, it possessed an acute sense of smell, and its short strong legs provided for a fair turn of speed. Yate also noted that kiwi skins were highly prized by Māori for cloak making,[8] but if he had plans to investigate the bird further he would be disappointed. In Sydney in 1836, before he could return to New Zealand, he was confronted by scandal and accused of sexual indiscretions with young Māori men in the Bay of Islands. He returned to England in disgrace and was dismissed by the Church Missionary Society.

For the attention of Richard Owen

By now an increasing amount of information on the kiwi was reaching England. Among the specimens received by the Zoological Society were those from a Dr Logan and George Bennett of Sydney, and these came to the attention of Richard Owen (1804–1902). A zoologist, palaeontologist and leading comparative anatomist, Owen was conservator at the Hunterian Museum at the Royal College of Surgeons in London's Lincoln's Inn Fields, and quickly began work on a series of papers on the kiwi. He was able to introduce recently discovered information on the bird into his Hunterian lectures, such as that of 29 May 1838 entitled 'Digestive System of Birds'. According to notes taken at the lecture, Owen described the feeding habits of the *Apteryx*, as had been observed by Dr Logan, and was obviously impressed by its accuracy: 'It was seen to invariably poise itself before making a strike. It never missed hitting the exact spot where the worm lay.'[9]

In a subsequent lecture, delivered on 30 April 1839, Owen drew attention to a few of the 'most novel and most interesting objects which have lately been contributed to the naturalist.' Among these the *Apteryx australis* stood 'pre-eminent in every point of view'. Owen explained why it was not like other birds, being 'utterly devoid of external wings',

Interior of the Hunterian Museum, Royal College of Surgeons, London, where in 1839 curator Richard Owen was presented with a fragment of moa bone for identification.

while, in his view, its feet were neither constructed for swimming like the penguin nor were they 'strong like the Ostrich tribe' and adapted for speed. Further, the bird was nocturnal, seeking its food by night and 'lying hid during the day in the burrows it forms from beneath the surface of the earth, where the process of incubation is formed.'[10]

One of the challenges facing the naturalist at this time was the preservation of specimens. But help was at hand, for at the 14 May 1839 meeting of the London Zoological Society Mr G. Smith exhibited several birds that had been successfully preserved by the injection of his patented 'antiseptic fluid'.

Another kiwi specimen, recently arrived in London and preserved in acetic acid, was also discussed at that meeting. It was presented to the society by Owen's 'esteemed friend', botanist and explorer Allan Cunningham, who took up the post of Colonial Botanist for New South Wales in 1837 and subsequently visited New Zealand. His paper accompanying the specimen bore the lengthy title 'Rough notes collected from the New Zealanders (by the aid of missionaries), on the habits of the *Apteryx Australis*, a bird of New Zealand, closely allied to the *Struthionidae* and named by the native inhabitants Kiwi', and was read to the meeting. It provided a full description of a 'most remarkable bird' that inhabited the 'densest and darkest forests', where it spent the day either beneath long grass or hidden in hollows at the base of trees. Cunningham also described the bird's solitary egg as being about the size of a duck's, and also related that Māori captured the kiwi during their 'frequent night-prowlings in the woods'. As a result, the bird had been 'extirpated … in some districts where it once abounded.'[11]

Alerted to the unusual bird life in New Zealand, Owen should not have been surprised when a bone fragment, purportedly from the same country, was brought to him for identification in 1839. The bringer of the bone was Dr John Rule, himself a qualified surgeon, who believed it to be part of the femur of a bird 'of the eagle kind' now thought to be 'wholly extinct' in New Zealand. Owen's first reaction was that it was bovine rather than avian, and dismissed it as nothing more than a piece of marrow bone. Rule persisted, drawing attention to the unusual and decidedly non-bovine texture of the interior of the bone.

Owen compared the bone with specimens of mammals in the Hunterian Museum collection. He was forced to eliminate his first hunch, the ox, as well as numerous others including the camel, buffalo, kangaroo, orang-utan and even human, until he came to the conclusion that it was the shaft of a femur, or thigh bone, from a bird similar in size to the adult male ostrich. John Rule returned the next day, as agreed, and received the happy news that the bone was indeed from a large bird. He now hoped to sell the bone to the Royal College of Surgeons, but his offer was declined. Owen, however, would now display his discovery to the world of European science at a meeting of the Zoological Society on 12 November 1839. He explained that his conclusion — that it was the bone of 'an unknown struthious bird of large size' from New Zealand

and presumed to be extinct — was supported by his knowledge that the same country was already home to 'one of the most extraordinary and anomalous' of such birds, a reference to what would soon be known as the kiwi. He concluded dramatically, putting his professional credibility on the line by postulating that on the basis of this small fragment of bone there had existed, if it did not still exist, in New Zealand a struthious bird 'nearly, if not quite, equal in size to the ostrich'.[12]

By now an increasing number of bones, apparently from a large and extinct bird by name of 'moa', were being found throughout New Zealand. A collection of 47 such specimens was sent to England by missionary William Williams, and when it arrived in 1843 it was directed to Owen, the obvious expert. With the opening of the crate his bold deduction of 1839, which had failed to convince certain members of the Zoological Society, was now vindicated; all doubt was swept away. Owen named the newly discovered bird *Dinornis* (meaning 'prodigious' or 'terrible' bird), and in a lecture to the Royal Institution in London concluded it was a gigantic version of the *Apteryx*. He referred to a kiwi in the collection of the Zoological Society, likening its long beak to the bill of a woodcock, its legs to those of a fowl and its trunk to that of a cassowary.[13] In a later lecture, Owen referred to New Zealand as 'the abode of the little Apteryx' and wondered how such a wingless bird, with webless feet and feeble swimming abilities, could have ever crossed stretches of ocean and made it to New Zealand in the first instance. The concepts of Gondwana, continental drift and the evolution of species would have to wait for another day.[14]

Owen would be forever associated with the moa's smaller extant cousin when in 1847 John Gould named a new specimen *Apteryx owenii*, now known as the little spotted kiwi. It was distinguished from other species of kiwi by its smaller size, 'transversely barred plumage' and slender bill. The specimen described by Gould was procured by a Mr F. Strange, and believed to have been another sourced from Stewart Island (Rakiura). As reported in 1862, further specimens and information to hand suggested this was the common *Apteryx* of the northern portion of the South Island where, according to geologist Ferdinand von Hochstetter, they were to be found in great numbers.[15]

Scientific endeavour in New Zealand

Thanks to the diligence of certain individuals in New Zealand, reports and specimens of that country's curious flora and fauna were dispatched to the headquarters of imperial science in England. And when it came to birds, extinct or otherwise, Richard Owen was the authority. Even so, the establishment of a scientific tradition in New Zealand was one of the aspirations of early settlers from Europe, who recognised public libraries, museums and other educational facilities as hallmarks of civilised society.

Auckland, founded on 18 September 1840, had a Mechanics' Institute by the middle of the following year, and sought contributions of books and specimens towards to the formation of a library and museum.[16] By then Wellington already had such a facility,[17] in the charge of a local surgeon, Mr F.J. Knox. Later that year a 'colonist' in Whanganui sent him a specimen of the kiwi, also referred to as 'the New Zealand emu' and, according to Knox, 'the most remarkable bird in New Zealand, and one of the most remarkable of the entire division of birds'.[18] It was a female, weighing 5lbs 8oz., and the fact that a local newspaper published Knox's extensive and exhaustive description suggests the bird was not at all well known to readers. Knox believed he had the honour of publishing the first comparative anatomy of the kiwi. With it he reprinted another account, attributed to Dr Dieffenbach, surgeon and naturalist with the New Zealand Company, which was included in *Information Relative to New Zealand* (1840), a publication Knox accused of being riddled with a great number of errors. Unsurprisingly perhaps, Knox's account was one of surgical precision and revealed such details as the lengths of the bird's upper mandible and each of its four toes, and the distance from the gullet to the stomach ('8 ins. 9 lines'). At the hands of Dr Knox the kiwi underwent a thorough dissection and internal examination, affording him such details as the weight of the heart ('90 grains') and the eye ('8 grains ... remarkable for its smallness').[19]

Knox's lengthy account was presented in two parts, the second including dimensions of the limbs ('or pelvis locomotion organs') and comment on the bird's culinary potential. He supposed the kiwi as an article of food to be 'excellent', with its muscles appearing 'delicate and fine in the fibre'. He had been assured by Europeans who had long been resident in New Zealand that the kiwi made a dish of soup 'equal to any turtle'. Knox explained: 'The fat is baked up with flour into balls and boiled with the soup, and the quantity of oil, which is very great, may be got rid of during the cooking to a greater or less extent, according to the taste of the consumer'.[20]

New Zealand's birds were now a matter of considerable interest to natural historians in Britain. In 1848 a Wellington newspaper reprinted an item from the English *Quarterly Review*, which noted that the kiwi was the remnant of a family of gigantic wingless birds, and now 'fast disappearing by the exterminating spread of the colonists'.

European science having been well furnished with (mostly) skins and skeletons of the kiwi, it was inevitable that live specimens would also be in demand. The first such export was made in 1851 when Edward John Eyre, Lieutenant-Governor to George Grey, presented a North Island kiwi *Apteryx mantelli* to the Zoological Society of London. The bird proved to be an object of much interest to fellow passengers on the voyage over, and on arrival at the society's gardens it was placed in an enclosure divided into five stalls. Presumably to make it feel at home there was a compatriot weka in the adjacent stall, while two neighbouring stalls were occupied by an antelope and an ostrich.[21] Some 18 years later that kiwi was still there, and this 'wonderful wingless bird of New Zealand' was now described as 'perhaps the most singular case of longevity among the birds in the Zoological Gardens.' Every year since 1851 the 'old bird' had laid her 'single enormous egg', which weighed 14 oz when fresh, and measured 4¾ inches in length and 9¾ inches in the smallest circumference. As was pointed out, the kiwi was about the size of a large hen and its egg — the largest egg in proportion to body size produced by any bird — was double the weight of that of a swan's egg. It was also reported in 1869 that after 'thirteen years of single blessedness' the Zoological Gardens' kiwi had been provided with a mate, 'but as yet has reared no progeny'.[22]

In the late 1860s further live kiwi were sent to the Zoological Society of London, but perhaps the largest consignment was one dispatched to naturalist and collector Lord Rothschild at Tring, Hertfordshire. It was described as 'the largest flock of live kiwis ever kept in captivity'. In 1893, at a meeting of the British Ornithologists' Club in London, Rothschild exhibited nine living specimens of different species of kiwi, along with nearly a hundred kiwi skins. By 1913 he no longer had any

Assembled skeletons of moa on display at Canterbury Museum, Christchurch, c.1870.

living kiwi, but his collection of its skins and skeletons was said to be the largest in the world; hardly surprising considering that there were 171 skins, 15 skeletons and 44 eggs in his museum, along with a pure albino chick, a white-faced chick and a silvery white adult. Rothschild had given 12 skins to other museums, and 10 or 12 skeletons to the British Museum (Natural History) in South Kensington. Illustrating the international nature of the kiwi trade, he had nine little grey kiwi eggs, four of which he had bought in Paris. In 1932 it was announced that Rothchild's collection of bird skins had been acquired by the 'United States National Museum' and taken to New York.[23]

Skeletons of the extinct moa would soon be eagerly sought after by museums around the world, and its smaller cousin would also play a part in the international trade in natural history specimens. Several live kiwi, along with a tuatara and other birds including weka, were sent by the New Zealand Government to Emperor Franz Josef of Austria in exchange for a number of chamois, which arrived in 1907. Released near Mt Cook, these eight animals were intended to enhance New Zealand's image as a 'sportsman's paradise'. On their arrival in Vienna the New Zealand kiwi contingent was placed in a 'magnificent aviary' belonging to Crown Prince Rudolf.[24]

Another major export of live kiwi took place in 1905, when 11 were sent to England on the *Kumara*. Of those, six were destined for Lord Ranfurly, former Governor-General of New Zealand, and the remainder were for the Zoological Gardens. According to one report, the birds were under the care of government veterinary surgeon Henry C. Wilkie, and special precautions were taken to ensure their safe passage. Several dray loads of New Zealand swamp soil containing buried grubs and earthworms were taken on board, while the birds were also fed small strips of meat. On the voyage over passengers helped source worms for the birds when the ship called at Rio de Janiero and Tenerife, and while passing through the tropics the kiwi were treated to iced water. One bird may have died *en route*, and five years later only one remained at the Zoological Gardens. When that bird also died, in 1920, it was suggested that there would probably be no further attempts to send live kiwi overseas, such experiments having not been especially successful.[25]

Inside our museums

New Zealand's first public museum was established in late 1852. Topping the list of the newly opened Auckland Museum's collections policy were 'Specimens illustrative of the Natural History of New Zealand — particularly its Geology, Minerology, Entomology, and Ornithology'.[26]

In 1861 the kiwi was the subject of a 'Report on the Present State of Our Knowledge of the Species of Apteryx Living in New Zealand', produced by Dr Sclater, Secretary to the Geological Society, and Austrian geologist Dr Ferdinand von Hochstetter, who had spent eight months in New Zealand in 1858–59. The report was read at the meeting of the British Association in London, and subsequently published in New Zealand. Of the four kiwi species detailed, *Apteryx owneii* has been mentioned earlier, and since the first was obtained and described by Gould in 1847, others had reached England. The first kiwi specimen known to science was *Apteryx australis*, conveyed to England on the *Providence*, and since then others had entered the British Museum and other collections. The third species, *Apteryx mantelli*, was smaller and darker than *Apteryx australis* and, among other distinctions, had 'more rufous colour' and 'long straggling hairs on the face'. This bird was believed to be restricted to the North Island. Finally there was *Apteryx maxima*, known to the 'Natives of the Southern Island [Rakiura] as the Roa-Roa'. As yet, no specimens of this bird had reached Europe.[27]

The report on the *Apteryx* concluded by drawing attention to the importance of obtaining further information regarding the recent species of this 'singular form of birds'. It was further noted that one of them, *Apteryx mantelli*, was 'fast disappearing, while its history, habits, mode of

OPPOSITE:
Scene in a New Zealand forest near Porirua, by George French Angas, 1844.

137549, Museum of New Zealand Te Papa Tongarewa

nidification [nest-building]' and many other details were still 'altogether unknown'. Members of the British Association who had friends or correspondents in New Zealand were urged to impress upon them the benefits that they will confer on science, by endeavouring to 'procure more specimens of, and additional information concerning the different species of the genus *Apteryx*.'[28]

The kiwi would soon enter the collection of another institution with the opening of the Canterbury Museum, under founder Julius von Haast in Christchurch in early December 1867. This display included 'the kiwi of the North and South Islands', along with skeletons of the 'gigantic moa, which is now supposed to be extinct'.[29] A decade later von Haast would initiate a major impact on the birds of New Zealand when he asked his friend, von Hochstetter, now of the Imperial Natural History Museum in Vienna, to find him a taxidermist. He recommended Austrian Andreas Reischek (1845–1902), who arrived in New Zealand in April 1877 and stayed for 12 years. During that time he personally shot, taxidermied and amassed a huge and near-complete collection of New Zealand birds, many specimens of which are still in perfect condition. No doubt the kiwi, which he described as 'one of the oddest birds peculiar to New Zealand', was among them. Reischek recounted how on one occasion in the bush in the King Country he 'shot a few pigeons and caught a young kiwi (*Apteryx owenii*)', and also claimed to have kept three types in captivity. All became 'quite tame' and the males would even eat out of his hand. The taxidermist also noted: 'This rare and unfortunate bird, which can neither run fast nor defend itself successfully against the ravages of man, and is indeed at home only in the sacred loneliness of the bush, is fast dying out. The European and his attendant dogs and cats destroy him and take him from his magnificent forest.'[30]

The Colonial Museum, which opened in Wellington in 1865, was the progenitor of today's Museum of New Zealand Te Papa Tongarewa. New additions to its collection in 1868 included a mounted specimen of the *Dinornis gigantea*, described as a 'striking object', while in one of the glass cases was a skeleton of the kiwi prepared by the aforementioned Dr Knox.[31] But obviously not all kiwi were in favour of the interest that science and a growing number of museums and collectors were now taking in them. In 1868 a rather extraordinary notice appeared in a

Wellington newspaper: 'Lost, from the Colonial Museum, a live Kiwi. The finder will receive one pound reward.'[32]

Up north, the curator of Auckland Museum, Thomas Cheeseman, was reported in 1882 having in his possession two kiwi, which he was preparing to send to an American museum. Such arrangements were described as a 'good deal', for by such exports New Zealand institutions were able to obtain valuable articles in exchange. Waitākere was identified as 'the great hunting ground for kiwis for scientific purposes', and despite suggestions that all native birds were 'dying out', kiwi were said to be 'about as plentiful' there as they were twenty years ago. As for payment, Cheeseman was offering between 5/- and 20/- for each bird, depending on its size and 'whether or not it has been mangled in the catching'. The same article explained that kiwi were caught at night by using small dogs, and that while rats had greatly contributed to reducing the numbers of native birds by destroying the eggs, they did not seem to affect the kiwi, which was said to be quite capable of driving off a rat. Because the kiwi laid only one egg at a time ('a monster compared with the size of the bird'), and remained on it in a well-concealed nest until it hatched, the kiwi egg was said to be 'worth much more than a bird'.[33]

Around this time the physical characteristics of the kiwi were a source of wonder at Otago Museum, which had in its collection three of the four known species of 'the most extraordinary and un-bird-like of all living birds'. In addition to its nocturnal habits the kiwi was distinguished by its 'queer walk, its apparent absence of wings, and its hair-like plumage'. Furthermore, the size of the egg was such that it had been thought 'quite impossible' that so small a bird could have produced it, but the matter had been finally settled when a kiwi at London's Zoological Gardens 'obligingly' began laying eggs. Visitors to Otago Museum were able to confirm that a brown kiwi egg was as large as that of an albatross, and about two-and-a-half times as long as that of a kākāpō.[34]

By 1912, in recognition of its increasing rarity, it became unlawful without special permission to take any kiwi out of its native country.

4

Settlement from Europe: The kiwi under threat

Hardly surprisingly, in 1840 the London-based New Zealand Company claimed there was 'probably, no part of the world which presents a more eligible field for the exertion of British enterprise … than the islands of New Zealand. The relative position of those islands, their soil, climate, rivers, harbours, and valuable natural productions, all invite Englishmen to settle there.' It was also suggested there could be a mutual benefit, whereby the introduction of 'the habits and arts of an orderly and civilized British community' would confer 'great benefits upon the natives'.[1]

Changing the landscape

The Polynesian and subsequent European settlers of New Zealand were not alone in modifying the landscape. Ever since leaving their African homeland, perhaps between 60,000 and 90,000 years ago, humans had been converting the world's forests into grasslands or open woodlands. In their evolution from hunter-gatherers to modern farmers, they had been setting fire to forests.

Early Māori were no exception to this practice, as was pointed out by

Rev. P. Walsh in a paper read before the Auckland Institute on 19 July 1896. He began by pointing out that no one who had lived any length of time in New Zealand could have failed to observe the rapid disappearance of the natural bush. Wherever one went, whether 'along the coast or inland, on plain or mountain', there were to be found 'unmistakable signs of destruction and decay'. Walsh argued that the advent of a population enabled the work of destruction to become 'much more rapid and complete'. He noted that the forest on the Akaroa Peninsula had now 'almost entirely disappeared within a comparatively few years', while Forty Mile Bush in Taranaki, and Seventy Mile Bush on the East Coast, would 'shortly exist only in name and in the recollection of the early settlers.' Walsh conceded that while much of the destruction of the bush was accounted for by natural causes and by several centuries of Māori occupation, the increase of European settlement had 'greatly precipitated matters'.[2]

Early Māori used fire to replace areas of forest with gardens, and also for hunting the kiwi's larger cousin, the moa. But such fires were liable to get out of control, and so by 1840 about half of the islands of New Zealand had been deforested, a process that would continue unabated.[3] This ongoing destruction was of course bad news for the kiwi, and flightless birds in general, but a quarter of a century before Walsh drew attention to the issue another concern was raised. It was suggested, rather presciently, that the denudation of the country had already had an unfavourable effect on the climate.[4] With the arrival and spread of Māori, the natural forest and tall shrubland cover was reduced, particularly in coastal areas.

Today, according to the Native Forest Restoration

PAGE 44: A taxidermied kiwi specimen, presumed to be from the nineteenth century. Curiously, it was originally referred to as 'The Kie Whie'.
PH-ALB-91-p5-3, Auckland Museum

OPPOSITE: A settler, two children and a dog watch as a raging fire consumes felled trees in this 1856 pencil and watercolour painting *Burning the bush, Taranaki*, by William Strutt.
E-453-f-008, Alexander Turnbull Library

Trust, native forests and shrublands cover approximately 9 million hectares in New Zealand, roughly 33 per cent of the total land area, which has been reduced from more than 80 per cent of total land area before the arrival of humans.[5]

The natural habitat of the kiwi suffered with the conversion of original bush into pastures and paddocks. Prior to the arrival of humans, about 5 per cent of this country's land area was grassland, and today grass covers more than 38 per cent. In addition to the unsuitability of pastureland as a habitat for a nocturnal bird, the clearance of bush cover presented several threats to the kiwi. As well as fire, birds could be killed by mechanical devices used to crush the vegetation, while the removal of selected stands of bush concentrated the kiwi — and their predators — into smaller areas. Kiwi are adaptable and manage to live in a wide range of habitats, from native forest and scrub to rough farmland and plantation forests, sand dunes, snowy tussocks and even mangroves, but they prefer habitats that include stands of trees running down to rivers, and pockets of wetland vegetation.[6]

If the disappearance of the forest wasn't bad enough, there had already been an even worse human attack on the bird's livelihood. In 1913 it was revealed that some 40 or 50 years earlier kiwi hunting was carried out to a 'scandalous extent', presumably to fuel the market for mounted (museum) specimens and feathers. One such hunter was known to boast that up to the end of 1871 he had killed no fewer than 2200 specimens of the little grey and Southern kiwi.[7]

Human settlement also brought another serious threat to the livelihood of the of the kiwi: predators. Both European and — to a lesser extent — the original Polynesian settlers, brought a range of terrestrial mammals to a country that previously had none. It was inevitable these new arrivals would either attack the kiwi directly, or indirectly interfere with its traditional food source.

It may have been under threat from several quarters, but one thing the kiwi didn't need to worry about was being farmed like the domestic fowl and bred for the table. During his visit to New Zealand in 1891 Rudyard Kipling admitted to having eaten, or helped to eat, a kiwi. In his own words, its flesh resembled 'a combination of string, cement and oil ...'[8]

🥝 Rats

From the early nineteenth century, those birds that had survived the predations of previously introduced mammals faced a new threat in the form of the ship rat (*Rattus rattus*), which went on to become the most uniformly distributed of the three rat species on the mainland. Described as 'one of the most successful mammalian weed species', the rat adapted readily to life in New Zealand. While it is difficult to determine its exact ecological damage, the spread of these vermin in the North Island more or less coincided with the decline of the bellbird, robin, stitchbird, saddleback and thrush.[9]

The Norway rat, *Rattus novegicus* (top), and the ship rat, *Rattus rattus*.
CCBY4.0 Auckland Museum

Unwelcome introductions

There was, of course, already a resident rat in New Zealand — kiore (*Rattus exulans*), brought by the Polynesians. It caused disruption to the existing native fauna, eating a wide range of smaller animals such as wētā, centipedes, spiders and snails and, less frequently, lizards and small birds.[10] A more serious impact was made by the first European rodent to become established here, the Norway rat (*Rattus norvegicus*), which probably came ashore from a visiting European or North American sailing ship in the late eighteenth century. The largest rat in New Zealand, it soon became a pest and by the middle of the following century was common in both North and South islands. It was a predator of native wildlife, in particular anything that lived, roosted or nested on or near the ground, while seabirds were particularly vulnerable.[11]

The possum problem

There could have been a much more serious potential threat to the kiwi in 1837 when a failed attempt was made to release the common brushtail possum from Australia into New Zealand. Successful liberation was achieved in 1858, in bush behind Riverton, Southland. The idea was that the animals' skins would form the basis of a valuable industry and, to preserve this valuable resource the government brought the possum under the Protection of Animals Act 1880. A further bill in 1905 consolidated existing legislation, specifying the season for killing native and imported game and outlining the penalty for taking game without a license. The 13 birds on the protected list naturally included the kiwi, along with the bellbird, kōkako, kōtuku, ruru and kākāpō, and while the huia was also there it may have been too late — the last accepted sighting of this bird was in 1907.[12] Interestingly, the only two mammals on the protected list were Australian imports: the possum and the wallaby.[13] Thus protected, the possum went forth and multiplied.

The common brushtail possum (*Trichosurus vulpecula*) was unleashed onto unsuspecting native New Zealand flora and fauna in 1858.

Flickr, Steve Olsen

Finally, in 1946–47, after much debate and concern expressed by conservationists, and by farmers and orchardists for whom the animal was proving a growing pest, all restrictions on the taking of possums were lifted and penalties for harbouring and liberating them were increased.[14]

Possums remain one of the greatest threats to our natural environment. Although mainly a plant eater, it can raid birds' nests and eat eggs and chicks, in particular those of forest birds such as kiwi, kererū and kōkako. As a result, few chicks manage to fledge in forests where possums are prevalent. They are opportunistic omnivores and, while leaves are the main part of their diet, they are also partial to buds, flowers, fruit, berries and nectar. By so doing they compete with native birds and reptiles for food sources, while the growth and life cycle of a tree or plant is significantly affected when all parts of it are eaten.[15] In the late 1980s, when the estimated national possum population was thirty million, it was discovered that these voracious marsupials were having a disastrous impact on the nation's stands of pōhutukawa, especially on the west coast of Northland.[16]

The introduction of the possum to New Zealand was bad enough for the kiwi, but it could have been worse. In 1877, in the hope of destroying rabbits, 15 mongooses were imported from India by a runholder, Mr C. Basstian of Dunrobin, in Tuapeka County, South Otago.[17] Escaped or released mongooses were later sighted in the wild, most recently around 1920, so they presumably died out.[18]

It was just as well Basstian's imports had not established — he was, after all, already responsible for creating a major problem in this country when he achieved the first successful liberation of possums in 1858.[19]

Other imported pests

Following the establishment of the possum, other introduced mammals would be contributing to the demise of local bird populations. In 1864 it was observed that 'The chorus of birds ushering the dawn now exists only in the pages of Cook', and the reason given was the 'progeny of the cat', brought by settlers from Europe.[20] Wild pigs and dogs were now also to blame for the 'almost total disappearance' of the kiwi in Waikato, eating the eggs and young birds, while a similar fate had also befallen the weka.[21]

The ferret was first introduced to New Zealand in 1879, in the hope that it would deal with the rabbit problem. It didn't, and instead became a major pest itself.

Malene Thyssen

The stoat — distinguished from the weasel by its white or cream coloured underbelly — had a significant effect on certain species of New Zealand birds including the kiwi, and can remove eggs from their nests.

Department of Conservation Te Papa Atawhai, CCBY 2.0

There was yet another imported animal that would prove a national pest, and while it did not directly affect the kiwi, the measures taken to control it most certainly did. The first European rabbits in New Zealand were a pair released by Captain Cook in 1777 on Motuara Island, Queen Charlotte Sound. It took about 30 years for the animals to become established, but by the 1870s they were proving extremely destructive to pastoral farmland, and thereby affecting the country's economy. Following the failure of all attempts at control, the government decided to introduce the rabbit's 'natural enemies', the mustelid trio of stoat, weasel and ferret. The release of stoats began in the mid-1880s, a decision since described as 'one of the worst mistakes ever made by

European colonists in New Zealand'. Of all imported mammals, it has since been labelled the most obvious threat to wild birds.[22] Stoats are widely regarded as the most significant predators of a number of New Zealand's most threatened and endangered native bird species, including the Haast tokoeka (one of the rarer South Island kiwi), North Island brown kiwi, Okarito brown kiwi, orange-fronted parakeet, black stilt, takahē and fairy tern.[23]

It may be fortunate that rats are food for stoats, but such is the food chain that when rats are plentiful, so too are (presumably well-nourished) stoats. In most parts of the country today stoats are responsible for approximately half of kiwi chick deaths. Without management, only 10 per cent of kiwi chicks survive to the age of six months, and chicks remain vulnerable to stoat predation until they reach about one kilogram in weight, at which time they are usually able to defend themselves.[24]

Weasels were introduced here in large numbers at the same time and for the same reasons as stoats. Their habits are similar but on a smaller scale, so are not currently considered a threat to any native species on the mainland.[25] The third mustelid, the ferret, first came here in 1879 and in such large numbers that by the turn of the century they were well established in the wild and soon regarded as pests. They failed to deal with the rabbit problem and fed mainly on other small mammals and, given the opportunity, small birds, eggs, lizards, frogs, eels and various invertebrates.[26]

While the above-mentioned animals can kill kiwi directly, others — such as rats, mice and hedgehogs — may not kill the bird but can still cause serious problems. They can degrade native forests by eating the fruit that native birds depend on, which also affects the birds' ability to distribute the seeds needed for natural regeneration. The same animals are also food for the kiwi's predators, such as the mustelids and cats, which means they inadvertently help maintain those populations.[27]

It has no doubt been to the kiwi's advantage that it is relatively difficult to catch, and not considered a delicacy. But by mid-1888 the kiwi was said to be becoming such a 'very rare and fast disappearing bird … which threatened to become extinct' that it would soon only be seen on Bank of New Zealand notes 'which are also becoming uncomfortably scarce'.[28]

5

Early symbols of identity: Kiwi in Fernland

With the country settled by Māori and an increasing number of Pākehā, the mid-nineteenth century saw an interest in the emerging identity of this young colony of Britain. Related to this was a growing appreciation of its distinctive features, such as flora and fauna, and birds in particular. Citizens also alighted on aspects of Māori culture to use — or perhaps misappropriate — for brand names, trademarks, symbols and decorative devices. The kiwi was just one of a number of possibilities from this rich mix of options, and in the face of stiff competition it eventually rose above all others to acquire a unique symbolic status and affinity with the people of New Zealand.

Taking the name of the kiwi

An early and popular use of the *Apteryx*'s common name was for a ship, not surprising given the importance of shipping to the young economy. In mid-August 1849 a new 120-ton brig, *Kiwi*, built at Kaipara, was expected at Auckland and would then sail for San Francisco.[1] Such vessels provided a vital service, and in 1860 the *Kiwi* brought 20 tons of 'prime eating potatoes' from Taranaki to Auckland.[2]

But it was another ship that would have the greatest impact, symbolically speaking. When the New Zealand Insurance Company (NZI) was established in Auckland in 1859 it undertook to take on marine risks in both the 'Coasting and Foreign Trade',[3] and its very first policy was for a cover of £200 for a 40-ton coastal trading schooner, also named *Kiwi*.[4] This connection continued, and on its policies and advertising the company used several distinctly New Zealand images, the kiwi in particular. Most frequently a pair of the birds were positioned beneath another popular symbol of New Zealand, the tree fern. The company enjoyed early success, opening a network of branches throughout the Auckland province and in the main centres of the country. It soon had agencies in Australia and Britain, and in the 1870s and 1880s it also expanded to Honolulu, San Francisco, Calcutta, Cape Town, Bombay, Hong Kong and Shanghai. Wherever the company went it took the kiwi, thereby raising the profile of New Zealand's unique bird around the world.

In 1959, to mark a century of service, NZI obtained its own coat of arms that, in heraldic terms, incorporated a 'tree fern couped proper' and a kiwi sharing supporters' duties with another popular symbolic bird, the tūī. A singular kiwi, holding a key in its beak, was retained as the usual company logo until 1987 when it sought a clean break with the past. All traditional references were dispensed with, and the new-look (and presumably internationally flavoured) logo now consisted of just three letters: NZI. Shortly after, the stock market crashed and the company motto 'Adversio Fortior' (Stronger in Adversity) was put to the test. Then in 2003 the company — and its kiwi — disappeared when NZI was acquired by Insurance Australia Group (IAG).

Back in 1861, two years after it was founded, a meeting was held in the Auckland office of NZI to establish what would become the Bank of New Zealand (BNZ), with branches throughout the colony.[5] With this link between the two enterprises, it may

A kiwi holding a key was the NZI Company logo used from 1859 until 1987.

CCBY 4.0, Auckland Museum

A kiwi shares the New Zealand £1 note with the Māori king, Tāwhiao, issued by the Reserve Bank in 1934.

PAGE 54:
Reproduction of poster advertising the sailing of the schooner *Kiwi* from Queen Street Wharf, Auckland for the Grey River gold diggings in the mid-1860s. This was presumably the same 40-ton coastal trading vessel that was the subject of the first policy undertaken by NZI after it was established in 1859.

not have been surprising that the new bank would also draw on the kiwi. However, the bird was not alone but one of a number of local images that graced the BNZ's banknotes. As well as being representative of the nature of the colony and its economy, the complexity of the design was no doubt intended as a deterrent to forgers. Thus the ornate £1 note issued in 1898 featured Zealandia, Britannia's youngest daughter, along with two Māori figures in front of a vertiginous smoking volcano, pastoral scenes with cattle and sheep, a mine representing industry, and a trio of kiwi in a fern-covered landscape.[6]

Kiwi continued to grace the nation's banknotes and coinage, appearing with King Tāwhiao on the £1 note issued by the new Reserve Bank in 1934. A left-facing kiwi was also on the florin (two shilling) coin, which was replaced by a bird facing the other direction on the 20 cent coin when New Zealand converted to decimal currency in 1967. Then, in 1991, the bird was relieved of its duties on lower denominations when promoted to the new $1 coin.

Despite the suggestion in 1888 that the BNZ's notes were becoming 'rare', those that were in

ABOVE LEFT: The kiwi was also called on to service smokers in the form of these ceramic ashtrays.

CENTRE: Among the many indignities the kiwi has endured, none may match being converted into a cigarette lighter.

ABOVE RIGHT: In the same way Kiwi polish was originally made in Australia, Kiwi safety matches were produced in Fiji by Pacific Manufacturers Ltd.

circulation surely helped popularise the kiwi. By then the bird — along with several other contenders — was also being recognised as a suitable name and image for commercial exploitation. Perhaps one of the first was a cigarette, manufactured by Christchurch hairdresser and tobacconist Jubal Fleming, who exhorted citizens to 'Smoke the Kiwi'.[7]

Trademarking the kiwi

The Kiwi cigarette may have been short-lived, but there was at least one other product with which the bird may not have wished to be associated: manure. It was not of course the bird's own excrement that was being marketed, but it marked the beginning of an association with drug manufacturers Kempthorne, Prosser & Co. The company began in Dunedin in 1869, and by 1886 was marketing its Kiwi brand artificial manures, while also acknowledging another local feature with its Zealandia sheep dip.[8] Kiwi manures were still going strong in 1913 — crops using them were said to 'always come out on top'[9] — and were on the market until at least 1938.[10]

A horse named Kiwi

'Kiwi' proved to be a popular name for racehorses. At the Wellington races in March 1855 the hurdles were won by Jack Fiskin, with Kiwi coming in fourth, although the latter performed better in the Beaten Stakes, running second to the appropriately named Leader.[11] Then at the Auckland horse sales in 1866 a brown mare and 'good steeplechaser' named Kiwi was sold for £40.9[12] Another horse named Kiwi was very active on the southern circuit in the period 1916–17, although at the Southland Racing Club's Invercargill meeting on 3 January 1916 it was scratched from the Makarewa Trot, along with Ridicule and Silver Shoe.[13] *Apteryx*-inspired racehorses competing on the nation's courses in the late 1960s included Ima Kiwi, Kiwi Lord, Kiwi Direct, Irish Kiwi, Kiwi Gentleman, Kiwi Hostess and Kiwi Express. But of all the horses to be given the name Kiwi, the most famous was the chestnut gelding owned by Mr 'Snow' Lupton of Waverley, which in 1983 achieved a remarkable double by winning both the Melbourne Cup and Japan Cup in the same year.

In 1983 New Zealand horse Kiwi won the Melbourne Cup, making a run from last place to first and executing one of the greatest Cup wins in history.

The Age, *Melbourne*

Kiwis as pets

If New Zealanders were becoming more aware of the kiwi in the latter half of the nineteenth century, some were taking this association to extraordinary lengths — by keeping the birds as pets. In August 1857 an Auckland newspaper carried the notice 'Strayed, A Kiwi', with the promise of the finder being 'amply rewarded' by its 'owner', a local homoeopathist.[14] The following year a 'tame' kiwi went missing from Auckland's Coburg Street (later renamed Kitchener Street),[15] while another was 'lost' in Napier in 1900.[16] In both cases rewards were offered for their return. 'Tame' kiwi also appeared at auctions,[17] and persons keeping them were advised that because the bird dug into soft ground for its food, it should not be fed on a hard floor because the banging of its beak could cause it to suffer from 'concussion'.[18]

Kiwi would insist on turning up in unexpected places. In August 1916 one was found 'probing' for worms in a lettuce patch in an Epsom garden in Auckland, and was presumed to have come from the bushy slopes on the eastern side of Mt Eden.[19] Four years later a resident of Carlton Gore Road in Grafton, Auckland, found a large tame kiwi and placed a notice in the 'Owners Wanted' column of the *New Zealand Herald*. It advised that anyone wishing to claim the bird needed to provide 'proof of ownership' and to cover expenses (presumably for the cost of the advertisement and the interim maintenance of the bird).[20]

PA   Auckland

A baby kiwi, found by four boys in the west Auckland suburb of Green Bay, is being cared for at Auckland Zoo.

Neither the zoo nor the Wildlife Service know how the kiwi came to be in Green Bay.

It was found on Christmas night by Damian Pivac, aged 10, his brother, Dwayne, and two cousins who were exploring a creek at the bottom of the Pivac property.

In a hole they saw what looked like a hedgehog.

A baby kiwi found in suburban Auckland in 1984, as reported in the Christchurch *Press*.

Papers Past, 28-12-1984 Press Association

Owners Wanted

KIWI, large, lame, found. Proof of ownership and expenses.—Apply No. 5 Carlton Gore Road.

An owner is sought for a kiwi, advertised in the *New Zealand Herald*, 2 December 1920.

Papers Past, 20-02-1920, NZ Herald

In the late nineteenth century Kempthorne, Prosser & Co. — otherwise known as the New Zealand Drug Company — did much to celebrate and raise the profile of the bird. But the company's registering of the first kiwi trademark back in 1877 would be the root cause of a bigger problem. Their trademark extended into three dimensions, for large models of the bird were prominently placed on the roofs of the company's buildings in the four main centres. Auckland's 'handsome' new warehouse was under construction in Albert Street in 1899, and mounted on the apex above the façade, some 90 feet (nearly 30 m) above the pavement, was the firm's trademark kiwi, measuring 6 feet by 4 feet (1.8 x 1.2 m).

Made of cement[21] and later adorned with 'gilt', it was to form a 'very conspicuous feature' of the building.[22] There the big bird remained for the next four decades, until 1941 when it was feared it could be a beacon for Japanese bombers and so the company had it removed. It was never replaced, ending its days as landfill at Auckland's Meola Road tip, and the city had to wait until 20 years had passed before its skyline was again graced by a giant kiwi. Another of the drug company's giant kiwi came under threat when the Wellington warehouse was destroyed by fire in March 1904. The conflagration was described as comparing 'in size, magnificence, awful grandeur, and absolute destructiveness' with any fires the city had previously experienced.[23] After the floors had fallen in, there was reportedly 'little left to burn but the brick walls and the big model of the kiwi … that stood clear-cut against the glare.'[24]

At this stage the symbolic kiwi was still competing with its larger extinct cousin. Around 1881 Sharland & Co. introduced their Moa brand baking powder, and one advertisement couldn't help itself, suggesting people should try the product because 'the moa (more) they use of it the moa (more) will their hearts expand …'[25] Less than a decade later Kempthorne, Prosser & Co. launched its 'pure and unadulterated' Kiwi brand. It too couldn't resist a touch of humour, explaining their product, unlike the kiwi bird that that 'has an awkward knack of sending pastry flying; won't be kept down'.[26]

By now an increasing number of products were trading on the kiwi, ranging from lubricating oil to linoleum reviver. There was also the Kiwi rabbit trap that was imported — presumably from Australia, along with the Kangaroo trap. It was available here from 1890,[27] and by 1895 was also competing with the Moa and Kea brand traps.[28] Some sense of the rabbit problem in 1891 was provided by a Dunedin ironmonger who took delivery of 500 dozen Moa traps.[29] The versatile Moa brand was also applied to beers and ales (from 1877), boots and shoes (from 1889) and coffee (from 1890).

Kiwiland?

In 1900 the Christchurch *Press* received several letters on the subject of changing the country's name. A correspondent identified as 'Rimu' suggested that few 'colonists' had much affection for the country's 'present Dutch name', and wondered whether 'Fernland' would be acceptable, being 'euphonious, appropriate and convenient.'[30] The matter came to the attention of the editor of another newspaper who identified some of the other suggested alternatives: Britonia, New Britain, Britannia, Maoriland, Moaland, New Idea Land, New Erin, Wikitoria, Tuiland, Britland, Pacifica, and Zealand. But none was considered 'sufficiently good to entitle it to supplant "New Zealand".'[31]

The debate continued and, interestingly, at that stage there was no mention of Aotearoa. In 1927 the suggestion of a subtle change to New Sealand caused an 'old identity' to counter that it should instead be Newzealland, 'in order to commemorate the zeal and courageous work of the early colonists.' However, neither offering was found worthy and the matter was concluded: 'Our country is variously called Maoriland and Kiwiland, but it will always remain good old New Zealand.'[32]

There was yet another alternative name for the country, immortalised by the Premier, Richard Seddon. Back in 1888, members of the Timaru

OPPOSITE:
Kempthorne, Prosser & Co. registered its kiwi trademark in 1877 and applied it to various products, including 'life salts', as in this advertisement from 1935.

F-126587-1/2, Alexander Turnbull Library, Wellington

Enjoy every minute of your life

Only the fit can really enjoy life. Keep the system functioning regularly with a daily sparkling glass of K.P. Life Salt—a mild and dependable natural aperient containing the product of health-giving fruit.

K.P. Life Salt promotes internal cleanliness, purifies the blood, clears the complexion, and gives you new vitality for work or play. Economical, too—large family size 2/6, smaller size 1/6, from all chemists and stores.

Effervescent
Refreshing
Cooling
Health-restoring

K·P. LIFE SALT

MADE IN NEW ZEALAND

"A Little a Day Keeps You Healthy and Gay"

branch of the Ancient Order of Foresters received a letter from friends in Australia referring to New Zealand as 'God's own country'.[33] Four years later that description became the title of a poem written by Thomas Bracken for the *New Zealand Herald*. His 96-line 'God's Own Country' offered an extensive coverage of New Zealand's scenic attractions from north to south, extending from the Bay of Islands ('bay of beauty!') to Lake Wakatipu with its 'deep, dark waters, walled by mighty mountains', and included such breathless couplets as:

> *Pleasure ground of the Pacific! Brightest region on the main!*
> *Land of many a rushing river, verdant valley, fertile plain*[34]

New Zealand Premier Richard John Seddon at the turning of the first sod of the Lawrence-Roxburgh railway works in Otago, around 1900.

1/2-058396-F, Alexander Turnbull Library, Wellington

But the most famous use of the phrase was by Seddon in 1906. About to return to New Zealand from Australia, he sent a telegram to the premier of Victoria, advising: 'Just leaving for God's own country'. Seddon would shortly die on board the ship and much publicity was given to that telegram, his last public utterance. Among other responses framed portraits went on sale, the manufacturer suggesting 'A copy should be in the home of every dweller in God's Own Country'.[35] The term was still used occasionally until the 1970s, while a variation, 'Godzone',[36] appeared around 1907 and was still seen in print in the 1980s.

The year of Seddon's famous utterance saw other significant appearances of the kiwi, particularly in Canterbury. The bird was depicted on a printed label advertising the Kaiapoi Woollen Mills, which had its origins in 1866 and became one of the most important industrial concerns in colonial New Zealand. In addition, the kiwi was included in a series of printed labels promoting the New Zealand International Exhibition, which was held at Hagley Park in Christchurch from November 1906 to April 1907.

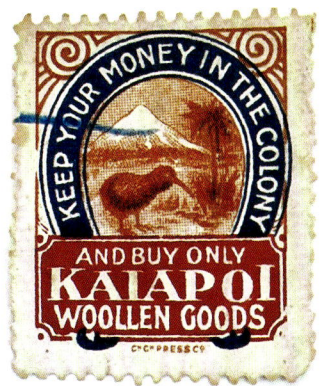

The kiwi, along with the tūī, was included in a series of cinderellas (labels resembling stamps but not issued for postal purposes) produced to promote the New Zealand International Exhibition held at Hagley Park, Christchurch, from November 1906 to April 1907.

Early symbols of identity: Kiwi in Fernland

6

'Rara Avis': A bird of the people

The new century saw an increase in popular references to the kiwi, ranging from brand names for products to symbolic embellishments for presentation to important visitors. In some instances, it was the bird itself — not its image — that was gifted to our overseas guests, frequently in the form of a feather mat.

Among the commercial products now bearing the brand name 'Kiwi' were cooking ranges, pumps and windmills, guns, cycles (built to order from parts made by Birmingham company BSA), and mouth organs. There was also Kiwi Kiwi writing paper, Kiwi tailor-cut suits, the Kiwi razor, Kiwi watches (8/6), the Kiwi (and Weka) alarm clock, Kiwi twine ('430 feet to the pound', made by the Wellington Cordage Company), the Kiwi hatpin protector (made of nickel, 4½d each), Kiwi bacon ('a man's choice'), the Kiwi pen (self-filling, 8/6), Kiwi butter (also Moa butter, both 1/2d per lb), and the Kiwi rabbit trap, with its unfortunate sales pitch: 'Get a Kiwi Every Time'.

The single most significant early adopter of the kiwi as a brand name was Kempthorne, Prosser and Co. Kiwi brand products began with its 'celebrated' manures and was followed by baking powder, culinary essences, flavouring essences (12 flavours) and asthma powder. There

PAGE 66: **In this highly imaginative scenario, a group of native birds including the kiwi and patupaiarehe (mythical Māori fairy folk), watch over the body of the last giant moa.**

Trevor Lloyd, Te tangi o te moa, *1907 Auckland Art Gallery Toi o Tāmaki*

was also their poisoned pollard (presumably competing with the imported Kiwi rabbit trap), which was a rabbit bait made of phosphorised wheat bran. The name *Apteryx* was also taken up by Kiwi Cycle Works in South Dunedin, and the Kiwi Cycle Manufactory in Hamilton.

In 1898 the New Zealand Post Office Department broke with the tradition of depicting the heads of reigning monarchs on postage stamps by opting for a set of pictorial images. They included the kiwi (6d), along with the huia (3d) and a pairing of the kea and kākā (1/-). Not everyone was happy with the illustration of the kiwi on the 6d stamp; the *Hot Lakes Chronicle* suggested the bird looked like it was 'evidently meditating suicide'.[1] Nevertheless, the same kiwi reappeared in another stamp issue in 1900, although now in green instead of the original red.

New Zealand's most famous bird on the 6d stamp issued in 1900.

Early protections proposed

While the first decade of the 1900s saw a proliferation of products happy to trade on the name of the kiwi, there were varying — and worrying — reports on the state of the bird itself. In certain districts its numbers were said to be 'rapidly diminishing',[2] and in August 1900 Parliament was told that the shooting and trapping of kiwi and kākāpō should be 'more rigidly put down' and that sanctuaries needed to be established.[3] But surely the most colourful comment on the present state of the kiwi — and the economy — was that it was becoming 'rarer and rarer before the triumphant march of frozen mutton'.[4]

When Member of Parliament James Allen visited England in 1913 he found 'much commiseration' for the huia, kiwi and other New Zealand birds, and was himself very sympathetic with the idea of increasing the protection of our native fauna.[5] He proposed to approach the Zoological Society of Wellington on the subject, which may have resulted in its deputation to the Minister of Internal Affairs, expressing concern that birds such as the Great spotted kiwi needed to be preserved from the ravages of the stoat and weasel.[6]

As the kiwi was becoming better known — although not necessarily any more visible to the general public — the country was being introduced to a fruiting vine that would, much later, be given the same name as the bird. The deciduous and sprawling *Actinidia deliciosa* is indigenous to South-East Asia, and originally found in the Hupeh (Hubei) and Szechuan (Sichuan) provinces of China, along the borders of the Yangtse River valley. Britain first became aware of it in 1847 when samples of what was named the Chinese gooseberry were sent to the Royal Horticultural Society, followed by seeds in 1900, and then plants were exported to the US in 1904.

There are various claimants as to who introduced the plant to New Zealand, among them the principal of Whanganui Girls' College, Mary Fraser. However, there seems to be agreement that Whanganui nurseryman Alexander Allison, who was given seeds by James McGregor on his return from China in 1906, was the first to fruit it, while both also passed plant material on to other growers.[7] Over the next decade or so growers did not entertain any high hopes for it, using the vine mainly for its ornamental value and to fill the odd gap in their nurseries.[8]

Patriotic duties and prestigious gifts

The kiwi (bird) assumed another commercial and extremely patriotic duty in 1909, when its image was printed on cards to be displayed in shop windows alongside New Zealand-made goods during a national 'Industries Week'. On this occasion it was a shared responsibility, for it was paired with the moa.[9]

The kiwi was also being called upon for more prestigious duties. In June 1901 the country was visited by the Duke and Duchess of Cornwall (later King George V and Queen Mary), ostensibly to thank us for supporting the Mother Country in the South African War. The casket containing the address of welcome presented to the royal couple was of 'true Maori design', being of greenstone slabs set in solid gold and surmounted by a kiwi in oxidised silver.[10] Among the gifts presented to the Duchess were at least one mat of kiwi feathers, which she wore over her shoulders, and another comprising both kiwi and huia feathers. One such item was described by the *New Zealand Herald* as 'a mantle of huia feathers … spun into a cloth of soft native flax'.[11] On their return to Britain the gifts accumulated by the royal couple were deposited in the British Museum. These so-called 'relics' included kākahu, one made of the plumage of the kiwi and said to be a garment that would 'certainly spring into fashion but for the fact that the feathers are almost impossible to procure.'[12]

As a result of such gift-giving it was claimed it would soon be 'as difficult to obtain a piece of greenstone and a kiwi mat as it would be to find a cave bear or a mammoth in the countries of Europe.' The same writer noted the current 'wholesale slaughter' of the kiwi, and that both Māori and Europeans were guilty of this 'foolish cruelty'.[13] There was now an 'unprecedented' demand for kahu kiwi, which was commonly referred to as the 'kiwi mat'. It was feared that as a result of the 'slaughtering' of birds taking place in the ranges near Taupo, along with the depredations caused by wild dogs and stoats, the North Island kiwi would become 'as extinct as the dodo.'[14] At the same time, the huia was under an even graver threat and there was reportedly a 'profusion' of the feathers of both birds, along with mats and ornaments, worn at a 'Maori wedding' in April 1903.[15] The last official confirmed sighting of the huia was made just over four years later, and the bird was declared extinct in the 1920s.

The unusual birds of New Zealand also went on show in the US at the 1904 World's Fair in St Louis. The kiwi was described as a 'strange … but inoffensive creature … tailless and wingless, and for all the world like a half-plucked and disreputable looking barn-door rooster'. The same commentator considered the 'most extraordinary bird of all' to be the huia, of which there were several mounted specimens on display.[16]

'Lowly' status

In addition to the kiwi's popularity as a prestigious gift and fashionable dress accessory, it was sought by scientists keen to get hold of a specimen of the 'lowest form of bird' in any condition.[17] The kiwi's 'lowly' status was referred to in a 1903 talk on the subject of 'Wings' at a church in Flemington, Canterbury, during which the audience was exhorted to 'rise above the sordid mess and the troubles of life'. It was suggested that, unfortunately, many folk were like the kiwi, having 'almost lost these uplifting powers through disuse'.[18] On the other hand, the kiwi was hailed 'the most notable living bird of New Zealand' and deserved to be classified among its 'most treasured possessions.'[19] The increasingly frequent reports of the kiwi disappearing from various parts of New Zealand led one newspaper to note: 'A live kiwi is a rara avis nowadays'.[20] But at least by 1905 the government was taking steps to preserve both the kiwi and the kākāpō in the south by placing them on an island under the protection of a caretaker.[21] In 1891 New Zealand selected its first sanctuary, Resolution Island in Dusky Sound, named after Captain James Cook's ship that landed there during its second voyage in March 1775. Richard Henry (1845–1929), who was born in Ireland and came to New Zealand in the 1870s, was appointed caretaker and curator on Resolution Island. He began studying the native birdlife, and became an expert on the natural history of flightless birds, especially the kākāpō. In 1908 he was relocated to Kapiti Island, and retired from government service in 1911. Henry produced many articles on natural history for newspapers and scientific journals, and in 1903 wrote a book on the flightless birds of New Zealand.

Another step towards the acceptance of the kiwi as a bird of the people was its selection for the title of the Auckland University College magazine, which first appeared in 1905. It may have been an obvious choice, for in 1887 the College had obtained its own shield,

THE KIWI

ABOVE: **Three kiwi surmount the shield of the coat of arms of the University of Auckland, which dates from 1887.**

50114249, Awcnz62, Dreamstime

TOP: **Masthead of the *Kiwi*, the magazine of what was then the Auckland University College, which first appeared in 1905.**

which featured three kiwi above an open book. As previously noted, the bird also appeared, surrounded by clematis, on a 'sticker' in conjunction with the New Zealand International Exhibition held in Christchurch in 1906–1907. Described as a 'sort of glorified postage stamp' and intended to be attached to envelopes to promote New Zealand overseas, it was the third in a series — following a map of the colony and a cameo of a rangatira — and depicted 'a contemplative kiwi, apparently looking for worms.'[22] Less well accepted by some was a new rail pass for Members of Parliament, a medallion that also showcased a kiwi, described as 'a very ordinary and solitary-looking fowl'.[23]

Back in the natural environment, the kiwi was not the only bird under threat. One reason given for there being fewer tūī was that 'tui-pie' was 'one of the daintiest dishes set before the early settlers',[24] while the huia was now 'seldom found anywhere, except in the mountains between Wellington and Hawke's Bay.'[25] As for the kiwi, a local newspaper repeated a popular description of the bird by English evolutionist Alfred R. Wallace, who considered it 'one of the queerest and most unbird-like of living birds.' Furthermore, '[h]is clumsy gait, his wretchedly defenceless condition, his family failings, his deformities and malformations, make him at once an object of ridicule, compassion, and affection.' So, while Wallace saw the kiwi occupying one of the lower rungs in the scale of evolutionary development — the bird having 'not grasped the principle of specialisation' and therefore needing to be content with 'a humble lot in life' — he may have also underscored the reasons for its growing popular appeal.[26]

Unusual specimens

James Drummond offered another perspective on the kiwi's treatment by evolution. He explained how an animal's lengthy isolation from the rest of the world could result in 'eccentricities in structure and habit', and how the absence of natural enemies could lead to 'indolence and sloth' and, in some cases, 'absolute degeneration.' In Drummond's view the kiwi was 'probably the most shocking living example in bird-life of degeneration', and he suspected Nature was in 'a very whimsical mood' when she made the bird.[27] He later described the kiwi as 'the most aberrant of all birds' and explained that he had used 'degenerate' in regard to the structure of the kiwi, 'not to its brain.' As he reassured his readers, the kiwi's brain was 'certainly not of a low type.'[28]

Another who categorised the kiwi as 'a degenerate' was teacher, writer and educationalist Edith Howes (1874–1954). In her words, this 'grey-brown bird of night … seems to have quietly discarded all elegance of form, all beauty of colouring, all advancement on primeval feathering, as things of nought', and 'superfluous beauties, superfluous powers, the strain after higher achievement, were but drags on his vitality'.[29]

This 'degeneracy' didn't appear to affect the kiwi's performance on the sports field. Around 1907 the *Auckland Weekly News* began to reproduce cartoons by Trevor Lloyd, which featured the kiwi as this country's national representative. The bird competed against the British lion and the Australian kangaroo and, despite its anatomical disadvantages, often managed to come out on top, inspiring such captions as 'The Kiwi Scores Again' and 'Another Win for the Kiwi'.[30] In 1913 the kangaroos reportedly found the kiwi 'a bird of questionable docility, and not at all the fragile creation he might have fondly imagined.' In fact, the kiwi proved to be 'tough, cunning and elusive' and on the wet conditions the kangaroo's dignity was buried in 'foreign mud'.[31]

Later that same year the All Blacks played (and won) 16 matches in North America, and their defeat of America 51–3 at Berkeley inspired

Cartoonist Trevor Lloyd was an early advocate of the bird as a national symbol, especially on the rugby field.

C-109-020, Alexander Turnbull Library, Wellington

the headline back home: 'Kiwi Scrags the Eagle'.[32]

Lloyd recorded another significant event in the life of the kiwi, its presence at the death of the last moa. In the 1907 watercolour *Te tangi o te moa* ('Death of a moa'), produced for the enjoyment of his family, the artist depicted the body of the giant moa being mourned over by the other birds, as well as the mythic Māori fairy folk, the patupaiarehe. As the denizens of the forest grapple with the significance of the passing of the *Dinornis*, a pair of kiwi are in close attendance, and no doubt aware that the mantle of responsibility for unofficial national symbol is about to be passed to them.[33]

The kiwi was also called on to represent the nation in a less vigorous sporting code when the Kangaroo and Kiwi Bowling Club was established for expatriate Australasians in London, in 1909.[34] If the kiwi's elevation in various public arenas reflected the claim that it was the most notable of New Zealand's flightless birds, one commentator went so far as to suggest it was 'the most notable bird known to man'.[35]

These were changing times, and in 1910 the 'old tattooed Maori stock' was now 'passing out' and said to be about as rare a sight as 'a kiwi in Lambton Quay'.[36] If the bird's call was being heard less frequently in parts of the country, at least on one occasion the call proved beneficial to law enforcement. In Palmerston North a kiwi giving vent to 'weird cries' enabled police to arrest (for drunkenness) a man prowling in the bushes.[37] As for the nature of kiwi's cry, it was now likened to a sound of the modern metropolis: the whistle of an electric tram.[38]

National representative

In 1907 New Zealanders were able to gain a sense of their evolving national identity. On 26 September, known subsequently as 'Dominion Day', the country graduated from being a colony of Britain to a Dominion within the British Empire. As a member of the Empire, it had used the British coat of arms, but to reflect its new status, in April 1908 the government decided to hold an open competition to select heraldry of its own. Entries closed in mid-June, whereupon a short list was dispatched for examination by the College of Arms in London.[39] The competition attracted entries from designers of varying skill, and suggestions for the two supporters on the arms included a Māori figure, Zealandia, farmers, soldiers, and even a pair of giant moa. Although some entries incorporated a kiwi, the bird didn't make the final cut.[40] After being passed 'under the cold criticism' of the experts in London, three designs were selected.[41] In anticipation of the final decision, and noting the tendency towards 'pretentiousness rather than modest nicety', one Wellington newspaper hoped that the Dominion would be 'spared from a kiwi rampant on a geyser and ejaculating "Ake, ake, kia kaha".' Instead, the authorities needed to adopt 'something solid that will wear well — not a tawdry thing that will date and tarnish and be offensive.'[42] A version of the new coat of arms appeared on the banner representing New Zealand and previewed at the Coronation of Edward VII at Westminster Abbey in August 1911. While the result was 'not unpleasing', its depiction of 'a very thin and wretched lamb' was not considered appropriate for a nation with a reputation for producing mutton.[43]

Finally, on 26 August 1911, New Zealand adopted its own coat of arms. On the winning scheme, tidied up by heraldic designers, the two supporters were 'Zealandia', wearing what has been described as a 'nightie'[44] and holding the national flag, and alongside a cloaked rangatira with a taiaha. On the shield between them were representations of New Zealand's industries: a woolly fleece, two crossed mining hammers and a wheat sheaf, and the four stars of the Southern Cross. This coat of arms saw 45 years of service before it was updated in 1956. Zealandia was now given a more modern garment and paired with a less threatening Māori supporter, and whereas they previously had diverging gazes they now turned to acknowledge each other. Local flora and fauna didn't get a look in on the original arms, but the supporters now stood on a bed of fern leaves, replacing golden curlicues; the kiwi was still conspicuously absent.

The fact that the kiwi was overlooked by its homeland's official coat of arms, perhaps because it was considered inappropriate and/or insufficiently elegant for such an important role. But the decision appears to have been to the kiwi's advantage, enhancing its growing identification as a bird of the people. The bird was recognised at certain levels of officialdom when a variety of government agencies and city councils gradually began adopting it in their crests and logos. Wellington's arms, adopted in 1878, paired a moa supporter with a British lion but Auckland's, in 1911, included not one but a pair of kiwi supporters. In 1922 Christchurch City adopted a design covering all the usual agricultural references and surmounted by a perching kiwi, but the motto 'Britons, Hold Your Own', drawn from Tennyson, caused some discussion.[45] The city's new coat of arms granted in 1949 carried a less imperialistic

OPPOSITE ABOVE: A pair of kiwi supporters on the coat of arms of Auckland City Council, granted in 1911.

OPPOSITE BELOW: A 'kiwi proper' on the crest joins a pair of pūkeko on Christchurch City's coat of arms, granted in 1949.

J. Nicholson

A league of its own

In 1905 New Zealand's national rugby union team, the All Blacks, toured Britain and became aware of the growing popularity of a professional (non-amateur) form of the game there. The New Zealanders brought the idea back home, leading to the formation of a professional team that visited Australia in 1907. Against objections from the New Zealand Rugby Union this team was also known, confusingly, as the 'All Blacks'.

Professionalism intended to insure players against accident and to pay their playing and training expenses — and perhaps a bonus at the end of a successful season — was a hot topic in New Zealand rugby circles at that time. While that first professional team was in Australia, the *Sydney Morning Herald* nicknamed them the 'All Golds', a play on 'All Blacks' that presumably referred to the payment received by the players.[46]

When New Zealand played New South Wales in a test match at Auckland Domain in 1912, the public were invited to 'Come and See the Kiwi and the Fern Leaf Make the Kangaroo Hop Along'.[47] The trans-Tasman rivals became frequently referred to as 'Kiwi(s)' and 'Kangaroos'.[48]

Because the New Zealand team's jersey featured a kiwi they were soon universally known as 'the Kiwis', and in 1938 the national rugby league team that toured Australia became officially known as the New Zealand Kiwis.

In 1995, 88 years after the formation of this country's first professional rugby league team, the previously staunchly amateur New Zealand Rugby Union decided that it would also turn professional.

2KED26A, Andrew Rowland, Alamy

and unambiguous inscription, albeit in Latin. The *Apteryx* survived the update unscathed, perched on the crest and described officially as: 'On a Wreath Or and Azure a Kiwi Proper'.

New Zealand was at the forefront of the suffrage movement, becoming the first self-governing country in the world where women had the right to vote in parliamentary elections, achieved by the Electoral Act of 19 September 1893. In 1911 a Suffrage March was held in London, winding from the Embankments to Albert Hall. A 'beautiful' silk banner was subscribed by New Zealand women in London featuring a central tree fern flanked by a pair of golden kiwi.[49] But it wasn't until 1918 that a law change gave women in the United Kingdom the same entitlement.

Back in its homeland the kiwi's popularity continued unabated. In 1912 Ponsonby Swimming Club revealed its new trophy, 'a triumph of the silver-smith's art' consisting of a large shield of mottled rimu surmounted by a silver kiwi and native shrubbery.[50]

The kiwi — entire or parts thereof — continued to be an obligatory gift for visiting dignitaries. When Lord Islington, this country's Governor from 1910–12, was presented with a kahu kiwi and also a kiwi beak, a local newspaper noted: 'As the kiwi is a bird which is almost extinct, the gift, therefore, is of more than intrinsic value.'[51] Since the exportation of kiwi — said to be growing 'rarer year by year' — was not readily allowed by the authorities, it was suggested that the birds were now probably as difficult to obtain as permits to remove them from the Dominion. Allegedly, they were still fairly numerous in 'dark sunless gullies' around the upper reaches of the Whanganui River.[52]

The kiwi's profile was enhanced when it featured in colour on the cover of the 1912 Christmas issue of the *Auckland Weekly News*.[53] A few months later two live specimens went on display in a Queen Street shop window.[54] Around the same time a pure white kiwi — a 'rara avis' indeed — was reported to have been 'captured' in the Taupō district.[55] The next year an amendment to the Animals Protection Act of 1908 was intended to combat the destruction of the country's 'fast-vanishing native birds.' Large numbers of bird skins were exported 'surreptitiously', and there was 'a great deal of slaughter going on'.[56] If that news wasn't bad enough, the kiwi may have been disturbed by another headline at that time: 'Kiwi Disabled/Broken Tail-Shaft'. Fortunately, the damage was not to a bird but to the Union Steam Ship Company's steamer of the same name.[57]

7

Kiwi at the Front: The patriotic *Apteryx*

On 5 August 1914 New Zealand joined Britain in declaring war on Germany. Six months later this country's forces saw their first combat, when they repulsed a Turkish attack across the Suez Canal. Before long, New Zealand soldiers overseas would begin to forge an association with their country's most unusual bird.

Long prior to hostilities breaking out in the Middle East and Europe, the country had security concerns of its own. The National League of New Zealand, established in 1906, advocated a system of 'universal defence training', which would involve rifle ranges in every township and sufficient rifles and ammunition to arm 'every capable citizen'.[1] The *Apteryx* soon became involved, with the formation of the Kiwi Defence Rifle Club in Otago in 1911. With the passing of the 1909 Defence Act the country's 52-year-old volunteer system was replaced with the Territorial Force, to be raised by compulsory military training. For further guidance, in 1910 the government invited Lord Kitchener, the British field marshal famous for colonial victories in the Sudan and South Africa, to report on our military preparedness. During his visit Kitchener was presented with a pure white specimen of the North Island

In 1910 the New Zealand Government invited British Field Marshal Lord Kitchener to visit and to report on our military preparedness.
AWNS-19100303-16-06, Auckland Libraries Heritage Collections

PAGE 80: *A kiwi, with the boot polish it inspired, featured on the cover of the* Times Weekly Edition *in 1921. The bird helpfully indicates the correct pronunciation of its name ('Kee Wee').*
Eph-C-CLEANING-1921-0, Alexander Turnbull Library, Wellington

brown kiwi, a very rare instance of albinism in the bird. When he learned that the Natural History Museum in South Kensington, London did not have such a specimen Kitchener deposited his, with a view to it going on public display.[2]

Then, a month prior to the declaration of war with Germany the president of the Kiwi Rifle Club spoke, somewhat ominously, of the value of such organisations if hostilities were to break out. He pointed out that all members of the Kiwi club were 'trained men and first-class shots' and he was adamant that rifle clubs should receive more government support; instead of currently allowing 150 rounds of ammunition free, and another 150 rounds at a reduced rate, it would be preferable if they each received 500 rounds at a reduced rate.[3]

The kiwi was becoming increasingly involved in the military. For 12-years' service in the old volunteer system, now replaced by Territorials, there was a silver medal of 'a neat kiwi and fern leaf design'.[4] Similarly, the badge of the 4th (Otago Rifles) Regiment (in the new Territorial system) depicted a kiwi flanked by fern fronds.[5] When citizens wondered about a suitable 'appellation' for the New Zealand soldier, one suggestion was 'Tommy Kiwi, in line with the English and New South Wales equivalents of Tommy Atkins and Tommy Cornstalk' respectively.[6] Another correspondent could only counter with 'Tommy Rot',[7] but Tommy Kiwi would not be too far off the mark. Before long a shortened version was adopted, thanks largely to a certain Australian tin of polish.

Kiwi connections can also be claimed with another British war hero, Lord Roberts, a household name after his actions in Afghanistan in 1880 and as Commander-in-Chief of British forces in South Africa in 1900. After retiring from the army he campaigned for national service (conscription) and preparation for war against Germany. In 1912 London's Natural History Museum mounted a display of rare birds including an albino kiwi that, according to the label, was presented to Lord Roberts by Colonel G.W.S. Patterson of Auckland. This was apparently a kiwi formerly housed in Auckland Museum, and its 'withdrawal' by Patterson was the subject of negative comment in some New Zealand newspapers.[8] But there had been some confusion, for the kiwi in question did not actually belong to the Auckland Museum, but to Patterson, who was 'well known in volunteering circles in Auckland'. It was Patterson who had presented the 'unique specimen' not to Lord Roberts but to Lord Kitchener when he visited New Zealand.[9]

In late July 1914, preliminary arrangements began for the raising of a New Zealand Expeditionary Force. On 16 October 1914, a group of 8417 volunteers, most of them ex-Territorials, sailed from Wellington for Alexandria in Egypt, arriving on 3 November. Their collar badge depicted a horse and was the subject of discussion, given that the badge of New Zealand in football, cricket and other sports was the fern leaf and prompted the question: 'Is the horse only found or first found in New Zealand like the Moa bird or Kiwi or Tuatara?'[10]

One effect of the war was to raise the profile of the kiwi, so it was perhaps appropriate that a new display of the bird was unveiled at Auckland Museum in April 1915. Representing a small open glade in a dense forest, it included specimens placed in various attitudes, with one in the process of swallowing a worm just extracted from the ground.[11] The kiwi's profile was also increased at Canterbury Museum when that institution received 50 skins, believed to be was the largest such collection in New Zealand, deposited by Dr B.M. Moorhouse along with 12 kākāpō skins. It was noted that Moorhouse had stopped adding to his collection when the birds were first protected, some 30 years earlier.[12]

Such voracious collecting surely had an impact on the kiwi population, despite the suggestion that the demise of native birds was not due to any 'ruthlessness on the part of man'. Rather, it was said to be the bird's own 'helplessness' in the face of imported animals, which made existence impossible for the 'leisure-loving feathered tribes of the New Zealand forest'.[13]

A sextet of taxidermied kiwi on display at Canterbury Museum, Christchurch, in 1880.

O.027201, Museum of New Zealand Te Papa Tongarewa

The patriotic bird

At home the kiwi was increasingly in demand for patriotic purposes. The Kiwi League, dedicated to the purchase — whenever possible — of locally-made goods, urged members to wear a small badge depicting the bird. As the League explained, the kiwi was 'a distinctly New Zealand production'.[14] A 'stuffed kiwi' and a tame pig were among items auctioned in Wanganui to raise money for the Belgian Fund (a charity that assisted Belgian civilian refugees),[15] while Wellington department store Kirkcaldie & Stains had handkerchiefs embossed with the kiwi, 'NZ's emblem', available in time for Christmas 1915.[16]

The kiwi's military associations were soon well underway. Along with depictions of Rangitoto and a nīkau palm, the bird featured on a badge issued by the Auckland RSA,[17] in addition to the badge of the 17th Reinforcements. While the latter were in camp at Featherston it was reported that 'many a hut door has this bird figuring on it in chalk'.[18] *The Kiwi* was also the name of an official troopship newspaper produced on a troopship en route to the conflict.[19]

Each New Zealand unit had its own badge, so there was no universal insignia equivalent to the Canadian maple leaf or South African springbok. This apparent oversight prompted the suggestion that a unifying device, such as a Māori, fern or kiwi, should have been adopted at the outset.[20] Nevertheless, the symbolic kiwi was now on a roll, and a patriotic citizen now suggested that New Zealand's equivalent of the slang term for the common soldier in the British Army, 'Tommy Atkins', should be 'Willie Kiwi'.[21] The bird was also visible in London on a flag during Red Cross Day in December 1917,[22] and for the benefit of New Zealand soldiers in that city there was a large hostel known as the Kiwi Club run by the YMCA.

Inevitably, obituaries were needed, and the following made at least two appearances in New Zealand newspapers:

> *Somewhere in France he's lying*
> *Somewhere in France he fell.*
> *Away from the land of the Kiwi,*
> *Where he bade his last farewell.*[23]

But if the news from the front was grim, Auckland cartoonist Trevor Lloyd provided some light-hearted distraction in the *Auckland Weekly News*. Cartoons depicted the Kaiser, John Bull and the bulldog, while New Zealand's part in the conflict was carried out by a caricatured kiwi. A provincial newspaper claimed a more objectionable human being than

In response to the Gallipoli campaign, which lasted from 19 February 1915 to 9 January 1916, Trevor Lloyd depicted the kiwi skewering a brace of turkeys.

AWNS-19150211-35-02, Auckland Libraries Heritage Collections

a Prussian officer would be 'hard to find'; as well as being a brute with a limited brain, he was, curiously, 'just as much a survival of past ages as the kiwi or tuatara'.[24]

In France in 1917 there appeared another manifestation of the kiwi, in the form of a theatrical party comprised of members of the New Zealand Expeditionary Force. Known as 'The Kiwis', they presented concerts in the New Zealand Divisional Theatre, a galvanised-iron clad building capable of accommodating up to 1000 men on the Flanders Front.[25] The troupe served a useful purpose, relieving the tedium of life in the trenches, and gave concerts in London and Paris. One audience at a pantomime in the latter city was reportedly astonished, responding with much cheering and bouquets for the 'lady performers' in the all-male troupe. It may seem hard to believe, but it was even suggested that this performance by The Kiwis, of male actors playing female roles, was the first of its kind to be seen in Paris.[26]

The last major action of the war for New Zealand Division was the capturing of the French fortress town of Le Quesnoy, on 4 November 1918. The Armistice came into effect a week later and on 25 March 1919, after three years of almost continuous fighting on the Western Front, the New Zealand Division was disbanded. Among the celebrations back in Auckland was a peace procession, for which shop windows in Karangahape Road were decorated in patriotic colours. In Rendells department store window, Zealandia stood serenely beneath the Union Jack and stars of the Southern Cross. She was flanked by 'pungas of the fern land', while a kiwi occupied the foreground.[27]

Kiwi for the return home

As service personnel were returning to New Zealand, there was unfortunate news regarding one kiwi who remained behind. It had been a resident at London Zoo for nine years and had died. The bird was said to have led such a 'secluded life' that the general public had very little opportunity of spotting it. The keeper would turn it out on occasions, but being nocturnal it would invariably scramble back into its box as soon as it was released. Even so, the Zoological Society wished to replace the bird, and wrote to the New Zealand Government asking if just one more kiwi could be spared from the 'island sanctuary of the Dominion.'[28] At least one more kiwi was sent, in the early 1950s.

Among the returning New Zealanders was what is now known as the Kiwi Soldier Concert Party. It had recently performed in England, Ireland, Scotland, Wales and France, and opened their New Zealand tour at Auckland Town Hall in December 1919. In their various manifestations — as 'The Kiwis', the 'Kiwi Quartette' and 'The Kiwi Boys' — the travelling troupe would raise large sums for patriotic purposes.

Just as King George V and Queen Mary had visited New Zealand in 1901, to thank the nation for supporting Britain in the South African War, during April and May 1920 the Prince of Wales (later King Edward VIII and Duke of Windsor) came to acknowledge our assistance during the most recent conflict. As was the custom, the Prince was presented with a kiwi feather mat at Rotorua, while his New Zealand souvenirs would also include a kiwi egg, sent to him by Mrs G. Perrott of Pokeno.[29] On his return home from his 'triumphal tour' of the loyal dominions, the Prince's accumulated gifts — over 500 separate items — went on public display at the Imperial Institute in South Kensington. New Zealand's contribution included a casket of tōtara 'surmounted by a kiwi' and a case of kākahu presented by 'the chieftains of Rotorua'.[30]

Another auspicious visitor to the country at that time was General Birdwood, who had been in command of the Australian and New Zealand Army Corps in the recent war. During his visit to Rotorua he too was presented with a 'handsome kiwi mat'.[31]

On a tin of polish

There were numerous associations between the New Zealander at war and the native nocturnal bird, but perhaps the most pervasive and unusual of all had an Australian origin. Around 1906 Melbourne-based William Ramsay developed a new boot polish, and needed a short, easily pronounceable name and a symbol that suited a small round tin. He alighted on 'Kiwi', in honour of the homeland of his wife, previously Annie Elizabeth Meek of Oamaru.

In 1909 Ramsay unloaded a large consignment of tins in Sydney, so his product had caught on. Two years later he introduced it to England, where sales continued to climb thanks largely to the maintenance of boots and saddles among the Edwardian middle class. The product received a further boost in 1917 when Ramsay's Kiwi Polish Company Pty Ltd received a massive order from the British Army. The Allied troops became familiar with the Kiwi's shine, and before long the connection was made between the New Zealand soldier and the bird on the tin.

Kiwi polish went on to enjoy international success and would be marketed in some 170 countries. Ironically, New Zealand was initially not one of them. The problem was the kiwi trademark, which had been registered in 1877 and used regularly since then by Kempthorne, Prosser & Co. for its range of household drugs and chemicals. Thus thwarted, in 1910 the enterprising Ramsay registered in New Zealand a trademark that bore more than a passing resemblance to the Kiwi product but with an image of a hand mirror in place of a bird. By at least August 1910 the 'new' Mirror polish for tan boots was available in shops, and by 1924 its range had been extended to include black and dark brown.

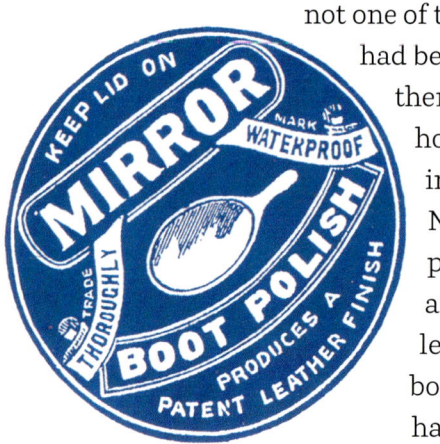

Kiwi by another name, Mirror polish was registered as a trademark in New Zealand in 1910.

Ramsay may have overcome the trademark issue with a cunning subterfuge, but perhaps a bigger challenge was competing with the already well-established Nugget line of polishes. Even when Kiwi polish was eventually able to market its product here under its real name, a generation or two of New Zealanders would, out of habit, 'nugget' their boots, and their patriotism never did extend to 'kiwi-ing'.

In 1920 Kempthorne, Prosser & Co. placed a notice in Otago newspapers advising that it understood Kiwi Polish Co. was putting boot polish under the device and word 'Kiwi' on the local market. If so, this would be considered an infringement of the drug company's registered trademark, and the notice warned that anyone found in possession of, selling or dealing with any such infringed goods, would be 'proceeded against at once'.[32] A succession of legal cases ensued, beginning at the Wellington Supreme Court in 1923 where it was found that it was not in the interests of the public for the drug company to hold a monopoly of the Kiwi trademark where it had not used it.[33] But eight months later the Court of Appeal held that there had been continuous bona fide use by Kempthorne, Prosser & Co. of its Kiwi trademark; Kiwi Polish Co.

A Kiwi Shoe Care Kit tin, c.1990.

was not entitled to register in New Zealand its trademark kiwi in respect of boot polish. It was determined that Kempthorne, Prosser & Co. had built up goodwill in respect of its kiwi 'emblem', and by attempting to register the term 'Kiwi' and use it to sell their boot polish, Kiwi Polish Co. was endeavouring to appropriate their goodwill.[34] The legal wranglings inspired some imaginative and alliterative headlines, in particular 'A Polish Problem: Trouble of a Trade Mark'.[35]

Kiwi Polish Co. therefore had to make do with Mirror, a Kiwi in disguise. Finally, in March 1927 it was able to announce that it was now permitted to market its polishes in New Zealand under the Kiwi brand. At the same time, the company proposed to continue producing Mirror.[36] Presumably it was a change in the restrictive categorisation of products — boot polish with household drugs and chemicals — enabled Kiwi polish to appear under this name. Still manufactured in Melbourne, it was advertised here as Kiwi and available in eight colours. Among other things it was the polish that 'resists the deepest puddles', and it was claimed that women liked it because it 'does not come off on their hose'. By 1929 the polish was available in its new airtight tin, 'opened in a jiffy by the twist of a penny in the specially designed slot.'[37] Five years later it was also being made here, by Kiwi Polish Co. (NZ) Ltd in Auckland's Durham Lane. There were frequent vacancies for workers, such as this advertisement from 1939: 'Girls wanted, for Lidding and Labelling.'[38] A couple of years later the bird in question might have enjoyed the lateral thinking required to solve a crossword puzzle in a London newspaper. The clue was 'Polish bird', but no amount of knowledge of the ornithology of eastern Europe would help here for the answer was, of course, 'kiwi'.[39]

In addition to Kiwi shoe polish there were also Kiwi brand non-slip 100% nylon 'Nylaces'.

A selection of KIWI shoe care products on sale in Italy, 2023.
Peter Dowling

Kiwi at the Front: The patriotic *Apteryx*

A giant kiwi

The concluding stages of the war saw the appearance of the largest kiwi of all, on a hill on the Salisbury Plain. As one newspaper announced: 'England is to have a memorial of a modern invasion which will be recalled with pleasure.'[40]

It took the form of a kiwi cut into the chalk of Beacon Hill, overlooking Sling Camp, which had been occupied by New Zealand troops since June 1916. It is highly probable that military authorities encouraged the men to undertake the project, perhaps in order to occupy them as they awaited arrangements for them to be shipped back to New Zealand. From the outset the plan was to leave an unmissable mark on the landscape, one that would last for 'hundreds of years' and qualify as an historic landmark like the famous white chalk horses. The design of the kiwi was the work of Sergeant Major Percy Blenkarne, of the Education staff, and based on a specimen of the bird examined at the British Museum.

The design of the planned Sling kiwi was transferred to the site by Sergeant Major V.T. Low. He adjusted for the slope of Beacon Hill and enabled the big bird to be seen and easily recognised from Headquarters Road, near what was known as YMCA corner. The task of cutting and removing turf to expose the white chalk beneath was completed on the morning of 28 June 1919, the day the Treaty of Versailles was signed, bringing peace after five years of conflict.

As for its size, the body of the Sling kiwi covered an area of 1¼ acres (0.5 ha), the height from the feet to the top of the bird's back was 420 feet (128 m), and the length of the bill was 150 feet (46 m).[41] Such a landmark needed regular weeding, and it was hoped that with 'a little attention from time to time' it would 'last for all time as a mark of the kiwi's glorious part in the war'.[42] In reporting the 'mammoth figure of a kiwi' above Sling Camp, the patriotic *Timaru Herald* advised that it 'easily dwarfed' the white horses and other hillside figures to be found elsewhere in Great Britain.[43]

A 1945 article explained that the land about the large kiwi consisted of about 12 inches (30 cm) of topsoil on a foundation of solid white chalk, and it was a matter of bringing the chalk to the surface. It may be hard to believe, but the same source claims that for the greater part of the operation there were as many as 2000 men working at the same time. A pile of coal, amounting to about five tons, formed the kiwi's eye. The bird was visible for many kilometres, and during peacetime was used by commercial aircraft from the Continent as a principal landmark when making for Britain, being 'plainly discernible' from aircraft over France.[44]

During the Second World War, the landmark was camouflaged and allowed to grow over, to prevent it becoming a navigational aid for German planes. In late 1945 it was restored by members of the Devonshire Regiment, who recut and cleaned it up.[45] Thereafter, responsibility for maintenance of the giant chalk kiwi was undertaken by the London-based Kiwi Polish Company. This arrangement lasted until 1950, whereupon the big bird fell into disrepair, reportedly becoming 'bedraggled' and 'threatened with extinction', with its outline ill-defined and eroded.

Fortunately, in 1981 members of a British Army unit based nearby at Bulford came to the rescue, and spent four days removing undergrowth and adding chalk to revive the now iconic image.[46]

The chalk kiwi constructed by New Zealand soldiers on the hill above their camp at Sling, on the Salisbury Plain in England, at the end of the First World War.

PAColl-6129-02, Alexander Turnbull Library, Wellington

8

Consolidation: The rise of kiwi symbolism in the 1920s and 1930s

The period following the First World War — and preceding the Second one — saw an increasingly widespread adoption of the kiwi, no doubt encouraged by its association with many of the returned soldiers. As for the bird itself, there were wildly varying reports as to how it was managing. But while its welfare and outlook continued to be matters of concern, both the kiwi's name and image were entering aspects of everyday New Zealand life.

Long recognised as one of the more unusual of birds, the kiwi had been subject to less than complimentary descriptions. It was, for example, described as both 'degenerate' and 'aberrant', although with reference to the bird's structure, not its brain.[1] More brutal was the observation in 1934 that the kiwi was 'a stupid wingless night prowler, easily captured in the glare of a fire.'[2] Then in 1935, on the subject of the choice of the kiwi as a national bird, ornithologist (and director of the

Dominion Museum from 1947 to 1966) Sir Robert Falla commented that it 'seems to have no special qualities to recommend it, unless they be modesty and retiring habits. It has no beauty of form, colour or movement. On the other hand it has an undoubted pedigree dating back to remote ages.'[3]

There was some vindication in 1932 with the announcement that tests conducted with a 'domesticated kiwi' indicated that its sense of hearing was so acute that, astonishingly, it could hear the ticking of a watch at a hundred yards.[4] Its sense of smell was also being reassessed. With nostrils at the end of its beak the kiwi was already unusual, but studies now suggested that an acute sense of smell played a more important role than vision when it came to sourcing food, thereby further setting the kiwi apart from most other varieties of birds.[5]

Kiwi at risk

Chief among the many threats to the livelihood of the kiwi were those posed, directly or otherwise, by humans. James Drummond recorded that before the bird was protected, the hunting of grey kiwi for muff-making 'became almost a vocation', while miners favoured grey kiwi 'for the pot'.[6] Humans, of course, brought dogs, which have been accused of being of most damage to kiwi,[7] although possum traps were also much to blame. In 1929 an 'ornithologist of repute' estimated that over 100 kiwi alone had been killed in this manner in the Rough River (also known as the Otututu River) valley on the South Island's West Coast during the previous possum-trapping season.[8] On a more positive note, kiwi were said to be increasing in the 'back country' of Whanganui, because they bred

PAGE 92: Sir Keith Holyoake's armorial crest, made of painted carved wood, and consisting of a kiwi holding a patu (club) with crown.

NPM2009.96.2, Nelson Provincial Museum

in damp places avoided by stoats and weasels,[9] while another glimmer of hope was that, despite being a 'helpless looking bird', it was said to be 'holding its own' elsewhere on the West Coast and able to 'look after itself very well'.[10]

At the same time there was concern that New Zealand was about to experience the 'vast silence' that was said to characterise the Australian bush and North American forest. The country was paying the price for the introduction of the rabbit, followed by the stoat and weasel: 'Gone are the kiwi, the weka, the kakapo, and the kakariki, the tui and the komako, and all the songsters of the bush ...'[11] New Zealand had long been warned of such consequences; in 1924 the *Auckland Star* reminded readers that some 35 years earlier it had published Austrian taxidermist Andreas Reischek's concerns for the threat to the kiwi and weka, in particular, by the introduction of stoats and weasels. Unbelievably, in 1924 there was still a protection on those two predators, which the New Zealand Forestry League sought to have lifted in the interests of encouraging bird life.[12]

Canterbury naturalist Edgar F. Stead warned that the munching of bush undergrowth by deer imported for the sport of stalking would have a serious effect on birds such as kiwi, weka and kākāpō.[13] Their foraging disturbed the moss and dead leaves that provided shelter for worms and other 'low forms of life'[14] on which the kiwi lived and, as was pointed out in a lecture in 1933, birds performed a valuable service by living off insects and helping to maintain Nature's 'wonderful balance' by cross-pollinating and seed distribution.[15]

In 1930 the Zoological Society of Auckland stated that the kiwi was in 'imminent danger of becoming extinct', being an easy victim to stoats, weasels and ferrets, and so urged the government to lift the protection of those three predators.[16] In 1932 it was reported that in just one possum-trapping season in the New Plymouth district, 100 kiwi were caught in traps, many killed outright or being so maimed that they had to be killed.[17] As well as the great 'wastage' of kiwi by such traps, there was reportedly still the illegal killing of the bird by humans, for both its plumage and flesh.[18]

The foothills and gorges of the Paparoa Range in the West Coast of the South Island had been 'kiwi country' for centuries, but by 1934 they were now also deemed 'opossum country'.[19] It was even suggested

Consolidation: The rise of kiwi symbolism in the 1920s and 1930s that some people regarded the native forests on the West Coast as ideal 'opossum farms'.[20] Back in the North Island, in 1933 it was claimed kiwi were being caught in traps at the rate of seven a day in the 'woods of Waikaremoana', and in many cases were suffering a lingering death. As was reported: 'What a pathetic fate for those birds in the forest, where their ancestors had peace, with no fear of enemies.'[21]

The kiwi had yet another threat to deal with in 1937 when it was revealed that poisoned grain laid for rabbits in Hawke's Bay accounted for the lives of 'many' such birds.[22] Dogs also posed a problem; until at least 1938 there were no restrictions on them being taken into the forest in game reserves. Whereas hunting had previously been limited to a period of about six weeks it was now continuous, with disastrous results for ground birds.[23] But there was some relief for kiwi in 1939, with the announcement of the Rotorua trout-fishing regulations for the next season. Among other restrictions, the use of feathers of the native bittern (matuku-hūrepo) or kiwi for the making of artificial flies was now prohibited.[24]

Continuing moves to protect New Zealand's native birds, a Bill introduced in 1921 and passed early the following year dealt with the powers of acclimatisation societies and regulated game shooting seasons. Among the 190 birds that were now 'absolutely protected' were the brown kiwi, great spotted kiwi (roroa), grey kiwi, spotted kiwi, and southern kiwi (roa).[25] Even so they were still under threat, as by bushmen — and their dogs — setting fire to the fallen bush, which the birds were reluctant to leave.[26] Although the kiwi was now protected, it was feared that extermination was only a matter of time.[27] This concern was well-founded, for a month after the 'capture' of a rare albino specimen near Eltham in South Taranaki in April 1922 it was killed by a dog.[28]

A tourist from Great Britain, who spent a month motoring around New Zealand in 1936, lamented that the only kiwi to be seen were 'stuffed ones' in museums. By comparison, back in Britain that elusive bird appeared in advertisements for this country and in sporting cartoons, as when the Kiwi team played the Lions in rugby.[29] As if in response to the tourist's disappointment, it was pointed out that the bird's rarity was one of its 'chief claims to fame. Are there any among us who would not welcome one pound for every New Zealander who has never seen a live kiwi?'[30]

Kiwi in unusual places

The kiwi could take heart from the fact that in addition to being recognised as one of New Zealand's 'exclusive possessions' it was 'world famous', and may have received more attention from ornithologists than any other bird.[31] Nevertheless, so unfamiliar was the 'hidden bird of Tāne' to the average citizen that an occasional sighting would make the newspapers.

Surely the most unlikely of these was on Wellington's Molesworth Street one night in September 1926. A pedestrian encountered the wandering bird and took it home for safekeeping, eventually handing it over to the Dominion Museum. Unfortunately it died before it could be placed in the zoo, but where it came from remained a mystery. The 'owner' of this stray bird didn't come forward, presumably not wishing to be identified because holding a kiwi in captivity was an offence against the law.[32]

There was another remarkable incident involving a kiwi one evening in 1931, when a resident of Auckland's Remuera Road found a bird bailed up by a dog in his back section. Not knowing quite what to do with it, he took it across the road to the Newmarket Police Station, where the officer in charge (the very appropriately named Sergeant Finch), secured it for the night in a 'warm box'. The following morning, Finch arranged for the 'jailbird' to be transferred to Auckland Zoo.

Unsurprisingly, the incident stimulated imaginative headlines in the nation's papers, among them 'Kiwi at Large' and 'Kiwi "Detained" by Police'.[33] The curator at the zoo believed the kiwi was the same one that had 'strayed' from the zoo about four months earlier. He thought it quite feasible that it had made its way to Newmarket without being noticed, being a nocturnal traveller.

In contrast, in January 1932 a perfectly preserved dead kiwi was found near the top of Taranaki (then known as Mt Egmont), lying near the edge of a snowfield.[34] Then the following year there was another 'extraordinary discovery'; of the perfectly preserved and frozen body of a kiwi was found on the ski grounds at Dawson Falls, almost 5000 feet above sea level.[35]

Doing business with the bird

The kiwi was obviously good for business. Existing brands maintaining a high profile during the inter-war period included Kiwi Manures, Kiwi Essences ('Eight Fruity Flavours'), Kiwi Binder Twine and the Kiwi Rabbit Trap. These were supplemented by a plethora of products, for there was little with which the kiwi could not be associated. There was another anti-rabbit device, the Kiwire wire spring trap, which also managed to mangle the bird's name, while the bird may also have wondered about the Kiwi chick raiser, a chicken feed made from grain. The Kiwi brand name was now applied to such new products as linoleum reviver, vulcanised suitcases, loose-leaf binders, geysers (for hot water), manicure sets, lever watches, wallboards, shearing machines, 4-valve electric radios (there were also Rangatira and Tui sets), paints, playing cards, exercise books, skinning knives, tennis balls, double-barrelled shotguns (made in Birmingham), tested seeds and an electric commercial oven, not to mention the Kiwi Auto-Bike, Kiwi Bru (cereal beverage), Kiwi Ale and the Kiwi Klick propelling pencil.

One of the kiwi's more unlikely associations was with bacon and ham. Morepork brand (which at least contained a porcine reference) dated from 1894 and Swan brand from around 1904, so perhaps the appearance of a third bird brand, Kiwi, in 1914 was not entirely unexpected. It was soon claiming to be 'the brand that made New Zealand famous',[36] and would later be responsible for one of the largest (three-dimensional) kiwi of all. But the kiwi itself might have winced at a 1925 promotion suggesting there was nothing nicer for breakfast than 'a choice Kiwi rasher sliced to perfection'.[37] Shortly the Kiwi range would also extend to sausages, saveloys, lard and even black pudding.

The early 1920s saw a proliferation of businesses acknowledging the kiwi: the Kiwi Dairy Company (Christchurch), Kiwi Grill Room and Delicatessen (Tauranga), Kiwi Tea Rooms (Lower Hutt), Kiwi Book Exchange (Newmarket, Auckland), Kiwi Colliery (Brunner), Kiwi Motor Bus Service (Waikato), Kiwi Gold Buyers (Wellington), Kiwi Taxis (Dunedin), Kiwi Bagwash (Auckland), Kiwi Fertilisers (Hawke's Bay), Kiwi Boarding House (Greymouth), Moller's Kiwi Service Station (New Plymouth), Kiwi Press (Wellington) and the Kiwi Cigarette Co. (Auckland). There were numerous Kiwi tea rooms and dairies around the country, and customers pausing for a cuppa at Hamilton's Kiwi

Tea and Luncheon Rooms in 1931 could, for 1/-, have their 'cup read by Madame Zara'.[38]

Of a more social nature were two organisations launched in 1930, the Empire-wide Kiwi Correspondence Club and the Kiwi Exchange Club, the latter designed for the swapping of stamps, coins and postcards. The bird also entered the musical instrument market with the Kiwi accordion and the Kiwi mouth organ, which was advertised as 'the king of harmonicas' and 'a regular pocket orchestra'. New Zealanders in the early 1920s could enjoy local spin-offs of the Kiwi Concert Party that had entertained the troops in Europe, among them 'The Famous Diggers' and 'Crimson Pierrots' who were touring the country's town halls and opera houses.[39] From Christchurch there was a group called the Kiwi Sunshine Players[40] in addition to the apparently short-lived Kiwi Sunbeam Concert Party in Ashburton. There was a Kiwi Orchestra in Taumarunui, a Kiwi Syncopated Orchestra in Wellington, and the Kiwi Five Melody Boys who presented the 'latest jazz hits' at dances in Auckland.[41] There was the Kiwi Jazz Band in Te Aroha, the Kiwi Dance Syndicate in Thames, variety entertainers known as the Kiwi Ramblers in Southland, the Kiwi Cabaret and Club in Wellington's Cuba Street, and the Kiwi Dance Club at Zealandia Hall on Auckland's Dominion Road.

Another obvious and extremely fertile field for the kiwi was the local souvenir industry, which provided images of the bird in a wide range of shapes and materials, and with overseas visitors mostly in mind. Watch-chains were popular at this time, and frequently embellished with a miniature tiki that, like the kiwi, was said to be 'almost an emblem of New Zealand'.[42]

The sporting kiwi

The kiwi was coming to the fore on the sports field. When the All Blacks beat South Africa 10–5 during the 1921 Australasian tour, a local newspaper announced: 'Kiwi Beats the Springbok'.[43] But the curious bird couldn't always manage it alone; a comment on a later match referred to the All Blacks as 'representatives of the Land of the Moa and the Kiwi'.[44] There was some discussion over the entitlement to use the term 'All Blacks' and the wearing of silver ferns on jerseys by the two rugby codes, union and league. New Zealand's representative league teams had always worn a kiwi badge over a silver fern, and it appears the matter was serious enough for it to be referred to the Minister of Internal Affairs for consideration.[45]

In 1934 a correspondent to a provincial newspaper suggested that 'All Blacks' was an unduly sombre image for a country 'favoured with sunshine', and that if the black uniform could not be changed then a large kiwi could be added to the silver fern on the jersey, and the team could be known instead as the Kiwis.[46] The idea gained approval from another quarter; that calling the nation's rugby team the Kiwis, and having one brand for all New Zealand produce sold in the United Kingdom would be a great boost for our exports.[47]

But the kiwi didn't have the athletics track all to itself; champion New Zealand runner Billy Savidan, competing in the 1930 British Empire Games in Hamilton, Canada was described as being from 'the land of the kiwi and pohutukawa'.[48] Back in its homeland, Kiwi became a popular name for sport teams. There was a Kiwi Football Club and a Kiwi Cricket Club in Hokitika, a Kiwi Swimming Club in Dunedin, several Kiwi hockey clubs around the country, the Kiwi Amateur Athletic Club and Kiwi Tennis Club in Wellington, the Kiwi Croquet Club in Huntly and Kiwi Miniature Golf in Dunedin, while Auckland's Carlton Club had a kiwi on both its badge and the gate to its bowling greens.

The sporting kiwi is also associated with a company that had its origins in Christchurch in 1880, when Alfred and Sarah Rudkin began making men's socks and cardigans in their own home. In 1904 Alfred joined forces with two former employees of the Roslyn Mills in Dunedin, John Lane and Pringle Walker, to form Lane Walker Rudkin and the associated Canterbury Clothing Company. In 1910 they began producing swimsuits and, following the First World War, rugby jerseys. The enterprise grew to become a twentieth century success story, manufacturing among other things Jockey underwear, Bob Charles shirts and Flexiwul socks. But the flagship brand was Canterbury leisurewear, and after major changes in 2000 production of this line was carried on by the newly named Canterbury of New Zealand. The company logo consists of three kiwi in profile, cleverly set against overlapping circles to create a trio of 'Cs' representing the initials of the Canterbury Clothing Company and its three founders.

🥝 Rarity value

Kiwi feathers were becoming increasingly difficult to obtain. A well-preserved kahu kiwi was said to be worth between £30 and £60,[49] and genuine examples were rare. There was 'a distinct want of the necessary feathers now that the kiwis are few and far between', and 1929 saw a prosecution in the Rotorua Magistrate's Court for the offering of such feathers for sale without lawful authority.[50] It was also noted that there appeared to be fewer feather cloaks and piupiu (flax garments) being used to decorate the interiors of wharenui (meeting houses).[51]

However, the lack of kiwi feathers appeared to have been solved by a weaver from Onehunga who used ostrich and pheasant substitutes. Emu and swan feathers were also substituted. Despite being illegal, one commentator suggested it was now necessary to 'chase the kiwi into the fastness of the upper Wanganui if his prized down is required.'[52]

Rare and precious offerings

The kiwi continued to provide for gifts for dignitaries and important visitors. In 1922 New Zealand Prime Minister William Massey was presented with a particularly fine kiwi mat, trimmed with white feathers, during a visit to a wharenui on the East Coast. Aware of its rarity and how difficult it would be to replace, Massey accepted the gift and then handed it back to his hosts, requesting that they 'keep it for him.'[53] One might wonder what became of the 'handsome and valuable kiwi mat' presented to Lady Alice Fergusson, wife of the governor-general, during her visit to Tikitiki on the East Coast four years later.[54] Then in October 1928 she made another visit to the eastern part of the North Island, becoming 'the first lady of title to go through the wild hinterland of the rugged country lying between Ruatoria and Waikaremoana'. Among the gifts she received en route was, predictably, 'a fine kiwi mat'.[55]

At the opening of the new wharenui, Te Poho-o-Rāwiri at Kaitī in Gisborne, in March 1930, the Minister of Lands and Agriculture, the Hon. C.W. Forbes, was presented with 'a beautiful kiwi cloak'.[56] The following year, also at Te Poho-o-Rāwiri, there was a reception for Governor-General Lord Bledisloe, at which Lady Bledisloe received a 'handsome and valuable feather mat, amidst applause'.[57] When Lord Bledisloe visited Ruatoki in the Bay of Plenty in October 1931, he received two mats, a spear and a kiwi cloak.[58] Four years later, at the farewell for departing Lord and Lady Bledisloe arranged by Princess Te Puea Hērangi at Ngāruawāhia, His Excellency was presented with a mat of kiwi feathers.[59] Little detail about the origins and makers of such prestigious gifts is available, and it is likely they remain in family collections or have been presented to public museums.

In late 1936 Te Arawa welcomed aviatrix Jean Batten to her birthplace, Rotorua. She was adopted as a member of Te Arawa, given the name Hine-o-te-Rangi ('Daughter of the Sky') and presented with a valuable kiwi feather cloak that had once belonged to a chieftain.[60]

But perhaps the most unusual story surrounding such gifts concerned British Admiral Sir Lionel Halsey. In 1913 he visited New Zealand on the battle cruiser HMS *New Zealand*, which this country's government had funded as a gift to Britain. A rangatira visiting the ship presented him with what was described at the time as a 'kiwi robe' and suggested that it would ensure his personal safety if he wore it when he took the ship into action, which Halsey did in the North Sea in August 1914 in the first Anglo-German naval battle of the First World War. Twenty-five years later he decided to send the garment back to New Zealand,

ABOVE: Her Excellency Lady Bledisloe wearing the kiwi feather cloak presented to her at the wharenui at Kaiti, Gisborne, during a vice-regal visit in June 1931.

AWNS-19310624-38-04, Auckland Libraries Heritage Collections

OPPOSITE: Jean Batten is greeted by guide Bella at Rotorua, 1936.

PAColl-8892, Alexander Turnbull Library, Wellington

on temporary loan for public display in the Centennial Exhibition.[61] The story of that now famous kiwi feather mat was recounted in 1957 when Lord Mountbatten, First Sea Lord, spoke at the New Zealand Society's twenty-fifth dinner in London. He noted that HMS *New Zealand* was the only ship not hit during the battles of Dogger Bank and Jutland.[62]

Kiwi in captivity

Kiwi symbolism was gaining traction; however, the real bird was having difficulty adapting. As noted elsewhere, kiwi had been previously sent to London Zoo by the New Zealand Government. In early 1928 it was reported the zoo had no examples of New Zealand bird life, and requests for kiwi, kākāpō, weka and tūī had been firmly opposed by Sir Māui Pōmare, New Zealand's Minister of Internal Affairs. That decision rankled one commentator, who compared Pōmare's refusal to allow a pair of live birds to be taken to 'the finest collection in the world for the instruction of millions' to the 'slaughter' of six kiwi that provided Lord Jellicoe (Governor-General from 1920 to 1924) with 'an appropriate souvenir for his smoke room.' It was also pointed out that sending another kiwi or two to London Zoo would 'help still further to advertise New Zealand.'[63]

Another notable kiwi-related event that decade concerned the display of a live bird at Auckland Game Fowl Club's national show in 1929, at the Municipal Hall in Newmarket. The bird in question had an interesting background, beginning when road workers in Northland disturbed an adult kiwi, causing it to abandon its nest. An egg was found and taken to the postmaster at Kawakawa, Mr G. Wilson, who warmed it over an oven. Several hours later, and with some assistance, a baby kiwi emerged. It was claimed to be the first kiwi hatched in captivity, and the chick was initially fed on egg yolk and breadcrumbs. It was offered to Auckland Zoo but was considered too young for public exhibition,[64] and in July was given a 'place of honour' at the Game Fowl show, in the company of some 360 other birds from around the country.[65] It was described as 'both a handsome and a lively bird' with 'a twinkle in his eye'. Although its 'short, red-brown appendages … could hardly be dignified by the name of feathers', it was 'altogether the most admired exhibit'.[66] After the show was over it was returned to its carer(s) in

Kawakawa but sadly did not survive for long. At six months old it crept under a piece of iron, which someone stood on and crushed and killed the bird.[67]

In early 1935, after residing on the Northamptonshire estate of Lord Lilford for 15 years, a kiwi was relocated to London Zoo, where its new home was the Ostrich House. This was believed to be the last live kiwi in Europe, and the first in London for 13 years. But visitors hoping to see 'the most curious bird in the world' were disappointed because it refused to come out of its box during daylight hours, vigorously resisting its keeper's efforts.[68]

A kiwi held at the Hawke's Bay Acclimatisation Society's game farm at Greenmeadows made the news in 1937 when filmed by a US cameraman. Some time later the Department of Internal Affairs advised the society that it was illegal to keep a native bird in captivity. The society responded that as a result of its association with many visitors their kiwi had become so tame that to release it would render it vulnerable to dogs. As a result, the department requested that the society retain custody until a decision could be made regarding its 'ultimate destination', although it is believed the bird remained at the society's farm.[69] The following year a kiwi was hatched from an egg at the game farm but around the age of six months it died, apparently as a result of illness following recent flooding.[70]

The emblematic bird

That the kiwi had become a 'national emblem' was apparent to Dr Robert Falla by at least 1924. He noted that the bird was 'the badge of a hundred clubs and the centre of a thousand trade marks', believing it was not as near to extinction as many people supposed, for it 'could be found wherever heavy bush remained'.[71] Further to Falla's observation, in preparation for their 1924 tour of Britain the All Blacks were presented with a full-grown kiwi mascot, which was caught 'up-river' in Whanganui and had been 'suitably prepared and mounted'.[72] One hopes this bird was not caught and killed for the purpose, as appeared to be the case with the gift for Lord Jellicoe. The *Auckland Star* objected to the killing of two specimens of the 'national bird emblem' and wondered how His Excellency, patron of a Bird Protection Society, might feel about receiving such an item.[73] 'It is reprehensible that live birds were sacrificed for the Vice-Regal gift, described as consisting of an illuminated address enclosed in a casket of native woods bearing Auckland City's coat of arms in gold and silver and supported on either side by a stuffed kiwi'.[74]

Strengthening the connection between the bird and the people, in 1924 the *Hawke's Bay Tribune* began a children's section for 'Young Kiwis', soon to be known as the 'Kiwi's Nest' and conducted by a 'Chief Kiwi'.[75] Although the bird was now a widespread national symbol, there was a suggestion that it was not an entirely happy choice, for the reason that in real life it was 'altogether too sluggish, retiring and nocturnal in his habits.' The weka was put forward as an alternative because it 'does not suffer from undue modesty or timidity' and 'is capable of asserting himself when necessary'.

As for the marketing of New Zealand goods overseas, while the kiwi was said to be a brand that 'no other country, no firm or organisation in another country, could possibly duplicate' — rather overlooking Kiwi Polish Company's Australian origins — the fern leaf was suggested as a preferred option. Admittedly it was not peculiar to New Zealand, but nowhere else did the fern grow in more 'splendid beauty and luxuriance'.[76] It was also felt that the nation could do better than both the fern leaf (which could be mistaken for 'a piece of English bracken') and the kiwi by following the lead of Denmark, which sold its butter as 'Danish butter'. In this case the only marketing device the country would need was the name 'New Zealand.'[77]

The kiwi's commercial potential was also recognised when the London-based Empire Marketing Board (founded in May 1926) decided to select an animal or bird representative of each British dominion or colony to promote Empire-made goods. New Zealand's kiwi joined a colourful menagerie that included the lion (United Kingdom), kangaroo (Australia), elephant (India), springbok (South Africa), alligator (West Africa), rhinoceros (Northern Rhodesia), turtle (West Indies) and tiger (Malaya).[78]

The kiwi was also on show at an Empire trade exhibition in Ottawa, Canada in 1932. In the sport and travel section, and against a painted mural of Mt Cook, the bird was depicted alongside a swordfish, rainbow trout and examples of Māori art and weapons.[79] When the peoples, industries, flora and fauna of the Dominions of the British Empire were represented on panels in the new headquarters of the Royal Institute of British Architects in London in 1934, the kiwi was there, along with a cow and a sheep, and what was identified as a 'Māori woven mat' and a fern.[80]

It was even suggested that the kiwi could play a part in international finance. It was proposed that each of the nine nations of the Empire to use the British pound be given a distinctive name for its own currency. The South African pound could be the Ostrich and that from Australia the Kookaburra, while the New Zealand pound could be, predictably, the kiwi.[81] While the Ostrich, Kookaburra and others didn't catch on, by the late 1930s the New Zealand pound was being dubbed the 'Kiwi' by some economists to distinguish it from Britain's pound sterling.[82] Another suggested name change was for New Zealand butter, then being sold in Britain under the Anchor brand. At least one citizen felt that Fernleaf, Kiwi, Tui, Zealandia or Kowhai would be preferable in terms of indicating the product's origin.[83]

Centennial celebrations

In 1936 New Zealand began planning a celebratory exhibition to mark its 100 years of 'organised settlement and government'. It was anticipated that the occasion would result in the proclamation of a national flower, the kōwhai being an obvious candidate. As for the ornithological equivalent, while the kiwi was usually considered the 'national bird' there was the question as to how many people had actually seen a live specimen, and for this reason it was suggested that many New Zealanders would prefer the tūī. The planting of kōwhai and other trees in the nation's gardens in recent years had attracted tūī, and as a result more New Zealanders were now able to see and hear this 'lovable' bird, said to be 'one of the world's best chanters'.[84] 'Scores' of newspapers reportedly supported the honour of national bird going to the tūī, which the *Auckland Star* described as a 'sunshine-loving songster'.[85]

Planning for the Centennial Exhibition, at Rongotai, Wellington, was well advanced when the Second World War broke out. While there were concerns regarding cost and that it might be a likely target in the case of an enemy attack, it was decided that the exhibition and other related events would be a tonic to national moral; the show must go on. The exhibition, which was at the heart of the celebrations, ran from 8 November 1939 to 4 May 1940, attracting a total of 2,641,043 visitors through the main gates. This was a time when the New Zealand population had not yet reached two million, so presumably many citizens made return visits. Each visitor could receive a personal Centennial Certificate of Attendance, the work of Wellington artist Leonard C. Mitchell. It was a complex composition, dominated by an updated figure of Zealandia embracing the future against a backdrop of images of physical progress. The design was rich in symbolism, including a border of traditional tāniko and decorative Māori carving patterns and the four stars of the Southern Cross on Zealandia's headband, while she was flanked by representatives of the nation's flora and fauna — a kererū in a rātā and (perhaps predictably) a tūī in a kōwhai. But more significant was the other bird standing in the centre foreground and in front of Zealandia's feet. Strategically positioned as if to show the country the way forward was a kiwi.

Near the main foyer of Government Court at the Centennial Exhibition was a case containing 11 New Zealand preserved birds, all of which, with the exception of the kiwi, were 'extremely rare'. Included were male and female huia, 'believed to be extinct'.[86] The kiwi had another significant role at the exhibition, providing transport around the 55 acres (22 ha) of grounds and buildings. The blue and silver 'Kiwi Train' was distinguished by a large model of the bird above the driver's cab, and it hauled trailers each capable of carrying 20 passengers.[87] Two years after the end of the Centennial Exhibition, the Kiwi Train went up for auction. Only a few buyers attended, and the locomotive and tender were sold for £60, the main value being in the 8-cylinder car engine that powered the train. The five carriages were bought for £16/10/— each by a Wellington coachbuilder.[88]

As well as entering the public consciousness, the kiwi was enriching the language. One usage that didn't take off was 'kiwi-ism', describing when a country lapsed from its national and international responsibilities, much as the bird itself had by retreating into the forest and neglecting its wings.[89] 'Kiwi' was taken up by the United States Army Air Force to refer to an officer in the service who couldn't fly, much like 'the bird with undeveloped wings.'[90] However in 1928, when it was

The Kiwi Train transported visitors around the New Zealand Centennial Exhibition.

E.001656/23, Museum of New Zealand Te Papa Tongarewa

suggested that US flying ace Charles Lindbergh should refrain from any further aerial risks, he retorted that he'd 'rather die in some pioneering flight than become an idolised Kiwi.'[91] This part of the world had its own aviation heroes. Australian Charles Kingsford Smith made the first crossing of the Tasman, also in 1928, from Richmond Airport near Sydney to Wigram at Christchurch, piloting the Fokker monoplane *Southern Cross*. During their subsequent triumphant tour of this country, 'Smithy' and his crew were presented with kiwi mascots and a floor rug for the cabin of the plane, its central design being a kiwi that was 'symbolical of the Dominion Aero Clubs.'[92] Six years later, for the first official trans-Tasman airmail flight, specially printed envelopes were graced with a kiwi and a kookaburra.[93]

Perhaps inspired by Kempthorne, Prosser & Co.'s statuesque three-dimensional birds — and certainly predating those erected by the Kiwi Bacon Company — University of Auckland engineering students set about constructing a mascot kiwi of concrete in 1929, with a 'plumage' in the

First day cover marking the inaugural flight by Qantas from Australia to New Zealand, by an Electra international aircraft, in October 1961.

Auckland colours of blue and white. We cannot be sure of the exact size of this bird but it was obviously portable enough to be taken to that year's University Easter Tournament in Christchurch, where it was subsequently destroyed during student 'festivities'.[94]

Postal kiwi

There was further evidence of the kiwi's popularity following the issue of a new penny postage stamp in 1926, although its depiction of King George V was dismissed as 'a very poor portrait'. Critics would have preferred a 'typical' New Zealand design and suggested, in the following order: a moa, kiwi, swordfish, hot lakes, a river or lake scene, or the Southern Alps.[95] The kiwi had made its first appearances on our stamps in 1898 and 1900, and would also feature on the 1d denomination — described variously as carmine or guardsman red — in a new set issued in 1935. At a meeting of the New Zealand Native Bird Protection Society, the design was criticised by W.R.B. Oliver, naturalist and director of the Dominion Museum (1928–47) on the grounds that the kiwi had 'no stomach at all, and had very thin legs coming out of its tail'.[96] In anticipation of the selection of designs for this stamp issue, it was suggested that in the past the country's publicity had made too much of the 'famous lizard', the kiwi and Māori figures, which were

The one penny stamp issued in the 1935 pictorial set was designed by C.H. and R.J.G. Collins.

'overdoing the primitive aspect', and that overseas people would prefer something more scenic.[97] Another opinion offered was that the preliminary designs showed a 'poor acquaintance with the subject', while the representation was seen as 'a libel on a bird famous throughout the world'.[98]

In 1938 it was pointed out that the moa was already extinct, from a philatelic perspective, and the kiwi was following suit as a result of the replacement of the 1935 kiwi penny stamp with a portrait of King George VI. It was conceded that the kiwi would missed — it had surely been a good advertisement for New Zealand when affixed to letters destined for overseas — but there was the possibility (unrealised) that it would reappear on a new stamp as part of the planned Centennial issue.[99] One newspaper correspondent was disgusted by the new penny replacement stamp, arguing that while the old kiwi design was 'not outstanding' it was preferable to its

CLOCKWISE FROM LEFT: A patriotic kiwi carrying the national flag sends greetings from New Zealand.

A kiwi surrounded by fern fronds features on this New Zealand postcard from the early 1900s.

A pair of kiwi are surrounded by images representative of Māori art and culture.

Consolidation: The rise of kiwi symbolism in the 1920s and 1930s substitute, a portrait that looked 'more like that of a Hollywood playboy than that of our beloved King'.[100]

Kiwi on currency

Following a suggestion that New Zealand should call its pound the kiwi, the shilling a tūī and the penny a huia[101] there came another; the pound could be called the 'tuatara'. The reason given was that the reptile was a creature of 'ancient lineage' and able to stay hidden for long periods, a facility that the pound was also believed to possess.[102] In a similar vein the idea that the New Zealand pound be renamed 'poundling' was floated.[103] While the kiwi remained a popular choice for the banknote, the moa was also put forward, 'because [the pound] is almost extinct'.[104] As for the lesser denominations, the country's new two-shilling piece (florin) was distinguished by what was described heraldically as a 'rampant kiwi'.[105] The Numismatic Society of New Zealand generally approved of the design, conceding that the kiwi was 'faithfully represented, but rather large'. On

The kiwi on the New Zealand ten shilling note, issued in 1940, kept a beady eye on the signing of the Treaty of Waitangi.

the other hand, the patu on the threepence was likened to a ginger beer bottle label.[106]

From August 1934 the new Reserve Bank of New Zealand began issuing its first bank notes, and the kiwi played a prominent part. On the 10/- note the bird was set at the forefront of a typical New Zealand landscape, and on the one pound note it accompanied King Tāwhiao, later replaced by Captain Cook.

In the name of the kiwi

In 1935 the Motueka Rugby Union elected as its president a local farmer who had been a popular player, and had represented Golden Bay for seven years as hooker. He had shown 'real executive ability',[107] which would come in handy in later life. Keith Jacka Holyoake was known since childhood as 'Kiwi' to distinguish him from a cousin, also known as Keith, and insisted: 'Call me Kiwi'.[108] He became vice-president of the Dominion Council (what later became the Federated Farmers of New Zealand), and in 1946 represented the country at the First World Conference of Farmers in London. Honoured at a farewell dinner at the House of Lords, he was presented with an etching of the Houses of Parliament, while a kiwi moulded in ice was wheeled in during the event.[109]

When delivering a speech in Christchurch in 1960, Labour Prime Minister Walter Nash referred to Holyoake, who would shortly lead a National Government. A voice in the audience called out, 'Call him Kiwi!', whereupon Nash replied, 'No, I won't call him a kiwi. A kiwi is a bird that walks quietly along. It has got a decent beak and can see things.'[110]

Knighted in 1970, Sir Keith was granted a personal coat of arms, for which there was no lack of suitably appropriate symbols. The design reflected his personal background and was a decidedly rural mix. The supporters were a bull and a ram, animals he had bred, and the shield bore a reference to his surname, a holly tree combined with an oak. Elsewhere were apples and grass, reflecting other agricultural interests, and on the crest a kiwi in recognition of the recipient's nickname. 'Kiwi' Keith had been prime minister of New Zealand briefly in 1957 and then from 1960 to 1972, and later served as Governor-General (1977–80).

Another distinguished New Zealander associated with the kiwi

Kiwi

was scientist Ernest Rutherford. On his personal coat of arms the shape of the shield represented the curves of radioactive bodies he discovered in 1903, the supporters were a Māori warrior and Hermes Trismegistus (representing knowledge and alchemy) and above all was the crest: a kiwi.[111]

By now 'Kiwi' was a popular *nom de plume* for letters to editors of newspapers, and for those preferring anonymity in the personal columns. But the name was not restricted to this country, for in 1938 we were visited by Dr M.L. Kiwi, a graduate of the University of Berlin.[112] As noted by Professor Arnold Wall in 1939, 'kiwi', along with 'kea' and 'moa', was included in the *Concise Oxford Dictionary* while 'tūī', 'tuatara' and 'huia' had, for some reason, been overlooked and would need to wait for a later edition.[113]

This plate features a kiwi in its natural habitat.

These small ceramic souvenirs of New Zealand combine 'Māori' decorative elements and images of kiwi.

Packing Chinese gooseberries for export.

NZME, NZ Herald

A transplant from China: Beauty and utility combined

The Chinese gooseberry's future in New Zealand became clearer when a 1921 meeting of the Auckland Acclimatisation Society reported a letter from a resident of Ōpōtiki who had successfully raised several plants from seed supplied by Mr J.W. Poynton of Feilding, some of which had grown 10 feet (3 m) high.[114] Shortly, Poynton reported that his plants had produced fruit 'about the size of a passion fruit' and had 'a most delicious flavour'.[115] The Chinese gooseberry was one of a number of plants new to New Zealand at this time, among them the avocado pear from California, the sugar beet from Denmark, various grasses from Australia, and the pecan nut from the US and Mexico.[116]

Awareness of the gooseberry plant was spreading, and a June 1923 meeting of the society heard its taste was likened to a mixture of gooseberry and apple, and that it could make 'splendid jam'. It was now also known that there were male and female plants, the latter outnumbering the former, and that flowers of both needed to be grown together in order to produce fruit.[117] Perhaps not everyone saw such a bright future for the plant, for when displayed

Watties' tinned Chinese gooseberries from 1959, before they became known as kiwifruit.

Eph-B-FOOD-Watties-1959-07, Alexander Turnbull Library, Wellington

at a national conference of nurserymen in 1924 it was described as 'valuable as fodder'.[118] But it was soon thriving in various parts of the country, recommended for use in jams, jellies and fruit salads, and a much-needed addition to the nation's fruit bowls when seasonal fruits were in short supply. Furthermore, the vine was considered to be of 'unsurpassed beauty' when used for covering arbors, pergolas and porches; in summary, it surely deserved the claim that it possessed 'beauty and utility combined'.[119]

The plant was recognised as 'a most delicious fruit and pretty climber,'[120] with a flavour now defined as a combination of English gooseberry and rock melon, and it also had great keeping qualities. The Chinese gooseberry had obvious commercial potential.[121] By the late 1930s, when there was growing concern for developments in Europe, a Waikato newpaper suggested that while there was a future here for the Chinese gooseberry grown on a commercial scale, a grape vine was better suited for small sections.[122]

Another recognised pioneer of the kiwifruit industry was Jim MacLoughlin who, after being made redundant at the Union Steamship Company in Auckland in 1933, bought a property in the highly productive farming area of Te Puke. He put in a pair of Chinese gooseberry plants as a novelty and liked the resulting fruit. The public response was also positive and so, in 1937, MacLoughlin planted out half an acre in his horse paddock, which has been hailed as the first commercial planting of Chinese gooseberry.[123]

In time, effort was put into improving the plant by selection and grafting, and as the fruit became larger, fleshier and tastier its popularity increased and the potential for a market, both locally and overseas, became apparent. Later, the Chinese gooseberry was rebranded as kiwifruit, and nowhere else in the world would it enjoy the commercial development and acceptance that it received in New Zealand.[124]

9

Back to the Front: The kiwi during the Second World War

The New Zealand soldier went off to what was then known as the Great War with a number of informal identities, the most prevalent probably being 'Digger'. If it had its origins in the gold- and gumfields of New Zealand, it may have seemed appropriate in view of the spadework involved in digging trenches on the battlefields of Europe. By 1917 the term was in common use among New Zealand soldiers, both in training camps and at the Front.[1] But as discussed previously, 'Digger' and all other such appellations were about to be supplanted by one inspired by a tin of boot polish. Not everyone was happy with the general adoption of 'Kiwi', and in 1944 a letter writer to the *New Zealand Herald* wondered why it was retained as a national symbol and why it had replaced the 'good old robustious name "digger"' to denote New Zealand servicemen overseas. Instead, the writer suggested the kea: 'There you have a bird! He may be bad mannered, noisy and given to thieving ... but what personality, what verve, what a symbol for a man's country!'[2]

Kiwi polish may not have had the same presence during the Second World War, but in New Zealand it took a military approach to advertising with the claims that it 'Serves the Services — Navy, Army and Airforce' and 'preserves the boots of our Armed Forces.' When asked in 1940 what a kiwi was, a Northland school pupil answered: 'A wingless bird found in New Zealand, and used for making boot polish'.[3]

On 3 September 1939 New Zealand joined Britain, Australia, France and India in declaring war on Germany. Two days later Prime Minister Michael Joseph Savage famously expressed this country's unswerving allegiance to Britain: 'Where she goes, we go. Where she stands, we stand.' At the time, Savage was recovering from an operation for colon cancer and spoke from his sickbed at his home in Wellington. He died just over six months later, on 27 March 1940, and at a ceremony in the vestibule of Parliament Buildings, the coffin of the much-loved and charismatic prime minister was draped with the New Zealand ensign and a kahu kiwi, the latter referred to as a 'kiwi mat'.[4]

Three months after the declaration of war it was announced that three small training vessels, not dissimilar to trawlers, were being specially built in Scotland for the Royal New Zealand Navy. Armed and equipped for minesweeping and anti-submarine duties, they would be named *Moa*, *Kiwi* and *Tui*. They were commissioned in 1941, and on 29 January 1943 the *Kiwi* distinguished itself when, with the assistance of her sister ship *Moa*, it rammed and wrecked a Japanese submarine in a fierce action near the Solomon Islands. The gallant HMNZS *Kiwi* served for another two decades, until 1963 when the Government Stores Board put it up for sale by tender, 'as is, where is', at the Naval Dockyard in Devonport. The ship was presumably sold for scrap.[5]

In October 1939, a month after the declaration of war, the cruiser HMS *Achilles*, serving with the New Zealand Division of the Royal Navy, was involved in the sinking of the German battleship *Graf Spee* in the Battle of the River Plate off the coast of South America. When the triumphant *Achilles* visited Auckland the following February, Captain Parry had a kahu kiwi placed around his shoulders at an official luncheon at Auckland Town Hall. Two months later, at another luncheon, Captain Parry was presented with a silver kiwi on a greenstone base.[6] In March

Watercolour by Official War Artist Russell Clarke of the battle between New Zealand minesweepers, HMNZS Kiwi and Moa, and the much larger Japanese submarine on 30 January 1943.

Archives New Zealand Te Rua Mahara o te Kāwanatanga

1941, when six vessels of the United States Pacific Fleet visited Auckland during a training cruise, another 'fine kiwi feather cloak' was presented to the commander, Captain Stone, at a civic welcome.[7] Around the same time a kahu kiwi was among the donations to be raffled to raise patriotic funds in Whangārei.[8]

The associations New Zealanders serving overseas had with the kiwi could begin before they'd left home. At Trentham Camp they were examined by members of the Dental Corps, whose badge featured representations of the British Crown and the bird.[9] Once overseas, there were memories of home; the hills of Greece, for example, reminded soldiers of Central Otago. Elsewhere they erected sign boards according to where their units had been drawn back in New Zealand, among them 'Kiwi Valley', 'Paekakariki Hill' and 'Khyber Pass'.[10]

An advance party of the First Echelon of the

Second New Zealand Expeditionary Force (2nd NZEF) arrived in Egypt on 7 January 1940, and were joined just over a month later by the main body, of 354 officers and 6175 other ranks. New Zealanders were in action by July, and for those convalescing there was the Kiwi Club in Helwan, Cairo, offering facilities for reading, writing, games and refreshment'.[11] During the Libyan Campaign the New Zealanders dug a tank trap, described as being 'of no small dimension' and known as the 'Kiwi Canal'.[12]

A remarkable and early example of kiwi ingenuity appeared in Cairo in early 1942 in the form of a yacht, 'home-made' by two members of the New Zealand Survey Battery. The 11-foot, 6-inch long craft was built on Z-class lines and could carry a crew of three. The total cost of construction was just £1, and the main material used was Oregon pine salvaged from motor truck cases and secured with straightened nails from the same source. The floorboards were of 'scrounged' cedar, while the sail was material rescued from a burnt tent and worked on by a tailor from among the Italian prisoners being held by the New Zealanders. Naturally the vessel was named *Kiwi*, with an image of the bird on its sail, and launched at a small beach on the Nile near the New Zealand camp at Maadi.[13]

In August 1942, the enemy acknowledged awareness of the symbolic kiwi when German planes dropped leaflets — referred to as 'bomphlets' — over the New Zealand lines in North Africa. Addressed to 'Men of New Zealand' they carried anti-English propaganda and claims of German success and, while not taken seriously, they became highly prized souvenirs. On the reverse side was what was described as 'an excellent reproduction' of

PAGE 118 & OPPOSITE: German propagandists attempted to discourage New Zealand soldiers from supporting Britain with this flier, which included a picture of a kiwi on one side.

EPH-B-WAR-WII-Propaganda-1942-01, Alexander Turnbull Library, Wellington

> **Men of New Zealand!**
>
> Have you ever asked yourselves why you are at war?
> For what ideals and for what motives have you left your native country to come and fight so far from home?
> Have you ever asked yourselves how many English soldiers there are in New Zealand ready to sacrifice themselves in the defence of your towns, your homes and your property?
> The English in New Zealand have one sole object; to take advantage of the natural wealth of your country and to make themselves rich at your expense.

a kiwi contemplating a landscape of flax bushes and cabbage trees.[14]

New Zealanders took their national game with them to the Middle East. As was pointed out back home under the headline 'Springbok and Kiwi', New Zealanders and South Africans were the 'keenest of rivals on the rugby field during times of peace, but were now close allies in time of war'.[15] In 1944, at Cairo's Alamein Club, a crowd of 16,000 watched the New Zealand Maadi Camp team beat the South African Armoured Division 13–4. According to a Cairo newspaper, 'Those Kiwi forwards were immense. They packed down like lions waiting for a meal of early Christian martyrs'.[16] For New Zealanders hankering for something quieter or more cultural in Cairo there was the Kiwi Camera Club, formed in late 1942. An exhibition marking its first anniversary consisted of more than a hundred photographs on a wide range of subjects, and over the same period the club's membership had grown from a nucleus of 9 to an astonishing 550.[17]

'Syncopation, Mirth and Melody'[18]

One of the best-known manifestations of the kiwi on active service was the so-named Concert Party. Carrying on the achievements of similar enterprises during the First World War, it had by early 1941 become officially part of the Entertainment Unit of the 2nd NZEF in the Middle East. The Kiwi Concert Party's talents were drawn from the troops and included vocalists and players of the piano-accordion, xylophone, violin and saxophone, while a feature that invariably drew 'prolonged

applause' was the female impersonators. The switch to comedy and farce was accomplished with 'ease', and performers were said to reveal 'a type of humour that is always in demand wherever the services gather'.[19] The Kiwi Concert Party followed the troops. It performed during air raids in Crete, where it had to leave behind all its costumes and instruments during the evacuation of New Zealand forces. But thanks to financial assistance from the National Patriotic Fund, it was soon fully re-equipped. Back in Egypt it worked through dust storms to erect the tent for its performances,[20] and later presented shows in Malta and Tripoli.[21]

In 1943 some 30 members of the Kiwi Concert Party, back home in New Zealand on furlough from the Middle East, undertook a national concert tour in aid of patriotic funds.[22] Calling themselves the Kiwis, they performed in all four main centres and other towns around the country, from Whangārei to Greymouth.

Performing in the Pacific

Mindful of the success that provisions made for the welfare of New Zealand troops in the Middle East, certain initiatives were now also brought to the Pacific. Following Japan's attacks on the US Fleet at Pearl Harbour on 7 December 1941, and then on the British in Malaya, a state of war existed with Japan, and New Zealand began planning its involvement in this new conflict. By the end of January 1943 New Zealand troops in New Caledonia were enjoying performances by a Pacific-based Kiwi Concert Party. The programme opened with a minstrel show and continued with sketches, stunts and solos of various kinds. One performer was billed as the 'mirth merchant', and a disclaimer on the printed

OPPOSITE, TOP:
New Zealand troops were treated to the first Italian performance of the Kiwi Concert Party during the Second World War on 12 May 1944 in the Volturno Valley, a mountainous area north of Naples.

DA-05773-F, Alexander Turnbull Library, Wellington

OPPOSITE, CENTRE:
New Zealand soldiers enjoy an outdoor performance of the Kiwi Concert Party at a military camp in Egypt during the Second World War.

PH-2020-1-1-21-7, Auckland Museum

OPPOSITE, BOTTOM:
Five members of the Kiwi Concert Party that performed throughout the Pacific during the Second World War. There were to be 12 permanent members – comedians, musicians and singers – who gave shows in New Caledonia, the New Hebrides, Guadalcanal, Vella Lavella and the Treasury Islands.

PA1-f-162-02-2, Alexander Turnbull Library, Wellington

programme explained that any reference to living persons was 'purely intentional'.[23]

The Kiwi Concert Party in the Pacific was in need of certain stage properties, and the National Patriotic Fund Board called on the public for donations. Among the items sought were tinsel glitter (gold, silver, and all colours), sheets of coloured cellophane, various shades of 'crepe hair', evening frocks and street dresses (worn but in good condition), evening shoes (size 6 or 7), grease paint and other make-up materials.[24] Until crepe hair became available, some kiwi ingenuity was called for and wigs were clipped from horses' tails.[25]

New Zealand forces in the Pacific also had their own newspaper, *The Kiwi*, published in Noumea and first appearing on 10 March 1943.[26] Further, early the following year New Zealanders had a newly built facility in Noumea, the Kiwi Club.[27] More kiwi ingenuity from the Pacific was on show in Dunedin, in the appropriately named Kiwi Gallery, in May 1944. It was a collection of artworks by soldiers based at Vella Lavella in the Solomon Islands, and made from material at hand, including metal from a wrecked Japanese bomber.[28]

Overall, the symbolic kiwi enjoyed increasing exposure during the war years, both at home and abroad. The local press frequently carried such references as 'Kiwi airmen' and 'Kiwi crew', while acts of bravery by New Zealanders in Italy were headlined 'Kiwi Courage'.[29] As mentioned previously, the kiwi had long been used to being depicted on badges and insignia associated with the armed forces, and an intrepid specimen even straddled a torpedo on the crest of the New Zealand Torpedo-Bomber Squadron.[30]

At home with the kiwi

Back in New Zealand, the unofficial emblematic bird continued to inspire businesses and new products. Recent additions included the Kiwi Cafeteria in Blenheim, the Kiwi Snack Bar in Gisborne, and Kiwi Furnishers in Hastings.

New products on the home market included Kiwi school exercise books, Kiwi Ale and Stout (16/9 per dozen in 1940) and, presumably capitalising on the interest in military matters, Kiwi water pistols ('popular and effective' and 4/6 each in 1945). For junior combatants who sought a more menacing weapon, 1947 saw the release of the Kiwi Potato Pistol (also 4/6). Meanwhile, certain shortages could be countered with another new product: 'Butter is Scarce — Safeguard yours with a Kiwi Butter Cooler'.[31]

The word 'kiwi' appeared on two war-related book titles: *Sing As We Go: The Story of the Kiwi Concert Party, 1941–43* by John E. Reed (1944); and *Kiwi Saga: Memoirs of a New Zealand Artilleryman* by Martyn Uren (1943).

The tradition of racehorses named Kiwi continued, with one taking part in the one-mile Wellington Guineas in October 1942, up against the intimidating-sounding Genghiz Khan and King Herod, and the aptly named War Effort.[32]

In 1944 the kiwi was described as 'the New Zealand emblem bird' (and 'the wingless wonder of the bird world'),[33] but despite its popular appeal and ubiquity there remained objections to its use. At an Auckland meeting in May 1940 it was suggested that because so little was being done in regard to such war-related issues as national service and the internment of enemy aliens, the national emblem should be changed from a kiwi to an ostrich, 'with its head buried in the sand'.[34] Similarly, even the Minister of Defence, the Hon. F. Jones, felt the choice of the flightless kiwi as a badge worn by New Zealand airmen was 'a poor one', for the men of the RNZAF had proved they were 'not only great flyers, but among the best airmen in the world.'[35]

The kiwi was now seen as a suitable symbol for promoting locally made goods. Back in 1931, the three finalists in a Manufacturers' Federation competition for a New Zealand trademark were the kiwi, fern and map of the country.[36] The intended design may not have eventuated, but at least the exercise showed a move away from the earlier emphasis of New Zealanders buying goods labelled 'Made in England' or 'British Made'. In 1943 another competition was held for an official patriotic symbol, with a first prize of £20. Around the same time a separate competition for a national slogan attracted 40,000 entries and was won by 'Well Made New Zealand'. The two concepts were then combined, to produce the silhouette of the kiwi surrounded by four stars of the Southern Cross, a couple of fern fronds and the slogan. The latter was copyrighted by the Manufacturers' Federation and was already in use by a number of local companies by January 1943.[37] The official campaign, using the symbol, did not survive the 1940s and while 'Well Made New Zealand' lived on, the slogan acquired a somewhat negative connotation.

The kiwi at large

There were still wildly varying reports as to the status of the kiwi population, which the *Manawatu Standard* described in 1940 as 'fast disappearing'.[38] The birds were 'still occasionally' spotted in Northland, where a person burning scrub caught sight of a particularly fine specimen half-dazed by the smoke and described it in ornithological terms as 'larger than a full-grown Orpington rooster'.[39] In 1940 a US tourist arrived in Auckland and announced his desire to obtain a live kiwi, for which he would pay £50. He was told there was 'nothing doing' and, further, that only about one-half of one per cent of New Zealanders 'had ever seen their national emblem in the flesh'.[40] On the other hand, a few months later a Javanese tourist had only been in this country for nine days when he spotted a kiwi, on the side of the road between Napier and Taupō. The car stopped and all passengers were able to closely examine the bird, which showed little fear of their approach.[41]

One kiwi luckier than many was discovered in July 1940 on the slopes of Mt Egmont by a ranger. It was injured, having apparently been caught in a possum trap, and the ranger took it home. He needed to amputate one of its big toes, but the bird made a 'splendid recovery'. Prior to being released

A kiwi was at the heart of the 'Well Made New Zealand' symbol, introduced by the Manufacturers' Federation in 1943 to promote locally made goods.

back into the bush it was presented at a meeting of the Egmont National Park Board in New Plymouth, and at least one member remarked that it was the first live kiwi he had ever seen.[42] At this time the kiwi population in the park was said to be growing rapidly and was now estimated at 100,[43] while the secretary of the Wellington Acclimatisation Society believed there was no danger of the kiwi becoming extinct from what he had seen of them along the Milford Track.[44]

Also, 1940 saw recognition of the kiwi's conservation role in the Tararua Ranges where, following the disappearance of native birds, noxious insects were attacking the young trees. The kiwi and weka were identified as probably doing most to conserve the forest by dealing with those insects, with the kiwi's long beak able to find pests and larvae living beneath the soil.[45]

According to Mr E.G. Turbott, zoologist and later director at the Auckland War Memorial Museum (1964–79), the kiwi was much more common in our native bush than most New Zealanders realised. This was due to its adaptability, which enabled it to exist under conditions that would have been foreign to its ancestors.[46] Another institution mindful of the kiwi was New York's Bronx Zoo, which announced its desire to acquire a specimen to add to its collection of rare animals. Aside from the fact that such collecting only added to the rarity of already endangered species, the Forest and Bird Protection Society of New Zealand expressed its hope that such a bird would not be made available for the zoo, one reason being that its life under unnatural conditions overseas 'would not be happy'.[47]

In 1942 dogs owned by deer cullers were accused of killing and threatening the survival of kiwi in Arthur's Pass National Park.[48] Some three years later the dog was singled out as the kiwi's worst enemy in open country, even though with its strong kick the bird was said to be 'more than a match for the weasel'.[49] Later that year, a survey was carried out by possum trappers, of vermin existing in native bush and caught in traps in the Grey District. Over the period of investigation the animals caught were: 58 stoats, 88 weasels, 32 cats, 992 rats, two hedgehogs, two dogs, 37 hares — and one kiwi.[50] That only one kiwi was caught can be considered good news, however the number of other animals that either threatened it directly or interfered with its habitat continued to be a major concern.

Back to the Front: The kiwi during the Second World War

Acclimatisation history may have been made at Hawke's Bay Game Park in Greenmeadows in September 1945 when a kiwi chick was hatched, allegedly the first in captivity in New Zealand.[51] The chick emerged fully fledged, weighing only ¾ lb, and was hatched by the male kiwi, which was still sitting on a second egg.[52] The news revived the claim that the first kiwi to be hatched in captivity was in fact the bird midwifed in Kawakawa by postmaster Mr G. Wilson in 1929, with a little help from his oven.[53] At ten days old the new arrival at Greenmeadows was described as a 'lusty active little bird about six inches high with an insatiable appetite for worms.'[54] In due course the second kiwi chick was hatched out, also by the male, which remained in charge.[55] The female seemed 'resigned' to her partner assuming responsibility for rearing their two youngsters, and remained 'aloof and disinterested for some weeks.' By night the two offspring were engaged in an 'eternal quest for worms', and spent the day nestled in the male's plumage.[56] Despite much care and attention, the second kiwi chick died at the age of just four months, suffering from paralysis of the neck.[57]

After the war

In early 1942 a hostel for New Zealand servicemen, Kiwi House, opened in London. Located near Albert Hall and formerly known as Rutland Hotel, it offered 35 beds and operated until December 1945 when there was a reduction in the number of New Zealanders needing accommodation.[58] Also in London, late 1944 saw the opening of the Fernleaf Club to cater for New Zealand servicemen, in particular liberated ex-prisoners of war arriving from Europe.[59] With the end of hostilities, that city anticipated a major influx of New Zealanders on leave and ex-prisoners from Europe. According to the *Auckland Star*, 'the Kiwi's reputation as a fighting soldier has long preceded him to London and his reputation as a decent, likeable, well-behaved fellow has been firmly established by the New Zealanders whom London has already met'. As a result, it was suggested that the city would take this 'invasion' both 'bloodlessly and calmly'.[60]

With the surrender of Germany on 7 May 1945 and the ending of offensive action against Japan on 15 August, New Zealanders serving overseas could look forward to returning home. This was cause for celebration, and hence a Kiwi Peace Ball at Te Karaka in Gisborne, and a Kiwi Victory Ball in Christchurch. But there could be a downside to such festivities; 'Disgusted Kiwi' complained to a Wellington newspaper about young people at the VJ (Victory over Japan) celebrations who were 'openly abandoning themselves to drunkenness'.[61] The kiwi played a prominent part in peacetime developments; in August 1944 citizens could enjoy a flutter on a forerunner of the Golden Kiwi, the 'Lucky Kiwi £5000 Art Union', promoted with a kiwi wearing a lemon squeezer hat and holding a bag labelled '1st prize £2000'. And the following year, with peace secured, New Zealanders could buy a ticket in the RSA Kiwi Victory Art Union.

The challenge of settling and providing employment for returned servicemen was a concern that the 2nd New Zealand Expeditionary Force Association claimed had spread 'through the four corners of "Kiwi" land'.[62] Initiative was shown by returned men; in late 1944 the *Auckland Star* noted that three young 'Kiwi' architects, home from the Middle East, had formed a company to design new homes,[63] while three others had got together and established the Kiwi Carrying Company.[64] A 'novel method of rehabilitation' was also adopted by some 20 ex-members of the Kiwi Concert Party who, after being discharged from the army formed a professional travelling variety company known as The Kiwis. Consisting of veterans who had served in the Mediterranean and North African campaigns, it was a cooperative venture with all members sharing in the profits. By late November 1945, when they were about to perform in Ashburton, the Kiwis had already visited 47 towns from Kaikohe to Invercargill.[65]

Among the opportunities the New Zealand public had to assist returned serviceman was a 'Kiwi Street Day' appeal in January 1945.[66] Later that year in Timaru it was decided that because there was an Anzac Square to 'honour the men of the Great War' there should now be a suitable honour for those who had served in the recent war. As a result, the street that was to be designated Kinsman Crescent was changed to Kiwi Drive.[67] Similarly, in 1946 Hamilton selected Kiwi Crescent for a new street name, it being 'synonymous with the troops of this war' and also in keeping with an existing Anzac Street.[68]

An alternative crop

While the years of the Second World War caused much disruption to the social life and economy of New Zealand, one positive horticultural development was progress in the planting and acceptance of what was still known as the Chinese gooseberry. In 1940 the New Zealand government imposed a ban in importing fruit, thereby prompting citizens to seek alternatives. During winter there were only a few apples available, but the Chinese gooseberry began attracting more interest, especially as it was recommended for its high vitamin C content. Following the war, returned servicemen who had gone into orcharding found 'it was an uphill struggle'. The price outlook for lemons, a popular crop in Te Puke at this time, was discouraging and so growers needed to diversify. As a result, the 1940s and early 1950s saw a steady expansion in the local market for the fruit yet-to-be-named kiwifruit.

Singing the Blues

As with the previous conflict, the Second World War offered New Zealanders an opportunity to see other parts of the world, albeit hardly under ideal conditions. But having seen it, they may have preferred what they knew back home, a sentiment expressed in a song composed by a New Zealand prisoner of war in Austria.

Sapper C.F. (Gus) Rayner, confined to Stalag XVIIIA, wrote to his parents in Auckland of a theatrical show put on by the prisoners, describing it as a 'Comedy in Low Latitudes' telling the story of three sailors whose ship went to New Zealand. Rayner explained that he wrote the lyrics and music for a number, *Kiwi Blues*, which also 'got a good reception'. By 1945 the sheet music for *Kiwi Blues* (copyrighted in 1944 and intended to be played 'not too fast') was available in shops for 2/-, along with another popular melody of the day, *Lili Marlene*.[69]

The opening four lines of *Kiwi Blues*, the lament of a homesick New Zealand soldier, are:

> *I've got the Kiwi blues,*
> *I've seen all I want to see,*
> *And the further I go, the better I know,*
> *That the islands of New Zealand will still do me.*

The sheet music for *Kiwi Blues*, composed by Sapper C.F. (Gus) Rayner in a German prisoner of war camp, and sold in the music stores of New Zealand by 1945.

10

Aftermath: The post–Second World War kiwi

With the return home of Kiwi servicemen, there were discussions with their compatriots from the previous war as to the distinction between 'Diggers' and 'Kiwis'. At the Ruāwai branch of the Northern Wairoa RSA it was suggested that the 'Kiwis' of the 2nd NZEF should be known as 'Diggers', because they had 'upheld the reputation' of the 1st NZEF. However, it was pointed out that members of the 2nd NZEF were originally known as Diggers, but when they arrived in Egypt they found that Australian troops were also referred to as Diggers, so the New Zealanders adopted the other name.[1]

At a 1946 Anzac Day ceremony in Ōpōtiki, the officiating minister spoke of the spirit of Anzac, noting that it belonged neither to 'Digger' or 'Kiwi' but was 'inherent to the New Zealand people'.[2] Unsurprisingly, the veterans of the recent war well outnumbered those of the previous one; in 1947, for example, the financial members of the Gisborne RSA comprised 2493 Kiwis and 987 Diggers.[3] It was agreed there needed to be more co-operation between the two and, in April 1948, Te Awamutu RSA saw the appointment of a Kiwi to the committee as 'an opportunity for a younger man to gain experience in the higher offices of the

Kiwi

New Zealand 'Diggers', forerunners of 'Kiwis', fit belts of cartridges to machine guns, near Bus-lès-Artois, northern France, May 1918.

1/2-013194-G, Alexander Turnbull Library, Wellington

PAGE 134: Colourful representations of kiwi began to be produced from a wide array of materials including glass, brass and plastic.

Association.'[4] With the passage of time, by mid-1950 it was anticipated that it wouldn't be long before Kiwis outnumbered Diggers in the RSAs of New Zealand.[5]

Among the challenges now facing the country was the provision of housing for returned servicemen. Low-interest (3 per cent) loans were made available through the State Advances Corporation, while in 1943 the Housing Construction Department became a branch of the newly constituted Ministry of Works, thereby facilitating the development of State housing. The resettlement programme also faced a shortage of building materials, which may explain a 1946 'Wanted to Rent' advertisement in a Gisborne newspaper: 'Browned-off Kiwi requires Self-contained Flat for himself and wife.'[6]

As for employment, the immediate post-war period saw a proliferation of new businesses trading on the kiwi. Among them were the Kiwi Mineral Stock Food Company and Kiwi Borer Exterminating Company (both in Gisborne), Kiwi Coal and Transport Company (Dunedin), Kiwi Construction Company (Westport), Kiwi Concrete Products (Gore), Kiwi Delicatessen (Waihi) and Kiwi Tyre Surgery (Ōpōtiki). Some more imaginative entrepreneurs took to alliteration and a fascination for the letter 'K', resulting in such enterprises as the Kiwi Dry Kleaning Company (Wanganui), Bell's Kiwi Kake Kitchen (Whakatāne) and Kiwi Karriers (Christchurch). In a similar vein, in early 1946 the local RSA organised a Kiwi Kan Kan Dance (with a Kiwi supper) at Edgecumbe Hall in the eastern Bay of Plenty.

The bird itself

1948 was a landmark year for ornithology in New Zealand with the rediscovery of the takahē, previously believed extinct. Two living specimens were found in a remote alpine valley in Fiordland by Southland doctor Geoffrey Orbell. That event appears to have raised the hopes for another species, for while the Director of the Dominion Museum, Dr R.A. Falla, believed there was little doubt that the huia had 'gone' he was not prepared to reject the possibility of its 'reincarnation'. At the same time, Falla identified the kiwi as New Zealand's 'most outstanding bird' and one that would 'probably remain for ever a puzzle to biologists', also noting: 'No New Zealand bird is less known, despite the fact that it is our national emblem.'[7]

Two specimens of our 'most outstanding bird' were in the news after being injured by possum traps. The first, caught on the slopes of Taranaki (then Mt Egmont), needed the amputation of a leg. When fitted with a bamboo replacement limb it became known as 'Peg-Leg Pete', inspired by a Walt Disney pirate. It was subsequently sent to Greenmeadows Game Park, but died in May 1949.[8] The second victim of a possum trap was from the Ōpōtiki district, and after having a leg amputated joined Auckland Zoo. Given the more conventional name of David, it was 'elevated to the ranks of war wounded' when the Servicemen's Re-establishment League agreed to make him an artificial limb. The zoo needed to establish its own worm farm to keep up with the bird's voracious appetite for about four cups of the wriggling invertebrates a day. Aged about one year, David was reportedly 'the only kiwi in any zoo in any part of the world', but unfortunately did not live long in his new home, dying in December 1949.[9]

Kiwi and their eggs were still in demand. In mid-1946 the Minister of Internal Affairs refused to allow Auckland City Council to send an egg to Australia in exchange for a duck-billed platypus.[10] The following year a shipment of natural history specimens from the United States passed through Auckland en route to Melbourne, in exchange for three of Australia's egg-laying aquatic mammals. This prompted the suggestion that New Zealand would miss out on obtaining the rare animals of other countries if it did not lift its restrictions on the export of kiwi, kiwi eggs and other rare forms of New Zealand life.[11] The ban had also been invoked following the suggestion that a live kiwi be sent to British prime minister Winston Churchill, presumably in recognition of his leadership during the recent war. Perhaps the idea was that the bird could grace the grounds of Blenheim Palace near Oxford, Churchill's birthplace. Unsurprisingly the Minister of Internal Affairs refused permission, reportedly because to do so would establish a precedent 'which would lead to all sorts of worries'.[12]

But while the dispatch overseas of either the bird or its eggs was prohibited, the kiwi continued to be associated with rare and special gifts. In 1947 the combined branches of the Royal Empire Society of New Zealand presented Princess Elizabeth with a jardinière decorated with elements of this country's flora and birdlife and a lid surmounted by a kiwi.[13] The following year, when the princess married the Duke of Edinburgh, the royal couple's wedding present from the Royal New Zealand Navy was a dinghy that they decided to name *Kiwi*. The 14-foot vessel was stored at the Sea Training Establishment at Southampton, and used for racing.[14]

'Kiwi' was now frequently used in connection with New Zealand sports teams abroad, and when the 2nd NZEF rugby team played in Glasgow in 1946 it was presented with a silver bowl with the city crest on one side and a kiwi on the other. In addition, each member of the team received a parcel containing two packets of cigarettes and a book of poems by Robert (Robbie) Burns. During this tour the team also attended a function at Buckingham House, inspiring the headline back home: 'Kiwi Team Meets King'.[15]

Kiwi over the Tasman

Surely the most popular — and successful — manifestation of the overseas kiwi in the post-war period was the eponymous and peripatetic concert party. After finishing its New Zealand tour in mid-February 1946, 40 members of the Kiwi Concert Party left for Australia, anticipating they would be there for a year and then spend a similar period in Britain.[16] They began in Melbourne, where they expected to play for about six weeks, but ten months later they were still going and enjoying crowded houses.[17] In April 1948 the troupe was described in the Christchurch *Press* as 'the rage of Melbourne'. Its run in that city had been 'phenomenal' and it was now into its second year, performing its third show.[18] By June it was estimated that more than 500,000 people had now seen them at the Comedy Theatre, at a time when Melbourne had a population of little more than one million. The concert party had created a record in Australia with more than 600 performances in an unbroken period of 18 months, and the Kiwis claimed they were 'nowhere near the end of their run.' Coincidentally, the previous record was also held by a company of New Zealand ex-servicemen — Pat Hanna's 'Diggers', who in 1924–25 played for 400 nights at the Cremorne Theatre, Brisbane.[19]

Finally, in early January 1949, the Kiwi Concert Party ended their phenomenal 114-week run in Melbourne, breaking all previous records for the length of season. In all they played 859 performances of five separate revues, to an estimated audience of over 800,000.[20] As reported in the *Otago Daily Times*: 'Nobody in the concert party knows why the show has been so successful in Australia, but they suggest that the secrets are in the non-stop variety style and the fact that there is something there to please everyone.'[21] On reflection, and quite apart from the sheer inventiveness and originality of the performers, perhaps the extraordinary success of the Kiwi Concert Party and the Diggers before them had much to do with the cross-Tasman bonds and common outlook (and sense of humour) forged during the two previous wars.

In May 1949, seven months before becoming Prime Minister of New Zealand, National Party politician Sidney Holland visited Australia and commented that no one was doing a better job of publicising his country than the Kiwi Concert Party, which was by that time playing to capacity houses in Sydney.[22] By September 1949 the Kiwis were in their thirty-fifth week in Sydney, still enjoying full houses, and since their Australian debut in April 1946 had performed in front of some 1,750,000 people.[23]

Helping out

The war in Europe ended in May 1945, but Britain would experience food shortages and restrictions for another nine years. The rationing of confectionery finally ended on 4 February 1953, and sugar in September, while the rationing of meat and all other items of food ended on 4 July 1954. Among New Zealand's contributions was a 'Kiwi Ball' (tickets 5/-), held in Gisborne in August 1947, to raise money for the RSA's Parcels for Britain Fund.[24]

The end of the war itself was followed by political tension between the United States and the Soviet Union and their respective allies, heralding the Cold War. The first major challenge posed by this international stand-off was the Berlin Airlift, which lasted for 15 months in 1948 and 1949, and was the effort undertaken by the United States, Great Britain and France to deliver essential supplies to their sectors in West Berlin, after the Soviet Union had blocked land access. New Zealanders assisted and in late 1949, in recognition of their contribution, the Royal Air Force (RAF) presented the Royal New Zealand Air Force (RNZAF) with a wooden shield depicting a kiwi with a coal scuttle in its beak. The New Zealand group had flown 420 round trips to Berlin's Tempelhof Airport, carrying 1400 tons of freight of which 700 tons (635 metric tons) was coal.[25]

Looking at ourselves

If soldiers of the 2nd New Zealand Expeditionary Force considered themselves Kiwis, they viewed their English comrades as Tommies. A New Zealander in Britain commented that the 'average Tommy' regarded the Kiwis as 'the salt of the earth and New Zealand itself as a minor paradise'.[26] The qualities of the New Zealand soldier were also commented on in 1947, on the fifth anniversary of the Battle of El Alamein. The latter was described as an event that should be regarded 'for all time as a landmark in New Zealand history' and one in which 'the fighting qualities of the Kiwi soldier were tested to the full'.[27]

The latter half of the 1940s saw the appearance of several war-related books with 'Kiwi' featuring prominently in the title. Perhaps the first of these was *Kalimera Kiwi: To Olympus with the New Zealand Engineers* by Chas. M. Wheeler (A.H. & A.W. Reed, Wellington, 1946), described as 'the informal recollections of one who was there'. It was also 'personal in style and vivid in impressions' and 'a useful supplement to official accounts on the subject'. The author was said to display 'the typical Kiwi attitude to work, war, and play, and cherishes a sense of humour more than a sense of dignity'.[28] This book was closely followed by *Chase Me a Kiwi: A Portrait of New Zealand* by Aldwyn Abberley (published in England in 1946). Describing itself as 'The Guide for Intending Settlers', it appears to have been aimed at residents of Britain who now wished to become Kiwis. Another book, *Kiwis on Tour in Egypt and Italy* by A.S. Helm (Whitcombe and Tombs, Christchurch, 1947), was described as likely to appeal to readers interested in 'travel, art, music, and the strange customs of far-off people'. The author had been in charge of what was described as the 'sight-seeing organisation' of the 2nd New Zealand Expeditionary Force, for the entertainment of soldiers on leave, so enjoyed 'unique opportunities' to visit such historical cities as Rome.[29]

Souvenir kiwi

As previously noted, in the late 1800s New Zealand was often referred to as 'Maoriland', particularly by the Australian press. At home, the alternative name evoked the early days of European settlement, as in the title of a lecture 'Memories of Maoriland, or Experiences in the Olden Times', given in 1899

OPPOSITE: This image of the kiwi, composed entirely of fruit and vegetables and with rhubarb stalks for its beak and legs, was issued by the New Zealand Department of Health in the period 1945–50. It was frequently on display in school dental clinics of the time.

at Devonport by William Webster of Kohukohu, Hokianga.[30] But in 1927, following discussions as to whether this country's name should be changed, it was noted that while it was variously referred to as Maoriland or Kiwiland, it would 'always remain good old New Zealand'.[31]

The country's name aside, the worlds of Māori and the kiwi — arguably two of New Zealand's most distinctive features — would become mainstays of the local souvenir industry, inspiring mementos for a growing tourist trade. Decorative elements of Māori culture and representations of the kiwi were often combined, although the bird also went it alone. As it became more embedded in the public consciousness, its profile raised by an increasing number of commercial and sporting applications, the kiwi was rendered in a wide range of materials and with varying degrees of anatomical correctness. Many of these manifestations of the kiwi were no doubt destined to gather dust on mantelpieces and sideboards, both at home and abroad.

11

Mid-century: The 1950s kiwi

Shortly after their involvement in the Berlin Airlift, New Zealanders were engaged in a much more serious phase of the Cold War. The invasion by the People's Republic of Korea of its southern neighbour on 25 June 1950 marked the beginning of the Korean War. New Zealand was quick to answer the United Nations Security Council's call for assistance for South Korea, and in late 1950 sent the 1056-man Kayforce. It comprised the 16th Field Regiment, which was headquartered near the Imjin River on 'Flagstaff Hill', also known as 'Kiwi Hill' and distinguished by a large image of a kiwi, in emulation of that created above Sling Camp 32 years earlier.

The Korean kiwi was initiated by Regimental Sergeant Major J. Dickinson of Auckland, who called in Regimental Survey Officer Second Lieutenant J. Hawkins of Rotorua. Using the kiwi on the tin of boot polish as his only guide, he surveyed a diamond shape with 50-foot (15 m) sides, and marked out the outline of the bird with 150 pegs. New Zealand gunners then dug out the kiwi to a depth of six inches (15 cm) and, after a considerable search, suitable stones — white for the kiwi and black for the background — were sourced from a nearby quarry. The sign was intended as 'a constant reminder to the Korean people that

Kiwi

The large kiwi symbol constructed on Flagstaff Hill, near the Imjin River in South Korea by members of New Zealand's 16th Field Regiment, which was headquartered there from late 1952 until July 1953.

1/2-121222-F, Alexander Turnbull Library, Wellington

PAGE 144: The half-tonne, revolving fibreglass kiwi installed above the Kiwi Bacon Company factory in Kingsland, Auckland around 1960 remained there until it was removed in the 1980s.

1726-010, Auckland Libraries Heritage Collections

New Zealand troops had served in their country', and when the 16th Field Regiment completed their withdrawal in late November 1954, following the signing of an armistice on 27 July 1953, they left behind what is believed to be the largest and most famous of the national emblems produced in the Commonwealth Division area. The kiwi's protection had been 'a matter of honour', as rival units frequently carried out 'alterations'. On one occasion it was modified overnight to resemble a kangaroo, and despite their protestations of innocence a party of Australian mortarmen were ordered to repair the damage.[1] Reinforcing the kiwi connection in Korea, in mid-1952 a New Zealand crew manning a British Centurion tank reportedly emblazoned the side of their vehicle with a kiwi, along with the name 'Ngapuhi'.[2]

Peter Fraser, the prime minister who succeeded Michael Savage in April 1940 and guided New Zealand through the years of the Second World War, died in 1950. Following the tradition, while his casket lay in St John's Presbyterian Church in Wellington, it was draped with a New Zealand ensign and a kahu kiwi.[3] Personal associations forged during that war were also recognised in 1952, when Major General Sir Howard Kippenberger and Captain C.H. Upham represented New Zealand at memorial observances in Athens. They took kiwi and tiki badges and pennants to present to key people in Greece who had assisted New Zealanders during the German occupation of that country.[4]

'The Queer, Eccentric Bird'

In early 1950 the warden of Tongariro National Park reported there were 'hundreds' of pigeons, tūī, bellbirds, parakeets and kiwi in the Urewera,[5] and Dr Falla, of the Dominion Museum, stated that the kiwi was in no danger of dying out. Whereas the population had vanished almost entirely from Wellington province, 'plenty' still remained in Northland, Taranaki, the 'back country' of the East Coast, Marlborough, Westland and Stewart Island (Rakiura).[6] On another occasion Falla observed: 'By a strange quirk of human nature New Zealanders have accepted the queer, eccentric, degenerate kiwi as a national emblem'.[7]

Getting caught in possum traps continued to be an occupational hazard for kiwi, and one victim known for obvious reasons as 'One Foot', lived with the permission of the Department of Internal Affairs on a poultry farm near Gisborne. The bird wouldn't touch diced or minced meat, but enjoyed half a pound of steak a day, necessarily cut into strips to resemble worms.[8] News of fatalities due to traps or on the road was not uncommon, but one late 1950 headline, 'Kiwi Dies', did not in fact concern the bird. Instead, it related to the ending of the publication of the *Kiwi*, official magazine of the 2nd New Zealand Expeditionary Force Association.[9]

The Department of Internal Affairs now allowed those kiwi suffering from a disability to be kept in captivity. In early 1956 another victim of a possum trap, also from Gisborne, entered a private zoo in Christchurch and on the flight south was fed on ox heart soaked in fish oil. Known as Sandy, the bird died later that year, and in March 1957 was replaced by another named Son.[10] Up north, the first-ever kiwi egg laid at Auckland Zoo appeared in September 1960, and later that year it had a kiwi population of four.[11]

The regulations regarding the exporting of live kiwi were apparently relaxed, and in the early 1950s two birds were sent to new homes overseas. In advance of this a kiwi made its first appearance on television, in Britain in 1952, as 'Kikki the Kiwi' in the children's programme 'Muffin the Mule'.[12] Back in the real world of natural history, an 11-month-old kiwi, originally from Whangārei, was sent to London Zoo as a Coronation gift. It flew on a Pan American clipper, stopping overnight at Nadi, Fiji, before going via Honolulu and San Francisco to New York, existing en route on a diet of New Zealand worms.[13] The bird's arrival at the zoo in September 1953 set keepers a challenge that they solved by offering gardeners employed in Regent's Park 2/6 for every flower pot full of worms. At first referred to as Peter, and later as Ngāpuhi, a name bestowed by the children of Auckland, it was known 'affectionately' to London Zoo staff as 'Percy'. He was said to be the 'first non-footballing kiwi' seen in Britain since 1934 when the zoo's previous specimen died. The new bird was soon thriving and had been bedded down in a straw-lined box in the Ostrich House.[14] Ngāpuhi attracted 'hundreds of visitors', even meeting the All Blacks during their tour of Britain,[15] and was hailed the most valuable bird in London's collection, worth £500. But by mid-1955 Ngāpuhi was 'off colour', suffering from what turned out to be a heart complaint, necessitating a course of pills. Shortly afterwards the bird died, whereupon it was to be taxidermied and sent to the British Museum.[16]

In 1958 another kiwi was sent from Auckland Zoo to London's Regent's Park Zoo, and had the distinction of being the first to fly over the North Pole. The plan was that it would travel in the honeymoon suite of Canadian Pacific Airlines DC-6B to Vancouver, where it would transfer to a Britannia flight. Unfortunately Britannias were not allowed to carry animals, so the kiwi had an unscheduled wait in Vancouver for the next DC-6B flight to London.[17] After arriving safely at London Zoo it was given the name 'Busby', on account of its habit of sleeping with its head and beak hidden in its plumage and thereby looking like a 'furry hat'. It also turned out that, pound for pound, Busby was the most expensive resident to feed at London Zoo. His diet of worms cost £1 per day, an expense that 'staggered' the curator of Wellington Zoo. A popular attraction known for his amusing antics, Busby died in 1961, reportedly of old age.[18]

The United States also gained a kiwi when in November 1954

🥝 Overdoing the kiwi?

The kiwi continued to be a popular choice for gift giving, although not without some controversy. A silver bird was the centrepiece of an inkstand mounted on polished greenstone, presented by the city of Christchurch to Queen Elizabeth, the Queen Mother, during her visit to New Zealand in early February 1958.[19] Two years later, New Zealand's proposed wedding present, of two silver-gilt kiwi, to Princess Margaret and Antony Armstrong-Jones was the subject of much debate. On seeing the proposed design, James Turkington, President of the Auckland Society of Arts, felt that the kiwi had been 'done to death', as had the silver fern and boxes inlaid with New Zealand woods. Another comment was that the kiwi should be allowed to live in its natural surroundings and 'not be reproduced in silver', and that a New Zealand landscape painted by a leading artist would have been a more suitable gift.[20]

Auckland City Council decided to donate one of Auckland Zoo's six birds to San Diego Zoo. The first kiwi to go to America, it travelled in a customised crate and was sent as 'an ambassador for New Zealand'.[21] In addition to these live exports, a taxidermied specimen was sent to Malaya in late 1957. New Zealand had become involved in the so-called Malayan Emergency, which had arisen when the Malayan Communist Party attempted to overthrow the country's British colonial administration. The newly formed 1st Battalion New Zealand Regiment was dispatched, taking as its mascot a kiwi made available by the Dominion Museum, and wearing a badge with a kiwi as its centrepiece.[22]

The end of the show

In late 1949 the Kiwi Concert Company completed its Australian tour with shows in Wollongong, Newcastle, Brisbane, Adelaide and, finally, Toowoomba. Having finished an 'extraordinary' record season, lasting

Programme for the 1950 New Zealand tour by The Kiwis Revue Company, who had performed in the Middle East during the war.

EPH-A-VARIETY-1950-01-cover, Alexander Turnbull Library, Wellington

over four years, they now made plans for a final tour of New Zealand, after which, according to one member, they will 'all go back to work'. Even so, there were still plans for another season in Australia and then tours of Canada, South Africa and possibly England.[23] The Kiwi's eight-year run finally came to an end and a month later, in February 1954, members of the party were spread around the country, while some had already left for overseas.[24]

Another kiwi-related entertainment in the early 1950s was the invention of a local dance, said to combine the rhythmic spirit of haka with the informality of the Canadian square dance and England's Lambeth Walk. Devised by members of the New Zealand Council of Ballroom Dancing, it was dubbed the 'Kiwi Polonaise', and hopes were expressed that on her forthcoming visit the queen might give it a whirl.[25]

The colloquial kiwi

The 1950s saw a rising recognition of national habits, referred to as 'Kiwi' attitudes or characteristics, such as the expressions 'She's right, mate', 'take it or leave it — don't complain' and 'She'll do'. It was also noted that 'laconic humour … characterises the Kiwi', and there was concern for the 'Kiwi' accent, as expressed in a letter to the Christchurch *Press* by 'Well Spoke, Noo Zillan'.[26]

There was now what might be identified as a forerunner to the 'Give 'em a taste of Kiwi' call at sporting events in the 1980s — the less aggressive 'Come on Kiwi', heard at Wimbledon in 1956, when Lynne Luxton of Christchurch was up against the top English player.[27] In a similar vein, when New Zealander Valerie Young mounted the rostrum to receive her gold medal for the shot put at the 1958 British Empire and Commonwealth Games in Cardiff, Wales, a shout went up around the ground: 'Good on you, Kiwi!'.[28]

From the early 1950s the kiwi began to grace the mantelpieces and sideboards of New Zealand homes in the form of a vase produced by Crown Lynn Potteries of Auckland. The bird, with its beak embedded in the ground probing for worms, was set against a hollowed tree stump that served as a handy receptacle for flowers.

The kiwi continued to infiltrate all aspects of New Zealand life. It appeared in book titles, such as Temple Sutherland's story of his leaving Scotland to live in New Zealand, *Green Kiwi* (published initially in London in 1956) and the story of boxing in this country, *Kiwis with Gloves On* by Brian O'Brien (A.H. & A.W. Reed, Wellington, 1960). Among the bird's appearances offshore, in 1951 the nation's Tourist and Publicity Department issued its overseas offices and travel agencies with a colourful baggage sticker bearing an image of the kiwi and the message 'Visitor to New Zealand',[29] then in 1959 a new 15,000-ton tanker, named *British Kiwi* (named

In the early 1950s Crown Lynn Potteries of Auckland began producing this popular kiwi vase, available in a wide range of colours. Kiwi also appeared in a diversity of other materials, including brass and painted plaster. The small glass specimens may have been made by Hokitika Glass in the 1970s.

Mid-century: The 1950s kiwi

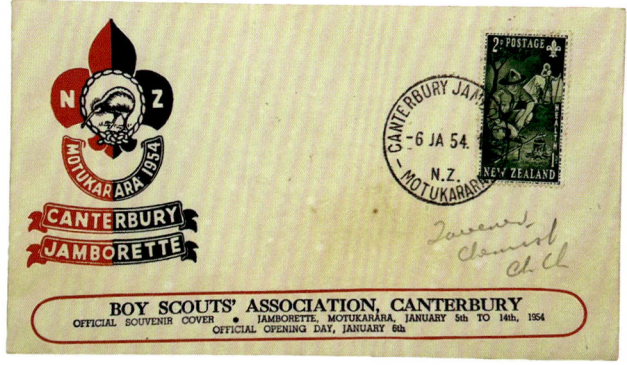

ABOVE: The cover of *Sing As We Go: The Story of the Kiwi Concert Party 1941-43* by John E. Reed, published in 1944.

RIGHT: The kiwi logo dominates on this envelope, printed to mark the 1954 Canterbury Boy Scouts Jamborette at Motukarara. (Postage is paid for by the previous year's Boy Scout Health Stamp.)

for British Petroleum), was launched in Britain.[30]

But surely one of the more unusual applications of the bird's name was by the Kiwi Lost Chord Club, formed in Auckland in late 1956 for persons who had undergone operations for the removal of the larynx.[31] Equally unlikely was the news in 1960 that the United States was planning to develop a nuclear-powered rocket, named Kiwi-A3, following earlier tests in Nevada, Texas.[32]

With talk of the adoption of decimal currency (which appeared in 1967), alternative suggestions for the name of the New Zealand dollar were zeal, tūī, fern and, of course, kiwi.[33] There was even the suggestion in 1958 that the kiwi would be preferable to the silver fern as an emblem worn by New Zealand athletes.[34] And when the nation's leading ploughman left for the world ploughing championships in Rome in 1960, he was presented with a pāua shell kiwi badge by Prime Minister Walter Nash.[35]

Another champion bird was the imitation kiwi affixed to the mast of the freighter *Crusader* after it made a record-breaking 11-and-a-half day voyage from New Zealand to Japan in 1958. Usually, a rooster was displayed to indicate a record had been achieved.[36] The kiwi

CLOCKWISE FROM TOP: An unlikely combination: 'Kiwi' was used as the name for a chimpanzee, 1968.

Souvenir shot glass.

The Ulster Society of Auckland was instituted in 1930, and a pair of kiwi appear on the programme for its 1970 conference.

The logo of the Hamilton-based company Kiwi Packaging was a stylised kiwi.

A kiwi as a petrol pump attendant on a blotter advertising Shell, from the 1950s.

A kiwi for Easter.

also appeared on another postage stamp, marking the Boy Scouts Association's Pan-Pacific Jamboree, held at Motukarara in Central Canterbury during December 1958 and the following January.

A rampant grower

By the 1950s the Chinese gooseberry was well established in New Zealand, recognised as 'a rampant grower and a very hungry feeder'. It could also have practical applications, as at the Awapuni racecourse in Palmerston North, where it was grown to provide 'living car-shelters'.[37] The first export shipment of Chinese gooseberry — ten 20 lb trays, grown in Te Puke — was made to London in 1952, through the New Zealand Fruitgrowers' Federation. The fruit accompanied a refrigerated consignment of lemons and tamarillos, and after a five week journey arrived in good order and created much interest.[38] Later that same year a shipment to Sydney also received a favourable reception, and by the end of the decade some 30 tons were being exported each year to England and Australia.[39] At the same time, vines of the plant were being exported in increasing numbers,[40] and one back in New Zealand appears to have achieved heritage status. In 1959, changes were made to the line of a fence associated with a road and rail development in Hamilton to save a 20-year-old Chinese gooseberry vine.[41]

During the 1950s New Zealand also began exporting the fruit to the United States. However there were problems with the name Chinese gooseberry, and so an alternative was needed. Auckland-based produce company Turners & Growers suggested 'Melonettes', but that was unsuitable because both berries and melons were subject to high import tariffs. The problem was solved in June 1959 when Jack Turner himself suggested 'kiwifruit', which was adopted.[42] But not everyone thought it was a great idea. No doubt mindful of the country's origins of Kiwi boot polish, the Australian news magazine *Bulletin* suggested kiwifruit sounded like something 'you might rub on your shoes' or, even less complimentary, 'something rolling unpleasantly from beneath the tail feathers of that unlikely bird.'[43]

The growth of the Chinese gooseberry sector was such that by 1967 New Zealand was exporting more than 400 tons per year — produced by about 130 acres (more than 50 hectares) under cultivation — to markets in Australia, Britain and the United States, while young vines were also being exported to California.⁴⁴ A spokesman for a party of nurserymen who visited California at that time did not think the sale of New Zealand plants would damage the US market for the exported fruit. In fact, exports that year, 1969, were a record at over 300 tons.⁴⁵

The kiwifruit received royal endorsement in 1975 when Queen Elizabeth, at the opening of the New Covent Garden Market in London, confided that it was her favourite fruit. On the other hand, Prince Charles always began his breakfast with an ugli fruit.⁴⁶

Perhaps the newly renamed fruit's first appearance overseas was in the supermarkets of San Francisco that, incidentally, has one of the largest urban Chinese communities outside China.⁴⁷ While the fruit began to extend into markets overseas, its culinary potential was being recognised back home, even if still referred to by its

In 1975 Turners & Growers celebrated the twentieth anniversary of the naming of kiwifruit. John (Jack) Turner (at right) came up with the new name for the Chinese gooseberry.

Photographer unknown, NZME

Mid-century: The 1950s kiwi

Turners & Growers' kiwifruit label.

old name. Thus, the 1961 recipe for Punga Pie consisted of an orange, grapefruit and Chinese gooseberry filling in a meringue shell, described as 'delicious and like eating sunshine'.[48] More imaginative dishes to follow in the early 1970s were Chinese Gooseberry Souffle, Chinese Gooseberry Chutney and Chinese Gooseberry Fool.[49] The fruit also had a practical application, following the discovery by New Zealand scientists that it contained an enzyme known as actinidain, which attacks and breaks down proteins, and could therefore be used to tenderise steaks.[50]

Along with the development of kiwifruit exports, there was a demand for the plants by fruit growers around the world. Inevitably, there was much discussion as to whether New Zealand should export its plants, one argument in its favour being that overseas growers supplying their local markets would in fact help increase demand for kiwifruit, and New Zealand would be able to supply it in their off-season. As it happened, by the late 1970s vines were to be found in commercial quantities in various countries including France, South Africa, Chile, Japan, Israel, Spain and the United States. All these plants were originally derived from the seedlings grown by Alexander Allison in Whanganui and, as noted in *The Kiwifruit Story* (by David Yerex and Westbrook Haines), it was entirely appropriate that 'the new fruit by then bore a name which belonged to the land which had adopted it, and then sent it out into the world.'[51]

For some reason the name kiwifruit was never patented. Perhaps it was not considered 'intellectual property', or it was just an oversight. But if it was a missed opportunity there was a positive outcome, for wherever in the world the fruit is grown or sold it is universally referred to as 'kiwifruit' or 'kiwi', which of course associates it with New Zealand. Had the name been patented, other countries would have been required to call the fruit by another name, in which case New Zealand's connection, and claim as originator, is not likely to have survived.[52]

An unpalatable association

If the original kiwi — the bird, that is — was impressed by the kiwi ingenuity that led to the renaming of a Chinese fruit, one wonders what it may have felt about a later suggestion relating to one of its natural enemies, the possum. In 1987 plans were announced to market in China the meat of that otherwise pestiferous marsupial as an 'exotic delicacy' under the name of 'kiwi bear', a change designed to avoid comparison with the 'rat-like' North American opossum (*Didelphis virginiana*).[53]

The rotating kiwi

Kiwi brand bacon had first appeared on the market around 1914, and seven years later Palmerston North ham and bacon curer Thomas Fenton registered his trademark depicting a kiwi browsing beneath a tree fern. Business boomed, and in 1937 when his company was taken over by the New Zealand Co-operative Pig Marketing Association (PMA), it had the biggest bacon turnover in the country. The PMA began a programme of expansion, acquiring Auckland's Nikau Bacon Company in 1940, and further processing plants and distributing depots around the country. Kiwi bacon had always enjoyed extensive national advertising, and around 1960 the PMA embarked on its most imaginative promotion, the installation of giant kiwi above each of its Kiwi Bacon Company facilities in Auckland, Palmerston North, Wellington, Christchurch and Dunedin.

The half-tonne birds, made of fibreglass over a steel frame, were designed by Auckland sign company Claude Neon, who subcontracted out their construction, which is believed to have taken place in premises in the Waitākere Ranges, west of Auckland. Once installed above the factories, the kiwi quickly become landmarks and part of local folklore.

Kiwi

ABOVE: Promotional pencil produced for the Kiwi Bacon Company.

TOP: The Kiwi Bacon Company's promotional material also included sets of playing cards.

OPPOSITE: The Kiwi Bacon Company's revolving kiwi on top of the Farm Products' building in Thorndon Quay in Wellington, December 1966.

EP-Industry-Meat retail-01, Alexander Turnbull Library, Wellington

In addition to their sheer size, they could rotate. In about 1980, electricity-saving measures ground the Auckland bird in New North Road, Kingsland to a halt, and ten years later observant members of the public were still advising the company that their bird had stopped.

The Kiwi Bacon Company was a victim of dramatic changes within the corporate world during the 1980s. It was taken over by its old rival Huttons, and during the subsequent reorganisation the big birds were removed from their perches.[54] The Palmerston North bird was initially housed at Pūkaha Mt Bruce National Wildlife Centre, before moving to its permanent home in Eketāhuna,[55] while the Christchurch specimen, known as Claude, went to Orana Wildlife Park.[56] The Auckland bird languished in storage at the Claude Neon signage company, but in 1990 was a main attraction at a Kiwiana exhibition at Auckland Museum. It was subsequently relocated to its current perch above the Kiwi International Hotel at Auckland Airport.

12

Cultural matters: Kiwi to the fore

The 1960s saw the kiwi give its name to an alleged national characteristic, the propensity for invention and improvisation. Such an ability would have been a very handy — if not essential — asset for this country's earliest settlers, both Polynesian and European, when confronted with unfamiliar resources, or the lack of them, in their new home. According to urban legend, New Zealanders are able to fashion literally almost anything from the proverbial No. 8 wire. But this ability did not begin with European settlement or even with the introduction of fencing materials. As pointed out by Bob Riley in *Kiwi Ingenuity*, the necessity for invention was confronted by this country's original arrivals from the Pacific, whose circumstances were 'even more uncompromisingly harsh than that faced by the European settlers'. With fewer implements at their disposal, Māori evolved highly sophisticated stone, bone and wood carving traditions, as well as constructing waka and nearly impregnable fortified pā, and developing sophisticated navigation skills.[1]

New Zealand's first Patent Act was passed in 1860 but was hardly followed by a rush of applications. Things picked up in the 1880s, reflecting both the growing agricultural economy and the very practical problems of making a living. That decade saw 120 patent applications connected with fencing and wire strainers, while others dealt with hedge-cutting, improved farm machinery, packing butter, dealing with blight in fruit trees, and the rabbit problem. One particularly popular challenge, the devising of suitable lead-headed nails for corrugated iron roofs, led to 14 applications from local inventors.[2] Another task confronting the farmer was scrub cutting, and in mid-1885 a large number of settlers 'interested in the destruction of Manuka' converged on a paddock at Bridge Pa in central Hawke's Bay to watch a trial of three machines, all of 'New Zealand invention and manufacture'.[3]

Perhaps the first published suggestion there was something special about local settlers was an 1864 reference to the 'inventive genius of a colonist of New Zealand' in regard to a new type of board game.[4] Eight years later another newspaper referred to 'young New Zealand's ingenuity' in the keeping of horses,[5] while a local invention known as 'Barrell's patent' may have provided welcome relief in the home, being a washing machine in which 'steam takes the place of knuckles and scrubbing boards'.[6]

Suggestions of New Zealand's invention and/or ingenuity continued, but it may not have been until 1965 when the first reference was made to 'Kiwi ingenuity', by the Christchurch *Press*. It was inspired by the following advertisement in the Agony Column of the *Times*: 'New Zealander new in London would caretake your London flat'.[7] The concept appeared to catch on; seven years later the senior vice-president of Federated Farmers of New Zealand informed a conference: 'We have a world reputation for 'Kiwi' ingenuity, so why not use it for further product development and new product research . . .'[8]

Encouraged by geographic remoteness — the 'tyranny of distance' (a term widely credited to Australian historian Geoffrey Blainey) — and a strong sense of individualism and practical know-how, New Zealanders like to see themselves as inventive, innovative and independent. These qualities have certainly served the country well in the past, whether atomic physics (Ernest Rutherford), aeronautics (Richard Pearse), or such social welfare innovations as being the first country to give women the vote, in 1893. But if there was some momentum associated with this Kiwi ingenuity, it may have faltered in recent years. By way of comparison, New Zealanders now file far fewer patents than Finland

Ingenuity across the Tasman

It should come as no surprise that there are similar claims for a native ingenuity in Australia. In fact, such abilities were surely in evidence whenever indigenous people established themselves in a new environment and, more recently, in the nineteenth century when many millions of Europeans left for new homes in North America, South Africa, Australia or New Zealand. If an early showcase for this country's inventiveness was agriculture, Australians had an even greater challenge, occupying the driest continent on earth, and one suffering from soils that were typically poor, shallow and rock hard. But the farming folk of Australia have been hailed as 'a special breed' and, according to *Made in Australia: A sourcebook of all things Australian*, have always been 'inventive, shrewd and flexible'. As a result, their struggle with adversity has bred 'a steely determination which has resulted in Australia becoming probably the most efficient and cost-effective primary producer in the world.' The same source advises: 'Australia was founded on the willingness to take risks; the readiness of millions of migrants to move to a new and perhaps hostile country. Risk taking, enterprise, is part of our history.'[9]

and Ireland, which have similar populations, or Switzerland, although it has a somewhat larger population of 8.7 million.[10]

Kiwiana

In early 1929 a horse named Kiwiana was unplaced in the Maiden Stakes at the Woodville summer races.[11] Sixty years later that *Apteryx*-inspired name would be adopted for a recently recognised aspect of this country's social history and popular culture. The stuff of 'Kiwiana' had of course been around for

PAGE 160: Postcard promoting 'Kiwi As', a 1997 documentary by Shirley Horrocks celebrating New Zealand's popular culture. The items on the trolley were no doubt produced with the assistance of the *Edmonds Cookery Book* and 'Sure to Rise' baking powder.

Cultural matters: Kiwi to the fore

some time but had yet to be identified as such.

Kiwiana refers to a collection of objects and ways of doing things that had come to characterise everyday New Zealand life and was seen as peculiar to this country. It is normally associated with the period of relative prosperity following the Second World War that gave rise to the baby boomer generation. Certain items and institutions, such as the pull-along Buzzy Bee toy, Plunket, and the tin of Edmonds baking powder, would become familiar to the majority of New Zealand households.

After years of comparative isolation and a heavy dependence on Britain for our imports, exports and way of life, the 1980s brought dramatic changes to the social landscape. The deregulation of the New Zealand economy meant that the country was now open to influence from the world at large. With the approach of 1990 and the 150th anniversary of the signing of the Treaty of Waitangi, there was an increasing interest in our history and sense of national identity. One response was to look back on our recent past, a nostalgic reflection on a way of life that had changed in the name of 'progress'. In 1989 the first compendium of those things that characterised New Zealand's popular culture was published,[12] and when it came to giving the phenomena a name it seemed obvious to acknowledge our unofficial national symbol and, following the lead of Australiana and Americana, call it Kiwiana.

Recognising the country's economic dependence on agriculture, the first book of Kiwiana naturally had a section on farming and sheep. At that stage the dominant animal was the New Zealand Romney, numbering some 29 million. Back in 1962 the retiring president of the New Zealand Romney Marsh Sheep Breeders' Association suggested that

OPPOSITE, CLOCKWISE FROM TOP: **The Buzzy Bee, a classic example of Kiwiana, first went into production around 1940.**
GH022590, Museum of New Zealand Te Papa Tongarewa

A tin of 'Sure to Rise' baking powder, another fine example of Kiwiana, which had its origins in 1879 when Thomas J. Edmonds left East London and set up business in Christchurch.
Thames Museum Te Whare Taonga o te Kauaeranga

The kiwi appeared to enter the fast food business in 1976 with the launch of the Kiwiburger.
Lcmortensen, CC BY-SA 3.0

the Romney ram would be a more meaningful national symbol than the kiwi, given that two-thirds of this country's exports came from the sheep, and an estimated 75 per cent of the nation's 48 million sheep had Romney ancestry.[13] Needless to say, the idea didn't catch on and the nation stuck with the symbolic kiwi. In fact, that same year the Labour MP for Lyttelton (and later Prime Minister) Norman Kirk suggested that New Zealand should adopt the kiwi as its only national symbol, and even include it on the flag.[14]

In 1990, 46 items of Kiwiana were namechecked in a jingle for the Kiwiburger, which had been launched in a McDonald's restaurant in Hamilton in 1976. Its kiwi-free contents included a beef patty, a fried egg, beetroot, tomato, lettuce, cheese, onion, mustard and tomato sauce on a toasted bun. Then in 1997, eight years after it was first identified and named, 'Kiwiana' entered the *Oxford Dictionary of New Zealand English* ('A Dictionary of New Zealandisms on Historical Principles'), where it was described, rather grandly, as 'any of many "collectible" items redolent of New Zealand life and culture'.[15]

Kiwi identity

In 1967 New Zealanders were informed that a 'real dinkum kiwi joker' could be characterised by 'monosyllabic language' and a slowness to patronise the arts.[16] At the same time, Mr J.D. Walker of the Master Builders' Federation advised that the days of 'the Kiwi bungalow — that stereotypical, dull, uniform group box-house' — were numbered. The organisation planned to make available several hundred architects' plans for houses that could be built for only slightly more than the 'Kiwi bungalow', believing people would 'gladly pay the extra for the better product.'[17]

Further to the kiwi giving its name to the nation's popular culture, New Zealanders of all types and persuasions appeared to identify with the bird. In addition to just plain 'Kiwi', the nom de plume adopted by letter-writers to newspapers during the 1960s began to include innumerable variations. They reflected the writers' origins ('Pakeha Kiwi', 'Kiwi by Birth', 'English Kiwi', 'Kiwi Pom' and 'Scottish Kiwi'), degrees of loyalty ('True Kiwi', 'Proud to be a Kiwi', 'Kiwi Born and Bred', 'True-Blue Kiwi' and 'An Average Kiwi'), age ('Young Kiwi' and

'Old Kiwi'), or state of mind ('Bewildered Kiwi', 'Concerned Kiwi', 'Sympathetic Kiwi', 'Disillusioned Kiwi', 'Angry Kiwi', 'Sad Kiwi', 'Two-Eyed Kiwi', 'Censored Kiwi' and 'Reticent Kiwi').

The connection between the New Zealander and the kiwi was further strengthened in 1967 following the country's introduction of new overseas currency restrictions. This inspired the suggestion that the wings of the New Zealand traveller had become vestigial — like the bird's — and 'if he can get off the ground at all his flight will be strictly limited. For the moment long distance travel is for other birds.'[18]

Golden Kiwi

New Zealanders had long enjoyed a 'flutter', a habit facilitated by the opening of the world's first totalisator at Ellerslie Racecourse in 1913, and a national 'art union' lottery that operated from 1932. Citizens also took part in overseas lotteries, in particular 'Tatts', an abbreviation of 'Tattersall's Sweeps' established by the licensee of the Sydney hotel of the same name in 1881. As an alternative to buying a ticket in 'Tatts', on 12 December 1961 New Zealanders had a lottery of their own, the appropriately named Golden Kiwi. It offered a top prize of £12,000, with a total prize pool of £30,000. The demand for tickets (5/- each) in the first Golden Kiwi exceeded all expectations, selling out within 24 hours, and the winner was an Auckland customs officer.[19] Within five months Mr Gotz, the Minister of Internal Affairs, recognised that the lottery was already 'too small', and was thinking of introducing a 'Golden Moa'.[20] In fact, the first of the proposed larger lotteries was held in July 1964 and was known as the Mammoth Golden Kiwi.

The stated aim of the Golden Kiwi was to raise funds for charitable, philanthropic and community purposes.[21] At the same time, and even though the government collected tax on overseas lotteries, it was saving more by diverting sales from Tatts. In September 1965 it was revealed that the revenue collected in New Zealand from the sale of tickets in Tatts had decreased by 40 per cent since the introduction of the Golden Kiwi.[22]

Although extremely popular with the public, and particularly handy for birthday and Xmas presents, the lottery was criticised by religious groups. The Bishop of Auckland, the Rt. Rev. E.A. Gowing accusing it of creating an attitude of mind that 'looks for huge monetary gain without effort', and feared it would have 'a very adverse effect' on the morals of the community.[23] Similar concerns were expressed by the President of the Methodist Church, who pointed out that the Golden Kiwi had drawn attention to the 'gambling craze which seems to have gripped the country.'[24] When it came to the distribution of funds from the sale of Golden Kiwi tickets, the Presbyterian Church declined to share in such moneys believing it conflicted with 'the moral drive toward direct sacrificial generosity'.[25]

In its first two years of operation, 131 Golden Kiwi lotteries paid out £4,023,000 to 242,310 prize winners.[26] News of its success was even reported in Canadian newspapers, along with editorials suggesting that Canada should 'borrow the idea'.[27] By 1967 there was admission that the Golden Kiwi was losing its lustre; in 1962 there had been 74 lotteries, but in 1966 there were only 44. It was suggested that 'saturation point' had been reached, while the fewer lotteries being held meant a reduction in grants to worthy causes.[28] The popularity of the lottery in its prime was reflected by the description of the nation's most sought-after sporting trophy, the Ranfurly Shield, as 'the Golden Kiwi of the New Zealand Rugby world'.[29]

A Golden Kiwi ticket from one of the 311 draws of the Golden Kiwi lottery, which lasted from 1961 to 1989 when it was superseded by Instant Kiwi and Lotto.

By the late 1980s, the now 'half millionaire' Golden Kiwi was offering a staggering $500,000 'guaranteed first prize' but the public appeared to be losing interest. After a run of 28 years and 311 lotteries the Golden Kiwi came to an end in 1989, although the name lived on with Instant Kiwi, which began in September that year.[30] By then New Zealanders were also being lured by the prospects of a brand new get-rich-quick scheme, Lotto, which also had the attraction of a live draw on prime time Saturday night television.

Symbols of service

The already well-established kiwi saw its application as a symbol gain further momentum in the 1960s. The Manufacturers' Federation had long shown faith in the bird, and in mid-1965 offered another version as a 'hallmark symbol to encourage the buying of New Zealand goods'.[31] The work of Christchurch designer Cees Leffelaar, this highly stylised outline of a kiwi encompassing the slogan 'New Zealand Made' was, after some criticism, supported by the Canterbury Progress League.[32] Within a month over a hundred manufacturing forms had agreed to incorporate the symbol on their labels and packaging material.[33] By the end of the following year that figure had risen to around 300, and by early 1968 it had reached 430.[34]

The new kiwi symbol was quick to make an impact overseas, and in June 1966 was reported to be widely recognised throughout Singapore,

The 'New Zealand Made' label was introduced by the Manufacturers' Federation in 1966.

Cees Leffelaar (left) at the presentation of the 'New Zealand Made' symbol at Christchurch, March 1966.

1072, Christchurch Star Archive

Cultural matters: Kiwi to the fore

Thailand and Malaysia.[35] There was also the suggestion that the kiwi should replace this nation's sporting emblem, the fern, accused of bearing a resemblance to a feather.[36]

The kiwi symbol was on prominent display throughout the New Zealand pavilion at Expo '70 in Osaka, Japan, leading to a request for a taxidermied specimen, supplied by the Dominion Museum.[37] The New Zealand delegation also distributed kiwi pin badges, which were said to have become one of the Expo's most coveted souvenirs. In addition, the announcement was made, fittingly by Prime Minister 'Kiwi' Keith Holyoake, that a pair of real kiwi would be presented to the Tennōji Zoological Garden at Osaka. The promised birds arrived in July 1970, although one took some time to recover from the long flight from Auckland.[38]

The kiwi was on the move in 1970, with the design of a new coat of arms for the Ministry of Transport. At the centre of the design was the first form of transport in New Zealand, a waka, in front of a Southern Cross. It was surmounted by St Edward's Crown and supported by Pegasus, the winged horse of Greek mythology, and a kiwi against a background of fern.[39] That same year the kiwi took to the skies following the retiring of the RNZAF roundel, which had consisted of three concentric circles of red, white and blue with a fern leaf on the central red disc. The new replacement roundel had a central red kiwi on a white disc with an outer circle of blue. The reason given for the change was that the fern was not readily identifiable as a New Zealand symbol overseas, and the kiwi was considered a more appropriate and generally recognised emblem of our nationality.[40] Today the kiwi is also used on the uniforms of navy and army personnel.

Unveiled in 1970, the new logo for the Ministry of Transport took inspiration from an immortal creature of Greek legend as well as from another, more local but by no means less legendary winged creature.

Knowledge Bank, Hawke's Bay Digital Archive Trust

Kiwi in confinement

In 1961 a remark by former British Prime Minister Winston Churchill, that he could not imagine anyone keeping a British lion as a pet, inspired an antipodean equivalent. The retiring president of the Canterbury Chamber of Commerce suggested New Zealand had become soft as a result of 'welfare state thinking' and needed to be more 'rugged' and 'resilient', especially when it came to promoting its exports. This call for the country to toughen up motivated one local newspaper to offer the headline: 'No One Will Keep Kiwi As Pet'.[41]

Following the decision in 1961 to send a kiwi — found on a North Auckland farm — to Edinburgh Zoo, a member of the Opposition in parliament asked if the country's finances could be improved

FROM LEFT: In 1970 the kiwi replaced the fern at the centre of the roundel on uniforms and equipment of the New Zealand Defence Force.

NZ Defence Force

The kiwi bids New Zealand good night

At 7.30 p.m. on Wednesday 1 June 1960, New Zealanders sat down to watch the country's first official television broadcast, transmitted from the AKTV-2 studios in Auckland's Shortland Street. The programme that evening included an episode of 'The Adventures of Robin Hood' and a performance by the Howard Morrison Quartet. By 1969 there were television stations in the four main centres, broadcasting for 65 hours each week, until 11 p.m. from Sunday to Thursday and until midnight on Friday and Saturday.

From 1975 the end of the evening's broadcast was marked by an animated short, featuring the Goodnight Kiwi. There were several versions, the best-known dating from 1980 that showed Kiwi in the control room, shutting down the screens before heading up the stairs to the studio roof. The bird then climbed to the top of the transmission mast and, after snuggling down under a blanket, went to sleep in a satellite dish. At that point New Zealanders turned off their sets and presumably went to bed themselves.

The Goodnight Kiwi repeated its nightly ritual until 19 October 1994 when it was made redundant, following the decision by Television New Zealand to begin broadcasting 24 hours a day.[42]

if a zoo took 'a particular New Zealand-bred kiwi', a reference to Prime Minister Holyoake. Unsurprisingly, the Speaker ruled out the question, which caused much mirth in the House.[43] Three years later, the now six-year-old kiwi at Edinburgh Zoo, known as Wiki, was reportedly proving a popular public attraction.[44]

The strain of receiving visitors proved too much for Auckland Zoo's sole kiwi in 1967, so it was decided that it should be given a two-month break from public exhibition. While it enjoyed its sabbatical, a taxidermied bird was placed in its pen. As a zoo official noted: the live bird 'slept all the time anyway and was always curled up'.[45]

Presenting the kiwi

A pair of silver kiwi, designed and made by Professor H.J. Simpson of Christchurch, constituted this country's wedding gift for Princess

Queen Elizabeth and the Duke of Edinburgh wearing kiwi feather cloaks at the national reception given in their honour at Nelson Park, Hastings, on 26 February 1986.

EP/1986/0899/37-F, Alexander Turnbull Library, Wellington

Margaret in 1960,[46] while Queen Elizabeth and Prince Philip wore the obligatory kahu kiwi at their reception at Rugby Park in Rotorua, during their tour in March 1970, coinciding with the Captain Cook Bicentenary.[47]

By now the kiwi was accustomed to being presented to visiting royalty and other dignitaries, and in 1964 the recipients included the Beatles. The group arrived at Wellington Airport for their New Zealand tour bearing a large kiwi made by Auckland disabled servicemen and presented to them in Sydney.[48] The kiwi even proved to be a suitable papal present in 1965 when its image, hand carved in kauri, was taken to Rome for presentation to the Pope by members of the Combined Irish Societies of New Zealand.[49]

Back home the kiwi continued to be a bird of the people when it was chosen to grace the 20 cent coin in New Zealand's new set decimal currency, released on 10 July 1967. According to one commentator, the image of the bird was 'slightly plumper' than its cousin on the florin, which it replaced.[50] Presumably totally unrelated to the forthcoming release of decimal coinage was the appearance of a counterfeit florin in Milford, Auckland, in 1966. The police noted that it was 'a fairly good copy' although thinner and lighter than the genuine thing, while the whiskers and feathers on the kiwi were 'not well done'.[51]

The kiwi on the 20 cent coin, which replaced the florin (2/-) when New Zealand became decimalised on 10 July 1967. Nearly a quarter of a century later, in 1990, the kiwi was upgraded and moved to the new $1 coin.

1967.188.1.3, CCBY4.0, Auckland Museum, Tamaki Paenga Hira

Kiwi inspired

The kiwi's place as the bird of the people was further consolidated when several new national organisations adopted its name. The first of these was in 1990 following the sale to private investors of state owned enterprise Telecom, which had replaced the Post Office in 1987. This 1990 sale prompted the 'Kiwi Share', a 'telecommunications service obligation', which was a contract between the government and Telecom requiring the latter to maintain certain practices of the former state entity, in particular those relating to unlimited local calling. In late 2000 the government decided to update Telecom's Kiwi Share obligations, aimed at improving access to basic telecommunications for New Zealanders. Then, in 2007, the Kiwi Share agreement was reviewed, to ensure it took account of fast-changing technologies.[52]

In 2002 the locally owned Kiwibank was launched, and by mid-year had 211 branches nationwide. It was the innovation of then-Deputy Prime Minister Jim Anderton, and the aim was to compete with the big four Australian banks that dominated the domestic market. A subsidiary of New Zealand Post, its branches were originally located within PostShops (previously known as post offices). Within two years of opening KiwiBank had attracted over 250,000 customers, and by the time it was 20 years old the figure had passed the one million mark. KiwiBank was the first bank to launch real-time mobile banking (in 2006–2008), and also the first to use recycled plastic in all its cards (in 2018–2021).[53]

The use of the kiwi to promote New Zealand-made goods continued with this promotion by Auckland Farmers in the 1980s.

But the kiwi-inspired initiative that has reached the most New Zealanders is KiwiSaver, a subsidised and voluntary contributing retirement savings plan offered by private sector providers. It began on 1 July 2007 and had the distinction of being the world's first national auto-enrolment savings scheme. To date only one other country — the United Kingdom — has committed to auto-enrolment on a national scale. By the end of June 2009, after just two years of operation, over 1.1 million Kiwis were members of KiwiSaver.[54]

Finally, in 2018 the kiwi gave its name to a government scheme designed to speed up the process of providing homes for its namesake compatriots. For the previous ten years, the supply of affordable homes had been overtaken by the growing demand, and many New Zealanders — especially first home buyers — were being priced out of the market. So KiwiBuild was launched with the aim of working with developers to

Cultural matters: Kiwi to the fore

increase the number of new homes coming on the market, and providing greater options for home ownership opportunities at more affordable prices. Unfortunately, the provision of modest and affordable homes for Kiwis was not so easily achieved. KiwiBuild's original targets, unveiled in 2018, were to deliver 1000 homes by June 2019, and 16,000 homes by July 2021. But while the government managed its first KiwiBuild target of 1000 homes, it did so two years behind schedule, reaching only 1058 homes by 31 May 2021. As one headline put it, by July 2021 KiwiBuild was 'two years late 15,000 homes behind schedule'.[55] The programme had been plagued by challenges presented by the COVID-19 pandemic and subsequent lockdowns, thereby adding to the ongoing problem of providing homes for Kiwis.

Taking (briefly) to the air

Somewhat ironically, the kiwi has given its name to several airlines that proved, perhaps predictably, short-lived. In 1992, following the demise of Eastern Airlines in the United States, a number of former pilots got together, calling themselves Kiwis because they were no longer flying. They decided to retain the name when they established a new venture, Kiwi International Airlines, which made its first commercial flights on 21 September 1992, using two refurbished Boeing 727-200s. The airline was based in Newark, New Jersey, and at one point had a fleet of four aircraft flying to six destinations. But Kiwi International was plagued by ongoing management and financial problems, and at the end of 1999 it was declared bankrupt, to be followed by liquidation and permanent grounding.

There was also, briefly, a Kiwi Travel International Airlines in New Zealand, founded in 1994 by Ewan Wilson, a qualified pilot and travel agent from Hamilton. It aimed to offer chartered flights within New Zealand, the first step in establishing an international airline. Although initial charter fights did not turn a profit, they provided good publicity and led to the decision to begin flights between Hamilton and Brisbane. But in doing so it came into direct competition with both Air New Zealand and Qantas, and the venture collapsed in 1996.

Continuing its relationship with flight, the kiwi has also given its name to an online travel agency, Kiwi.com, which began in 2012 and is headquartered in Brno in the Czech Republic. Until 2016 it was known as SkyPicker.com, a name that might suggest a reference to the kiwi. The company enjoyed rapid growth, becoming one of the largest online air ticket sellers in Europe. However, it has been embroiled in controversy concerning refunds and customer service practices. Meanwhile Kiwi.com claims 'We Hack the System/You Fly for Less', and despite being named after a nocturnal bird with limited daytime vision, it 'finds cheap flights other sites can't see'.[56]

Another unlikely overseas adoption of New Zealand's bird was by a quarterly French comic collection, *Albums Comiques de Kiwi,* which first appeared in 1964. The character 'Kiwi', the subject of several strips in each 80 page collection, had been partly anthropomorphised, with human hands and arms in place of vestigial wings, but retained his bird-like beak and feet. He obviously had a beak for trouble, getting himself into precarious situations, which necessarily brought his aggressive streak to the fore. His unlikely (mis)adventures took him to some exotic locations, while he also appeared capable of time travelling.

But the enterprise that made the kiwi world famous was of course the Australian boot polish, which received a massive boost when bought up in large quantities by the British army during the First World War. A century later, however, it was announced that the product would no longer be sold in Britain, a result of the growing popularity of casual shoes that don't require polishing. The current owners (since 2011) of the polish, S.C. Johnson, announced their plan to focus on its range of other products. Meanwhile, Kiwi polish continues to be sold in New Zealand, available in major supermarkets.[57]

Covers of the quarterly French comic collection, *Albums Comiques de Kiwi* showing the eponymous main character on his journeys to faraway places.

Cultural matters: Kiwi to the fore

Zespri green kiwifruit, SunGold and RubyRed.
Zespri Limited

13

The high-flying kiwi(fruit)

If the kiwi, symbolising the New Zealander, had gained in confidence in the latter decades of the twentieth century, the same was true of the country's rapidly developing kiwifruit industry. In 1977 there were fewer than 500 kiwifruit growers, about 200 of whom were in the Te Puke region, and with fewer than half a million vines covering less than 4000 acres (5260 ha). Three years later they were covering 13,000 acres, and by 1985 the figure was expected to reach 40,000 acres (16,187 ha).[1]

In 1974 Te Puke proclaimed itself 'kiwifruit capital of the world', but it wasn't until the region's natural cobalt deficiency was dealt to in the 1920s that agriculture was able to develop. By 1950 there was nothing to suggest that what were still known as Chinese gooseberries would play such an important part in the region's future, the emphasis then being on lemons and tree tomatoes. At first the gooseberries attracted little interest, but when early planting suggested their potential the change, in the words of kiwifruit historian Roly Earp, 'swept like a bushfire through the No. 3 Road area and beyond.' The No. 3 Road has been described as the 'Kiwifruit epicentre of Te Puke', and within the space of 15 years not only had established orchards switched to kiwifruit but all other suitable land was taken up by the new crop. Initial progress may have been unspectacular; nevertheless a change came in 1964 with the introduction of the Hayward variety of kiwifruit.[2] Developed in the 1930s by pioneer horticulturalist Hayward Wright, who has been credited with being the person responsible for the start of the kiwifruit industry as we know it,[3] the Hayward kiwifruit would become the main green variety produced for the world's markets and dominate production in most growing areas. Described as moderately hairy and more rounded than other kiwi varieties, it claims to have the best eating quality of the existing green varieties, mainly due to its higher levels of sweetness.

'A Strange New Zealand Phenomenon'

A major step forward for the kiwifruit industry was the coining of the name in 1959, and a decade later exports had reached 102,000 trays. The lack of organised grower control and the need for a joint marketing effort saw the establishment in 1970 of the Kiwifruit Export Promotion Committee (KEPC), and its first challenge was the need for public education. As summarised by Earp, the main issues were: 'What was this hairy little object, when was it ready for eating and how could it be used?' The campaign began with posters and the publication of recipes using kiwifruit, and in 1979 the KEPC produced a glossy booklet that introduced it to the world. Entitled *Kiwifruit — A Strange New Zealand Phenomenon*, it included a history of the fruit in this country and a cover photo of the bird that had inspired its name.[4]

There were still matters to be sorted out, and 1972 saw the formation of a steering committee representing growers with the aim of establishing a kiwifruit export licensing authority. Hopes for a quick resolution were soon dashed, but a positive development was the election in 1975 of a National Government and the appointment of a new Minister of Agriculture, Duncan McIntyre. At another meeting of the steering committee in December 1976 it was agreed that some form of controlling or organising body was essential for the industry and, finally, the Kiwifruit Marketing Licensing Authority was established in 1977. This had the rights to set market standards such as fruit size, quality and packaging for export markets, and was intended to enable growers to take control of their own industry.[5]

Aerial view of kiwifruit orchards in the Bay of Plenty in March 2012.

Karl Johaentges, Alamy

The kiwifruit boom

By now kiwifruit was being recognised as 'the high flyer on the agricultural scene', the cause of a 'gold rush' that peaked in the period 1979–82. Farmers from around New Zealand were said to be selling up and acquiring 15 acres (6 ha) of kiwifruit in the Bay of Plenty and other suitable growing districts. Non-farming types, such as doctors and lawyers, were also getting in on the action, encouraged by tax laws (amended in 1982) that allowed the claiming of the costs of developing such businesses against income from other sources.[6]

The boom in this new industry led to the creation of what David Yerex and Westbrook Haines have identified as a 'kiwifruit aristocracy', who benefited from getting into kiwifruit by the mid-1970s. Then came a 'second wave', hoping to capitalise on the popularity of the new crop. As a result, the town of Te Puke experienced rapid growth; where there was once a single family on a dairy farm, there were

Kiwi

In 1974 Te Puke proclaimed itself 'kiwifruit capital of the world', and in 2015 announced plans to erect an enormous kiwifruit in front of the railway station in the middle of the town.

now several families growing kiwifruit. The crop also inspired a kiwifruit-themed festival, with a Kiwifruit Queen contest and a Kiwifruit Cooking Competition.[7] To further celebrate the horticultural connection, in 2015 plans were announced to erect an enormous kiwifruit in front of the railway station in the middle of Te Puke.[8] Eighteen months later the landmark was completed when two enormous kiwifruit slices were lowered into position, creating a striking impression at the western entrance to the town.[9]

In the years following the formation of the Kiwifruit Authority, a major concern for some growers was the on-going supply by New Zealand nurserymen of kiwifruit plants to overseas growers. In the period 1979–82 New Zealand was, on an annual basis, supplying up to 11 countries with plants, and a total of up to 745,000 plants were being sent, mainly to Argentina, Chile, Japan and Korea. The US Government was advised that plants might be sold to overseas growers who could later provide competition for the New Zealand-grown product, but no action was taken. It was feared that there could well be retaliation if New Zealand were to prohibit the export of kiwifruit material.[10]

Creating Zespri

Unsurprisingly, a number of other countries were now growing kiwifruit, thereby increasing competition for global exports. In addition, New Zealand growers found themselves competing with each other, and the resulting pricing battle caused a reduction in their profitability. As a result, in 1988 growers voted to move to a 'single-desk' system and the New Zealand Kiwifruit

Marketing Board was created, to enable the industry to make better use of economies of scale, set universal standards for high fruit quality, develop new markets, and invest in research and development. Nine years later, in 1997, the New Zealand Kiwifruit Marketing Board was renamed and this new co-operative of kiwifruit growers in New Zealand became Zespri International Limited.[11] Just as there are several species of kiwi, kiwifruit have also diversified, with the first gold kiwifruit variety, Hort16A — developed with Crown research partner Plant & Food Research — released to growers as a commercial variety in 1999; Zespri SunGold Kiwifruit, licenced initially with a small number of New Zealand growers in 2010; and Zespri RubyRed™, which was developed in 2019 and received an enthusiastic response during sales trials in New Zealand, Singapore, Japan and China, prior to its commercial launch in 2022.

But just as the original kiwi bird continues to weather a succession of threats to its livelihood, the kiwifruit has also had its fair share of challenges. In November 2010, the kiwifruit bacterial canker disease *Pseudomonas syringae* pv. *actinidiae* (Psa), which had been sweeping kiwifruit producing regions around the world, was first detected in a Te Puke orchard and subsequently identified in numerous growing regions across New Zealand. It causes leaf spotting and extensive vine death, and had a devastating impact on Zespri's original gold kiwifruit, Hort16A.[12] Either by good management or by good luck, Zespri SunGold proved to be more tolerant to Psa so the decision was taken to cutover all the Hort16A to Zespri SunGold. This provided an immediate pathway for recovery with Zespri SunGold proving to be a far superior variety than the original Hort16A from a growing, post-harvest and global sales perspective. Further to the Psa outbreak, in the early 2020s the kiwifruit export industry experienced 'a horror couple of years', plagued by various COVID-19 related challenges including labour shortages and supply chain issues.[13] In 2022 adverse weather conditions and ongoing labour shortages contributed to fruit

The logo of Zespri International Limited, formed in 1997 with the renaming of the New Zealand Kiwifruit Marketing Board.

quality problems on and off shore, impacting grower returns. Then in October 2022 the North Island suffered a major frost event leading to a significant reduction in the 2023 New Zealand kiwifruit season volume, exacerbated by cyclones that hit key growing regions in early 2023. The industry made positive progress on fruit quality throughout 2023 with a significant increase in volume in 2024, enabling it to meet the strong demand for its fruit.

A primary export

In terms of the outputs of individual countries, in 2017 China was the world's leading producer of kiwifruit followed by Italy, New Zealand, Iran and Chile.[14] However, Zespri International is the world's largest marketer of kiwifruit, selling in over 50 countries. Today it works with 2800 growers in New Zealand and 1500 internationally, with licensed growers in Italy, France, Japan, South Korea and Greece. As a result of a limit placed on it by its New Zealand growers, Zespri is restricted to a total of 5000 hectares overseas growing limit for the SunGold kiwifruit, so needs to focus on achieving maximum production from this. It also procures 20 million trays of green fruit across its many supply regions.[15] Kiwifruit is currently a $4 billion-plus industry for New Zealand, and regulations such as the Kiwifruit Industry Restructuring Act 1999 and the Kiwifruit Export Regulations 1999 have established Zespri as the primary exporter of New Zealand-grown kiwifruit to all countries other than Australia.[16]

It is a curious fact, and perhaps not entirely coincidental, that the single largest market for Zespri's fruit is the country of origin of the Chinese gooseberry, followed by Japan. Twenty per cent of New Zealand kiwifruit is sold in China, and in the seasons since 2021 annual sales have been around 40 million trays. The product is available in more than 60,000 stores in the region and is in competition with such other fruit as blueberries, durian and cherries, which have also grown in popularity in the Asian region in recent years. Another challenge for Zespri is the alleged unauthorised production, sale and promotion in China of New Zealand-bred Gold3 fruit, which is marketed as Zespri SunGold and is New Zealand's best global seller. By Zespri's estimation there are around 8400 hectares of 'rogue' Gold3 growing in China.[17]

In what may be seen as another parallel with the 'real' kiwi, in a joint venture in 2021 Zespri and Plant & Food Research established the Kiwifruit Breeding Centre (KBC). Based in Te Puke and operating out of Kerikeri, Motueka and Mt Albert, Auckland, it is dedicated to improving kiwifruit breeding and cultivation.[18] So just as the bird itself is being nurtured in sanctuaries and on off-shore islands, the small fruit that adopted its name is also being closely attended to and looked after, all the better to deal with any future threats to its livelihood.

Levitating kiwifruit

The story of how an unprepossessing small, brown and hairy fruit from China was subject to kiwi ingenuity and subsequently sold back to that country in large quantities is remarkable enough, but there was a much more fanciful tale associated with kiwifruit. In 1978 it was revealed that a Hawke's Bay fruit distributor had offered to pay $200,000 in England for the construction of a saucer-shaped 'spaceship' or 'levity disc' that, its inventor claimed, would be able to travel the 20,000 kilometres to New Zealand in just 30 minutes! The offer was made on the condition that on its return trips to London the craft would carry kiwifruit and tangelos to be forwarded to the distributor's agents at Covent Garden. By such means the fruit would reach the UK market cheaply and in the best possible condition.

Construction of the prototype three-seater craft was apparently already underway. It would be powered by 'self-generating magnetic power', a system its inventor stumbled across in 1946. As a result, he began building model levity discs, described as looking 'remarkably similar to the traditional flying saucer'.

The inventor claimed that one such disc, after lifting off, hovered and then 'shot off' never to be seen again, while another was tracked by radio 'well on its way to the Moon'. He claimed that several of his craft had reached speeds of 251,000 km/h and, even more astonishingly, could see no reason why they could not exceed the speed of light — a suggestion that would surely have raised the eyebrows of one Albert Einstein.[19]

14

In survival mode: Conserving the kiwi

In the early 1900s Trevor Lloyd's cartoon kiwi exhibited an aggressive streak, both on the sports field when competing with the Australian kangaroo and the British lion, and on the battlefield when dealing with Germans and Turks. This proactive attitude reappeared with a vengeance in the 1980s when the bird started punching above its weight and challenging for the America's Cup, with support from media campaigns promoting 'Kiwi Magic' and 'Kiwi Pride'. Also associated with yachting was an image known as the 'Fighting Kiwi', of a fierce wild-eyed bird brandishing a taiaha (short staff). New Zealanders competing in various sporting codes were urged to 'Give 'em a taste of Kiwi', an exhortation that was taken quite literally in the form of Dominion Breweries' new international product, Kiwi Lager. The patriotic symbol of this brew achieved the remarkable design feat of combining the letters 'NZ', the fern and the kiwi. But while the kiwi was frequently to be seen going on the attack in support of New Zealand, in real life the bird was fighting for its survival.

Kiwi

Dominion Breweries' Kiwi Lager, introduced in the 1980s, managed to combine several distinctively New Zealand elements. At left a can label, at right a coaster.

PAGE 186: Fierce 'Fighting Kiwi' like this have long been associated with New Zealanders in sporting competitions and on battlefronts around the world.

The aristocratic kiwi

As documented here, since the time of European settlement of this country there have been widely varying views on the outlook for the kiwi. With the spread of population and the growth of newspapers and other publications in the early twentieth century, general awareness of the bird and its welfare also became more widespread. In 1924 a commentator noted that our land birds were 'remarkable for their distinctness from those of any other country', the kiwi being 'exclusively a New Zealand production'. At the same time: 'It is to be regretted that it has now became a truism that the rarer birds of New Zealand are passing away, and will soon be extinct.'[1] Fourteen years later, a writer in the *Otago Daily Times* advised that the kiwi belonged to the 'oldest house of living birds, the Apterygeidean' and, as a result, New Zealand could 'justly claim possession of the most unique and aristocratic bird in the world.'[2]

As for what the kiwi was up against, by the mid-twentieth century, as the problems posed by introduced predators became more apparent, the possum was identified as 'the very worst of all foreign foes in our bush'. The destruction of the bush was bad news indeed for our native birds while the bush — allegedly more so than in any other country — depended on the birds for their incidental distribution and propagation of seeds. It was revealed that the seeds of 65 per cent of the forest plants and trees, including every timber tree (except the kauri and the beeches), were dispersed solely by birds. Without the presence of birds the New Zealand bush would be non-existent, while the kiwi's contribution to its preservation was its diet of insects. At the same time, the bird was the subject of a 'tragic paradox': 'the hidden bird of Tāne' had lived in the forest gloom for untold years, unknown and undiscovered until caught in a possum trap.[3]

Banking on the kiwi

It is believed this country was once home to millions of kiwi, however it is now estimated that only 68,000 remain.[4] There had been plenty of prior warning, but it was not until the population dropped to around 100,000 several decades ago that it became apparent the kiwi really was following the moa down the road to extinction. Appropriately, one of the first companies to adopt the image of the kiwi was also one of the first to undertake a significant initiative to save the bird.

The Bank of New Zealand was formed in 1861 by directors of another company, New Zealand Insurance, which had begun only two years earlier. From its beginning the organisation had a close association with the kiwi, as would the new Bank of New Zealand, which featured the bird on its early banknotes. In 1954 the bank was granted its own coat of arms, consisting of a shield dominated by the stars of the constellation of the Southern Cross and surmounted by a kiwi, described in heraldic terminology as 'Standing on a Mount of Earth with Ferns proper growing there.' When the coat of arms evolved into a logo known as 'the chevron' in 1969 the kiwi had disappeared, replaced by the Southern Cross and representations of five gold coins. But while the bank preferred the Southern Cross to the kiwi as a local symbol the bird lived on in other forms, as when carved into bank furniture and on building ornamentation.[5]

Nevertheless, the Bank of New Zealand (which would officially abbreviate its name to BNZ in 2008) had not forgotten its historical connection with the kiwi. In 1991 it formed a partnership with the Department of Conservation (DOC), together with Forest & Bird, to help prevent the extinction of the bird on the mainland. Further to this, in 2002 a partnership of BNZ and DOC established the BNZ Save the Kiwi Trust, with the aim of increasing the kiwi population, protecting its natural habitat and maintaining its genetic diversity. Related to this was BNZ Operation Nest Egg, a programme involved in taking kiwi eggs from the wild and hatching them in order to increase the bird's chances of survival. Once the birds had reached a weight of 300–400 g they were released on predator-free islands. By the time a kiwi attained the 'magic weight' of one kilogram it was considered quite capable of fighting off such predators as stoats and feral cats.

In February 2008, the thousandth BNZ Operation Nest Egg chick was hatched at the National Kiwi Hatchery Aotearoa in Rotorua, the only purpose-built kiwi conservation centre in the world open to the public. In 2015, after 22 years of support, BNZ sponsorship for kiwi came to an end, having raised more than \$12 million for the bird's conservation.[6]

Another organisation, and one with a kiwi association going back to at least 1914, came to the bird's rescue at this time. In 2005 Kiwi Bacon announced its plan to contribute to the conservation and management of kiwi throughout the country, by sponsoring the BNZ Kiwi Recovery Trust to the tune of at least \$150,000 over three years. A Kiwi Bacon spokesperson noted that when the company began, there were about seven million kiwi but now there were only about 70,000, 'so we felt we simply had to do our bit to help.'[7] The decline in the kiwi population has accelerated in the last 30 years, and the number of kiwi in unmanaged areas is halving every ten years; at this rate the bird will be extinct on the mainland in our lifetime.[8]

Māori and kiwi conservation

The kiwi is a taonga (treasure) to Māori, who have strong cultural, spiritual and historic associations with the bird. As the holders of traditional knowledge, tangata whenua have a vested interest in its welfare and are therefore working alongside conservation groups, communities, and the Department of Conservation Te Papa Atawhai to reverse the national decline of the kiwi population. For a number of iwi and hapū throughout New Zealand their relationship with kiwi has been formally recognised as part of their Treaty of Waitangi settlement claims, such as the Ngāi Tahu Claims Settlement Act 1998. Kiwi have become the flagship species for conservation, and today more than 90 community and iwi-led groups actively protect the bird over a combined area estimated to be 230,000 hectares, which is similar to the amount of public conservation land protected by DOC for kiwi.[9]

Lake Waikaremoana Hapū Restoration Trust is one such conservation group. The kiwi population around Lake Waikaremoana, Te Urewera National Park had declined by 90 per cent in the 70 years from 1920–90, and in order to restore the birds' numbers the local hapū worked with Dr John McLennan of Manaaki Whenua Landcare Research and DOC. Together, in 1992 they created an inland island along the shore of Lake Waikaremoana by fencing off the Puketukutuku Peninsula, which covers about 750 hectares and is surrounded by water on three sides. The fence was designed to keep kiwi chicks safe from pests, and electrified on the outside to deter pigs and deer. Lake Waikaremoana Hapū Restoration Trust also runs a trapping programme designed to eliminate stoats. Traps have been laid since after 1995, contributing to the remarkable 56 per cent survival rate among brown kiwi chicks. In the adjoining bush area, where no trapping takes place, kiwi chick survival rates are less than 10 per cent.[10]

The Kiwi Rescue research programme, which received funding from the Ministry of Business, Innovation & Employment, ran from October 2016 until March 2021, collaborating with various groups and organisations to develop new and cost-effective ways of helping everyone assist the kiwi. As part of the programme Kiwi Rescue worked with tangata whenua to identify kiwi on their land, assist with management and restoration decisions, and to determine whether existing science modelling and monitoring techniques were suitable for the bird's needs.[11]

In 2010 two kiwi, named Ngati Hine Rua and Ngati Hine Tahi, were blessed by Māori and given to the Smithsonian Conservation Biology Institute (SCBI) in Virginia. In 2016 the female laid an egg and after 'much attentive incubation' by her mate it hatched on 10 May. This birth of a healthy kiwi chick at SCBI was heralded as another step back from the brink of the bird's extinction.'[12]

Hatching survival plans

National Kiwi Hatchery Aotearoa continues to play a vital role in the preservation of our national bird. In the wild kiwi eggs get eaten by predators, and out of every hundred kiwi eggs laid in burrows in the forest only five chicks will make it to adulthood. By hatching the eggs in safety at the hatchery the birds have a 98 per cent survival rate, while releasing them when they're at least one kilogram in weight increases their survival rate in the wild from 5 to 65 per cent.[13]

It is believed that the kiwi population declines by two per cent every year. Of those kiwi which hatch in the wild, an appalling 95 per cent are killed before they reach adulthood. Around 20 kiwi are killed every week.[14]

Despite the grim outlook there is some positive news. Several current initiatives around the country demonstrate that when predator threats are removed and a community assumes responsibility for guardianship, people and kiwi can successfully live together. In the last decade Whakatāne's kiwi population has gone from eight to 300, and at Whangārei Heads from 80 to 880, while during a similar period a couple of dozen kiwi reintroduced to Rimutaka Forest Park have produced a population that now numbers 150. Also, the Capital Kiwi Project has undertaken efforts to restore a large scale and sustainable wild kiwi population to the Wellington region, the hillsides to the south and west of the city being prime habitat for the bird, providing plenty of shelter and food.[15] Overall, in terms of saving our national symbol, in 2016 DOC announced that it hopes the number of kiwi will be restored to around 100,000 by 2030, with species populations of 35,400 brown kiwi, 35,000 tokoeka (southern brown kiwi), 2900 little spotted kiwi, 19,900 great spotted kiwi and 900 rowi (Ōkārito brown kiwi).[16]

Almost bird of the century

But for an unlikely interloper, at the end of 2023 the kiwi would have been voted the Bird of the Century. In 2005 Forest & Bird — Aotearoa New Zealand's leading independent conservation organisation — inaugurated what has been hailed 'the world's favourite avian election', the Bird of the Year competition, which was won by the tūī. To celebrate its one-hundredth birthday in 2023 the organisation decided to determine which bird had 'captured New Zealanders' hearts over the last century'. There were 75 bird species in the competition, five of which were extinct and therefore a salutary reminder of the biodiversity this country has lost. (In fact, currently an appalling 82 per cent of our living native bird species are threatened or at risk of extinction.)

But if the kiwi — voted Bird of the Year in 2009 — had ideas of now being voted Bird of the Century, it hadn't counted on a global campaign conducted on television by British-American comedian John Oliver. It resulted in the top honour going to the pūteketeke, the Australasian crested grebe, a lake-dweller known for its eye-catching courtship and for carrying its chicks on its back. The pūteketeke obviously caught the public imagination and won with a massive 290,374 votes. While the North Island brown kiwi had the distinction of coming in (a distant) second, with 12,904 votes, it only just managed to head off the kea, which received 12,060.[17]

Robo-Kiwi

One region bucking the national trend of declining kiwi numbers is the Bay of Islands, where its kiwi population has been increasing by 3 per cent a year. This is despite the fact that within four months in 2023, 20 wild-hatched kiwi were killed in suspected dog attacks.[18] It is now recognised that uncontrolled dogs cause 70 per cent of kiwi deaths in the wild, and it seems entirely appropriate that kiwi ingenuity is now being tested to address the problem. A group of Canterbury University engineering students have joined forces with Scion (New Zealand Forest Research Institute Limited) and the National Kiwi Hatchery to develop a new tool, known as Robo-Kiwi, designed to deter dogs from attacking and killing the birds. Previously, taxidermied kiwi were used to train dogs to avoid the birds, but apart from such specimens being difficult to obtain, some dogs did not interact with static objects. However, the new Robo-Kiwi model, consisting of a 3D printed shell with moving legs propelled along a rail, is much closer to the real thing and so provokes a stronger reaction in dogs.

Depending on its response to the device, the trainer is able to give the dog an 'uncomfortable feeling' by means of a collar. By receiving such 'corrections' the hope is that the dog will quickly learn to leave the

Robo-Kiwi, with its moving feet propelled along a rail, was designed to replace a static kiwi as a training aid.

Scion

real bird alone. The rail is lightweight and easily transportable, and the intention is that Robo-Kiwi can be taken to areas where the birds are present, and dog owners can enrol their animals in kiwi avoidance training sessions.[19]

In late 2023 concerns were expressed that efforts to conserve the kiwi could be compromised by the sale of a stuffed toy for dogs, in the shape of the bird and wearing a Santa hat. Although it did not 'strongly resemble a real-life kiwi', and was unlikely to train dogs to attack birds, the chief executive of Save the Kiwi, Michelle Limpey, said it was a 'bad look', especially since several kiwi had been killed in dog attacks in recent months. It was also pointed out that kiwi have a strong smell — presumably not something replicated in the toy — which dogs find attractive and so hunt kiwi for game rather than eating. As it turned out, Mitre 10 agreed to remove the kiwi-shaped toy from its shelves, and so the real bird may have been able to rest a little bit easier over Christmas 2023.[20]

Conclusion

After millions of years of splendid isolation in primordial Aotearoa New Zealand, the kiwi was confronted by the arrival of humans. Over the next thousand years the 'hidden bird of Tāne' was the source of feathers for prestigious garments and, more recently, became an unofficial national symbol. Unlike any other bird, it was probably the kiwi's curious features that ensured both the rise in its public profile and enduring popularity. As a result, the name and likeness of the bird found their way into all aspects of New Zealand life and commerce. But humans settlers also introduced pests and predators to this country, raising the prospect that the kiwi might be following its larger cousin, the moa, to extinction. However, recent campaigns have raised awareness of the kiwi's plight, and suggest that populations are now recovering. For that, and other reasons, New Zealanders need to look after its unique nocturnal and flightless bird. While there is no other bird quite like it, there may be no other creature on Earth that has had such an impact on the culture and identity of its homeland.

Notes

1   A land of birds: From Gondwana to Zealandia

1. Craig Robertson, 'Gondwana, How it got its name', March 2008, www.thestudy.net.au/projects/gondwana-name.html
2. 'Golden Westland/Survey Results/An Ancient Continent', *Grey River Argus*, 28 November 1908.
3. collections.tepapa.govt.nz/topic/1326
4. E.M., 'Mystery of the Moa', *Taranaki Daily News*, 4 June 1932.
5. www.britannica.com/animal/kakapo
6. www.aucklandmuseum.com/discover/stories/blog/2015/did-the-kiwi-ever-fly

2   The hidden bird of Tane

1. www.bbcearth.com/news/who-really-discovered-new-zealand
2. Elsdon Best, *Forest Lore of the Maori*, E.C. Keating, Government Printer, Wellington, 1977, pp. 165–66.
3. A.W. Reed (Illustrations by Roger Hart), *Maori Legends*, A.H. & A.W. Reed, Wellington, 1972, p. 6.
4. www.polynesia.com/blog/maori-legend-how-the-kiwi-bird-lost-his-wings
5. Carolyn M. King (ed.), *The Handbook of New Zealand Mammals*, Oxford University Press, Auckland, 1990, p. 177.
6. Te Rangi Hiroa (Sir Peter Buck), *The Coming of the Maori*, Maori Purposes Fund Board, Wellington, 1958, pp. 93, 99.
7. www.doc.govt.nz/nature/conservation-status/threatened-birds
8. *New Zealand Mammals*, pp. 281–87.
9. Elsdon Best, *Forest Lore of the Maori*, E.C. Keating, Government Printer, Wellington, 1977, pp. 167–68.
10. J.S. Polack, *New Zealand: Being a Narrative of Travels and Adventures During a Residence in that Country Between the Years 1831 and 1837*, (originally published by Richard Bentley, London, 1838), Kiwi Publishers, Christchurch, 2000, pp. 135, 138–39.
11. Jock Phillips, 'Kiwi — Kiwi and people: early history', Te Ara — the Encyclopedia of New Zealand, www.TeAra.govt.nz/en/kiwi/page-4 (accessed 17 July 2023).
12. Elsdon Best, *Forest Lore of the Maori*, p. 170.
13. Mick Pendergrast, *Te Aho Tapu: The Sacred Thread*, Reed Methuen Publishers Ltd, Auckland, 1987, pp. 6–10, 108.
14. https://nzetc.victoria.ac.nz/tm/scholarly/tei-Bea01Bank-t1-body-d7-d6.html
15. A.H. McLintock, *An Encyclopaedia of New Zealand*, R.E. Owen, Government Printer, Wellington, 1966, Vol. 2, p. 791.
16. J.S. Polack, *New Zealand: Being a Narrative of Travels and Adventures During a Residence in that Country Between the Years 1831 and 1837*, p. 138.
17. John Ward, Secretary to the New Zealand Company, *Information Relative to New-Zealand Compiled for the Use of Colonists*, John W. Parker, West Strand, London, 1840, pp. 51–58.
18. 'In Touch with Nature/Notes on Natural History in New Zealand/(By James Drummond, F.L.S., F.Z.S.)', *Otago Daily Times*, 18 November 1911.
19. 'Account of an Exploring Expedition to the S.W. of Nelson', *Nelson Examiner and New Zealand Chronicle*, 7 March 1846.
20. 'Account of an Exploring Expedition to the S.W. of Nelson', *Nelson Examiner and New Zealand Chronicle*, 14 March 1846.
21. Elsdon Best, *Forest Lore of the Maori*, pp. 114–15.

3   'A perfectly new genus': Discovered by science

1. www.canterbury.ac.nz/news/2021/unfolding-the-mystery-of-the-first-kiwi-specimen.html
2. www.newzealandantiqueprints.co.nz/gallery/birds/shaw.html
3. George Shaw; Frederick Polydore Nodder, illustrator; and Elizabeth R. Nodder, publisher, *Vivarium Naturae* or *The Naturalist's Miscellany*, printed by Buchanan McMillan, London, 1812–13, vol. 24, plates 1057 and 0058, www.biodiversitylibrary.org/bibliography/79941
4. www.canterbury.ac.nz/news-and-events/news/unfolding-the-mystery-of-the-first-kiwi-specimen.html
5. teara.govt.nz/en/artwork/10186/early-european-engraving
6. Michael Lee, *Navigators & Naturalists: French Exploration of New Zealand and the South Seas (1769-1824)*, David Bateman Ltd, Auckland, 2018, pp. 382–94.
7. J.L. Nicholas, *Narrative of Voyage to New Zealand*, (originally published as Narrative of a Voyage to New Zealand, printed for James Black and Son, London, 1817), facsimile edition, Wilson & Horton, 1971, Vol. 2, p. 255.
8. William Yate, *An Account of New Zealand and of the Church Missionary Society's Mission in the Northern Island*, 1835 (facsimile edition by A.H. & A.W. Reed, Wellington, 1970), pp. 58–61.
9. Richard Owen, 10th lecture, 29 May 1838, 'Digestive System of Birds'. Notes made by Wm. W. Cooper, later revised and corrected by Owen. Collection of Royal College of Surgeons, 42C.26.
10. Richard Owen, 1st lecture, 30 April 1839, 'Introduction to the Course'. Notes made by Wm. W. Cooper, later revised and corrected by Owen. Collection of Royal College of Surgeons, 42C.27.
11. *Proceedings of the Zoological Society of London*, 1839, 7:63–65.
12. Richard Owen, 'Exhibition of a Bone of an Unknown Struthious Bird from New Zealand', *Proceedings of the Zoological Society of London*, 1840, 7:169–71.
13. *Tasmanian Journal of Natural Science*, vol. 2, 1846, no. 6, pp. 239–40. Reprinted from *Athenaeum*, no. 850, p. 138.
14. *The Annals and Magazine of Natural History*, vol. 1, Second Series, 1850, pp. 147–52.
15. *New Zealander*, 24 May 1862.
16. 'Mechanics' Institute', *New Zealand Herald and Auckland Gazette*, 24 July 1841.
17. *New Zealand Gazette and Wellington Spectator*, 7 August 1841.
18. *New Zealand Gazette and Wellington Spectator*, 20 November 1841.
19. 'Remarks/On the Natural History and Comparative Anatomy of the Kiwi', F.J. Knox M.D., *New Zealand Gazette and Wellington Spectator*, 1 December 1841.
20. 'Remarks/On the Natural History and Comparative Anatomy of the Kiwi', F.J. Knox M.D., 'Concluded From Our Last', *New Zealand Gazette and Wellington Spectator*, 4 December 1841.
21. J. Drummond, F.L.S., F.Z.S., 'Nature Notes', *New Zealand Herald*, 11 September 1920.
22. 'The English Mail/New Zealand Affairs', *Daily Southern Cross*, 18 August 1869.
23. J. Drummond, 'In Touch with Nature/Notes on Natural History in New Zealand', *Otago Daily Times*, 24 May 1913; 'Nature Notes', *New Zealand Herald*, 11 September 1920; 'In Touch With Nature/At Home in Captivity', *Otago Witness*, 7 June 1932.
24. J. Drummond, 'Anglo-Colonial Notes', *Otago Daily Times*, 30 May 1907.
25. J. Drummond, 'Nature Notes', *New Zealand Herald*, 11 September 1920; *Taranaki Daily News*, 30 October 1929.
26. *Daily Southern Cross*, 29 October 1852.
27. 'Report on Apteryx in New Zealand', *Otago Daily Times*, 5 June 1862.
28. Ibid.
29. 'The Museum at Christchurch', *Otago Daily Times*, 9 December 1867.
30. Andreas Reischek, *Yesterdays in Maoriland* (originally published as Yesterdays in Maoriland: New Zealand in the 'Eighties, Jonathan Cape, London, 1930), facsimile edition published by Wilson & Horton Ltd, Auckland, 1970, pp. 177, 218–21.
31. *Wellington Independent*, 12 May 1868.
32. *Evening Post*, 29 January 1868.
33. *New Zealand Herald*, 18 May 1882.
34. 'Museum Jottings / II The Flightless Birds', *Otago Daily Times*, 25 May 1888.

4   Settlement from Europe: The kiwi under threat

1. John Ward, Secretary to the New Zealand Company, *Information Relative to New Zealand Compiled for the Use of Colonists*, John W. Parker, West Strand, London, 1840, p. 1.
2. Rev P. Walsh, 'On the Disappearance of the New Zealand Bush', *Transactions and Proceedings of the Royal Society of New Zealand*, Vol. 29, 1896, pp. 490–96.
3. Bronwyn Dalley and Gavin McLean (eds), *Frontier of Dreams: The Story of New Zealand*, Hachette Livre Ltd, Auckland, 2005, pp. 49–50.

4. 'News of the Week', *Otago Witness*, 22 July 1871.
5. www.nfrt.org.nz/the-facts/
6. savethekiwi.nz/about-kiwi/threats-to-kiwi/loss-of-habitat/
7. 'The Comical Kiwi', *Auckland Star*, 12 June 1913.
8. *Otago Daily Times*, 5 August 1925.
9. Carolyn M. King (ed.), *The Handbook of New Zealand Mammals*, Oxford University Press, Auckland, 1990, pp. 206–225.
10. Ibid, pp. 192–206.
11. Ibid, pp. 206–225.
12. nzbirdsonline.org.nz/species/huia
13. 'New Zealand Game Laws', *New Zealand Herald*, 23 August 1905.
14. King, *The Handbook of New Zealand Mammals*, pp. 68–78.
15. www.doc.govt.nz/nature/pests-and-threats/animal-pests/possums/
16. projectcrimson.org.nz/
17. 'News of the Day/Importation of Mongoose', *Globe*, 15 May 1877.
18. King, *The Handbook of New Zealand Mammals*, p. 280.
19. 'New Zealand Birds/Their Beauty and Rarity', *Hawke's Bay Tribune*, 10 October 1934.
20. 'Cats the Destroyers of Game and Song-Birds in New Zealand', *Colonist*, 12 August 1864.
21. 'Game Laws', *Daily Southern Cross*, 13 June 1867.
22. King, *The Handbook of New Zealand Mammals*, p. 310.
23. www.nzgeo.com/stories/the-menace-of-stoats
24. www.doc.govt.nz/nature/native-animals/birds-a-z/kiwi/facts/
25. King, *The Handbook of New Zealand Mammals*, pp. 313–20.
26. Ibid, pp. 320–30.
27. savethekiwi.nz/about-us/what-we-do/predator-control/
28. *Thames Advertiser*, 6 July 1888.

5 Early symbols of identity: Kiwi in Fernland

1. *New Zealander*, 23 June 1849.
2. *Daily Southern Cross*, 25 September 1860.
3. *Daily Southern Cross*, 9 October 1859.
4. *Daily Southern Cross*, 7 June 1859.
5. 'State of Trade', *Daily Southern Cross*, 14 June 1861.
6. teara.govt.nz/en/object/37131/trading-bank-banknotes-bank-of-new-zealand-note
7. *Timaru Herald*, 2 August 1881.
8. *Otago Witness*, 20 August 1886.
9. *Wairarapa Age*, 9 August 1913.
10. *Wairarapa Times-Age*, 26 April 1938.
11. 'Wellington', *Nelson Examiner and New Zealand Chronicle*, 24 March 1855.
12. 'Monetary and Commercial/Auckland', *Daily Southern Cross*, 12 March 1866.
13. 'Sporting/A Big Pacing Feat', *Mataura Ensign*, 3 January 1916.
14. *Daily Southern Cross*, 11 August 1857.
15. *Daily Southern Cross*, 19 November 1858.
16. *Daily Telegraph*, 28 June 1900.
17. 'For Sale', *Auckland Star*, 13 June 1878; *Hawke's Bay Herald*, 4 July 1887 and 6 August 1887.
18. 'The Flightless Birds of New Zealand', *Hokitika Guardian*, 15 December 1917.
19. 'In Touch with Nature', *Lyttelton Times*, 18 August 1916.
20. *New Zealand Herald*, 21 February 1920.
21. *New Zealand Times*, 22 December 1900.
22. 'Kempthorne, Prosser & Co.'s New Warehouse', *New Zealand Herald*, 4 November 1892.
23. 'Destructive Fire in the City', *Evening Post*, 25 March 1905.
24. 'The Wellington Fire', *Manawatu Standard*, 25 March 1904.
25. *Observer*, 8 October 1881.
26. *New Zealand Times*, 25 February 1890.
27. *Southern Cross*, 14 March 1914; *Otago Daily Times*, 6 March 1916.
28. *Otago Witness*, 8 September 1892 and 19 December 1895.
29. *Otago Daily Times*, 6 November 1891.
30. *Press*, 30 April 1900.
31. 'The New Railway Policy', *Hawke's Bay Herald*, 30 May 1900.
32. 'Random Notes', *Western Star*, 24 May 1927.
33. 'Banquet', *Timaru Herald*, 23 March 1888.
34. 'God's Own Country, by Thomas Bracken', *New Zealand Herald*, 28 May 1892.
35. *Evening Post*, 16 June 1906.
36. 'The Critic', *NZ Truth*, 4 May 1907.

6 'Rara Avis': A bird of the people

1. 'Random Shots', *Auckland Star*, 30 April 1898.
2. *Hawera and Normanby Star*, 27 September 1900.
3. 'Parliament/Yesterday's Sittings', *Evening Post*, 17 August 1900.
4. 'Anglo-Colonial Notes/The Kiwi', *New Zealand Herald*, 19 June 1901.
5. 'More Protection/The Native Fauna/A Sympathetic Minister', *Star* (Christchurch), 17 June 1913.
6. 'New Zealand Fauna/Threatened Extinction', *New Zealand Times*, 16 July 1913.
7. 'The Garden/The Late Mr Alexander Allison', *Manawatu Standard*, 23 September 1932.
8. David Yerex and Westbrook Haines, *The Kiwifruit Story*, Agricultural Publishing Associates Limited, Masterton, 1983, pp. 11–14; P.R. Sale, *Kiwifruit Culture*, V.R. Ward, Government Printer, Wellington, 1983-85, pp. 8–9.
9. 'Industries Week/Will Begin Today', *Lyttelton Times*, 27 April 1909.
10. *Evening Post*, 5 June 1901.
11. *Poverty Bay Herald*, 15 June 1901; *Evening Star*, 24 June 1901; 'With the Royal Tour', *New Zealand Herald*, 31 May 1902.
12. 'Anglo-Colonial Notes', *New Zealand Herald*, 9 March 1903.
13. 'Maori Curios', *Hawke's Bay Herald*, 21 June 1901.
14. *Lyttelton Times*, 6 January 1902.
15. 'Maori Wedding', *Fielding Star*, 11 April 1903.
16. 'New Zealand as a Tourist Resort/Wonders of England's Colony in the Southern Seas Displayed at the World's Fair', *Hawera & Normanby Star*, 7 September 1904.
17. 'Science Notes/A "Link" Not Yet Missing', *New Zealand Mail*, 7 October 1903.
18. 'Flemington Presbyterian Church', *Ashburton Guardian*, 9 October 1903.
19. 'Our Own Animals/The Ancient House of Apteryx/A Bird of Many Parts', *Lyttelton Times*, 29 April 1903.
20. 'Local and General', *Wairarapa Daily Times*, 14 November 1908.
21. 'Acclimatisation/Aims of the Societies', *New Zealand Times*, 31 July 1905.
22. *Oamaru Mail*, 28 February 1906; *Temuka Leader*, 3 March 1906; *Free Lance*, 3 March 1906.
23. 'The Fretful Porcupine', *Observer*, 21 July 1906; *Auckland Star*, 3 July 1906.
24. 'Girl Guide Notes', *Manawatu Times*, 3 November 1934.
25. 'The Natural History Court/Birds, Beasts and Plants', *Lyttelton Times*, 6 November 1906.
26. Ibid.
27. 'Bird Life/The New Zealand Avifauna', *Lyttelton Times*, 7 April 1908.
28. 'Nature Notes', *New Zealand Herald*, 17 October 1914.
29. Edith Howes, 'The Kiwi', *New Zealand Herald*, 28 November 1911.
30. *New Zealand Herald*, 4 March 1908 and 10 June 1908.
31. 'New Zealand V. Australia/Notes on the Game', *Grey River Argus*, 12 September 1913.
32. 'The "All-Star" Match', *New Zealand Times*, 20 December 1913.
33. www.aucklandartgallery.com/explore-art-and-ideas/artwork/5907/te-rangi-o-te-moa
34. 'Bowling', *Evening Post*, 21 May 1909; *Otago Daily Times*, 3 June 1909.
35. 'Local and General', *Wairoa Bell*, 16 March 1909.
36. *Free Lance*, 9 July 1910.
37. *Manawatu Times*, 15 January 1909.
38. 'In Touch with Nature', *Lyttelton Times*, 1 April 1911.
39. 'Dominion Coat of Arms', *Poverty Bay Herald*, 12 February 1909.
40. See Hamish Keith (text) and William Main (picture research), *New Zealand Yesterdays: A Look at Our Recent Past*, Readers' Digest Services Pty Limited, NSW, 2020, pp. 31–33.
41. 'Local and General News', *New Zealand Herald*, 31 August 1909; *Poverty Bay Herald*, 16 April 1910.
42. *Evening Post*, 30 September 1910.

43. 'New Zealand Arms', *New Zealand Herald*, 22 August 1911.
44. Denis Glover, 'Zealandia' in A.H. McLintock (ed.), *An Encyclopaedia of New Zealand*, E.R. Owen, Government Printer, Wellington, 1966, Vol. 3, p. 701.
45. 'City Coat of Arms/Design Adopted by Christchurch', *Ashburton Guardian*, 15 August 1922.
46. 'Topics of the Day', *Press*, 15 August 1907.
47. *New Zealand Herald*, 5 September 1912.
48. 'Kiwi and Kangaroo/Should Know One Another Better', *Auckland Star*, 29 June 1914.
49. 'A Suffrage March', *Star* (Christchurch), 9 September 1911.
50. 'Swimming', *Auckland Star*, 7 Match 1912.
51. 'Local and General', *Wanganui Herald*, 4 October 1912.
52. *Southland Times*, 13 January 1913.
53. The 1912 Christmas issue of the *Auckland Weekly News*, with the kiwi on the cover, was advertised in the *New Zealand Herald*, 19 October 1912.
54. *New Zealand Herald*, 21 February 1913.
55. *Auckland Star*, 18 March 1913.
56. 'To Protect the Birds/Illicit Slaughter', *Dominion*, 8 October 1914.
57. 'Kiwi Disabled/Broken Tail-Shaft', *Nelson Evening Mail*, 10 October 1914.

7   Kiwi at the Front: The patriotic Apteryx

1. 'Universal Defensive Training/A National League of New Zealand', *Evening Post*, 25 August 1906.
2. *Wanganui Herald*, 23 August 1910.
3. 'Kiwi Rifle Club', *Evening Star*, 16 July 1914.
4. 'Volunteer and Defence Notes', *Evening Star*, 28 January 1903.
5. *Evening Star*, 18 July 1911.
6. *Taranaki Herald*, 16 November 1911.
7. 'The Critic', *New Zealand Truth*, 13 January 1912.
8. 'London Personals/Doings of New Zealanders Abroad', *New Zealand Times*, 9 April 1912.
9. 'In Touch with Nature', *Lyttelton Times*, 23 December 1911.
10. 'Our Readers' Opinions/The Country's National Badge', *Gisborne Times*, 17 September 1914.
11. 'Home of the Kiwi/New Museum Exhibit/Reconstructed Forest Scene', *New Zealand Herald*, 16 April 1915.
12. 'Scientific Collection/Valuable Bird Skins and Eggs/Deposited at Canterbury Museum', *Lyttelton Times*, 12 April 1916.
13. 'Our Dying Native Birds', *Woodville Examiner*, 17 November 1916.
14. 'German Trade', *Sun* (Christchurch), 22 May 1915.
15. 'Tale of a Pig/And a Stuffed Kiwi', *Wanganui Chronicle*, 26 May 1915.
16. *Evening Post*, 29 November 1915.
17. *Wairarapa Daily Times*, 6 April 1916.
18. 'Local and General', *Wairarapa Daily Times*, 25 July 1916.
19. *Thames Star*, 4 October 1917.
20. 'Our Badges', *Ellesmere Guardian*, 5 September 1917.
21. 'With the 29ths/The Poor Tommy Atkins', *Ohinemuri Gazette*, 23 November 1917.
22. 'Women Folk', *Star* (Christchurch), 22 December 1917.
23. 'In Memoriam', *Ashburton Guardian*, 12 October 1918.
24. *Taranaki Herald*, 25 April 1917.
25. 'Anzacs' Christmas/How the New Zealanders Spent the Day', *Ashburton Guardian*, 16 February 1917.
26. 'In the Off Season/New Zealanders in Paris', *Dominion*, 18 May 1918.
27. 'Off the Line of Route/Private Decorative Efforts', *Auckland Star*, 18 July 1919.
28. 'General News', *Press*, 12 August 1920.
29. 'Local and General News', *New Zealand Herald*, 13 May 1920.
30. 'The Prince's Tour/Valuable Collection of Presents/Gifts From New Zealand', *Otago Daily Times*, 6 May 1921.
31. *Oamaru Mail*, 6 July 1920.
32. 'Notice to the Public', *Evening Star*, 30 August 1920.
33. 'Trade Mark Dispute/Similarity of Design', *New Zealand Times*, 7 August 1923.
34. 'Court of Appeal/Judgments Delivered', *Auckland Star*, 16 April 1924.
35. 'A Polish Problem: Trouble of a Trade Mark', *New Zealand Times*, 2 April 1924.
36. 'Commerce and Finance/Merchandise Market', *Otago Daily Times*, 7 March 1927.
37. *Auckland Star*, 25 September 1929.
38. *New Zealand Herald*, 26 October 1939.
39. 'Local and General', *Horowhenua Chronicle*, 24 September 1930.
40. *Colonist*, 1 September 1919.
41. 'On Beacon Hill/New Zealand Emblem at Sling/The Giant Chalk Kiwi', *Marlborough Express*, 26 September 1919.
42. 'Entre Nous', *Free Lance*, 8 October 1919.
43. *Timaru Herald*, 29 May 1920.
44. 'Making Giant Bird', *New Zealand Herald*, 30 August 1945.
45. 'Huge Kiwi/Memorial at Bulford', *Ashburton Guardian*, 29 August 1945.
46. 'Chalk Kiwi Restored', *Press*, 28 July 1981.

8   Consolidation: The rise of the symbolic kiwi in the 1920s and 30s

1. James Drummond, 'The Kiwi's Brain/Nature Notes', *Star* (Christchurch), 14 March 1932.
2. J.H.S., 'Maori Memories/Art of Bird Catching', *Taranaki Daily News*, 3 November 1934.
3. *Manawatu Standard*, 13 May 1935.
4. 'Maori Nature Notes', *Manawatu Times*, 16 January 1930.
5. 'New Zealand Birds/Kiwi's Sense of Smell/Lecture by Mr. Edgar F. Stead', *Press*, 14 November 1934.
6. James Drummond, 'Nature Notes/Grey Kiwis', *New Zealand Herald*, 9 July 1932.
7. 'Nature Notes/Extinction of Birds', *Evening Post*, 15 January 1927.
8. 'Bird Food Supply', *Evening Post*, 29 May 1929.
9. 'News in Brief', *Otago Daily Times*, 28 January 1926.
10. 'West Coast Sounds/In the Country of the Deer', *Otago Witness*, 3 May 1927.
11. 'Out in the Sunshine/The Vast Silence', *Manawatu Times*, 3 January 1924.
12. 'Stoats and Weasels', *Auckland Star*, 28 May 1889; *Auckland Star*, 1 February 1924.
13. 'Deer Menace/Effect on Plants and Birds/Damage by Chamois', *Auckland Star*, 8 March 1930.
14. 'The Destruction of Deer', *Otago Daily Times*, 18 December 1935.
15. 'Man's Friends/Defence of Native Birds', *Evening Star*, 30 August 1933.
16. 'Protecting the Kiwi/Society's Suggestion/Danger from Weasels', *Sun* (Auckland), 29 August 1930.
17. 'Opossums in the Bush', *Evening Post*, 17 December 1932.
18. 'Still Time to Save the Kiwi', *Evening Post*, 23 July 1934.
19. 'Opossum Traps/Menace to Kiwis/Remedy Sought', *Dominion*, 8 September 1934.
20. 'Nature — And Man/The Battle for Beauty', *Akaroa Mail and Banks Peninsular Advertiser*, 11 September 1934.
21. 'Nature — And Man/Pity the Kiwi', *Hawke's Bay Tribune*, 10 November 1933.
22. 'The Kiwi/Loss by Poison', *Evening Post*, 1 November 1937.
23. 'Loss of Native Birds/Free Slaughter Alleged/Withdrawal of Protection', *New Zealand Herald*, 5 July 1938.
24. 'Fishing Regulations', *New Zealand Herald*, 11 October 1939.
25. 'Animals Protection and Game/New Bill Introduced', *Otago Daily Times*, 27 September 1921; 'Game Protection Bill/In Legislative Council/Some Important Amendments Made in Measure', *New Zealand Times*, 25 January 1922.
26. J. Drummond. 'In Touch with Nature', *Otago Daily Times*, 21 March 1922.
27. 'An Albino Kiwi', *Stratford Evening Post*, 15 April 1922.
28. 'Local and General', *Waikato Independent*, 11 May 1922.
29. 'General News', *Press*, 4 March 1936.
30. X.Y., 'By the Way', *Evening Star*, 14 March 1936.
31. 'Nature Notes/New Zealand Birds', *Evening Post*, 12 December 1925.
32. 'Kiwi in Molesworth Street', *Evening Post*, 16 September 1926; *New Zealand Times*, 17 September 1926; *Evening Star*, 18 September 1926.
33. 'Kiwi at Large', *Evening Post*, 2 October 1931; 'Kiwi 'Detained' by Police', *Dominion*, 2 October 1931.
34. 'Local and General', *Taranaki Daily News*, 27 January 1932.
35. 'Dead Kiwi Found', *Bay of Plenty Times* and 'News of the Day', *Taranaki Daily News*, 26 September 1933.

36. *Manawatu Standard*, 17 December 1921.
37. *Manawatu Standard*, 7 February 1925.
38. *Waikato Times*, 23 June 1931.
39. *Ohinemuri Gazette*, 30 March 1921.
40. *Press*, 26 October 1921.
41. *Auckland Star*, 14 August 1922.
42. R.S.D., 'Lost and Found/Notes by a Pakeha Maori', *North Canterbury Gazette*, 26 August 1932.
43. 'Kiwi Beats the Springbok/Fast Forward Work', *Evening Star*, 15 August 1921.
44. 'Without Prejudice', *Dominion*, 17 September 1921.
45. 'Sports of All Kinds', *Otago Daily Times*, 18 June 1925.
46. 'Points of View/"Kiwis" or "All Blacks"', *Waipa Post*, 19 June 1934.
47. 'Local and General', *Ellesmere Guardian*, 22 June 1934.
48. 'British Empire Games/How New Zealanders Fared', *Southland Times*, 15 September 1930.
49. 'Unprecedented Scenes', *Dominion*, 5 October 1926.
50. 'Kiwi Feathers for Sale', *New Zealand Herald*, 9 July 1929.
51. 'Rarer Every Year/Maori Mats and Ornaments/Shortage Now Noticeable', *Auckland Star*, 11 March 1927.
52. 'Ostrich and Pheasant Supplant Kiwi Feathers', *Sun* (Auckland), 5 May 1927; *Gisborne Times*, 5 July 1927.
53. 'Gift of Valuable Kiwi Mat', *Gisborne Times*, 7 March 1922; *Poverty Bay Herald*, 7 March 1922; *Manawatu Standard*, 14 March 1922.
54. 'Comrades of "Diggers"/Governor and Premier', *Auckland Star*, 17 February 1926.
55. 'A Unique Trip/Through the Urewera', *Evening Post*, 12 October 1928.
56. 'Poho-O-Rawiri/Meeting House on Kaiti', *Gisborne Times*, 12 March 1930.
57. 'Maoris Welcome/Reception to Governor', *Poverty Bay Herald*, 19 June 1931.
58. 'His Excellency's Tour/Maori Lands Inspected', *Auckland Star*, 19 December 1931.
59. 'Native Settlement/Prime Minister Impressed', *Otago Daily Times*, 31 January 1935; 'Maoris' Farewell/The Governor-General', *New Zealand Herald*, 2 February 1935.
60. 'Personal', *Poverty Bay Herald*, 31 December 1936; 'A Spell in New Zealand', *Evening Post*, 28 June 1938.
61. 'Mascot Mat/Chief's Gift to Admiral', *New Zealand Herald*, 2 March 1933; 'Maori Robe/Historic Garment/Worn at Jutland', *Auckland Star*, 29 April 1939.
62. 'First Sea Lord Gives Haka at London Dinner', *Press*, 15 February 1957.
63. 'Nightingales Singing/Export of Kiwis Prohibited', *Taranaki Daily News*, 16 January 1928.
64. 'Kiwi Hatched in Oven', *Taranaki Daily News*, 19 April 1929.
65. 'Game Fowl Club/First Dominion Show', *Auckland Star*, 24 July 1929.
66. 'Down Petticoat Lane/True Blue New Zealand', *Wanganui Chronicle*, 26 July 1929.
67. '1930 kiwi hatched naturally', *Press*, 15 January 1977.
68. 'Last Kiwi in Europe/Bird at London Zoo', *Hawera Star*, 18 February 1935; 'In London Zoo/Kiwi is Strangest Bird', *Gisborne Times*, 20 March 1935.
69. 'Kiwi in Captivity/Retention Not Legal', *New Zealand Herald*, 8 April 1937.
70. 'Young Kiwi Growing', *Thames Star*, 19 March 1938; 'Kiwi Chick Dead', *Otago Daily Times*, 21 June 1938.
71. 'Our Native Birds/Many Unique Species', *New Zealand Herald*, 12 August 1924.
72. 'News of the Day', *New Zealand Times*, 18 June 1924.
73. 'Random Shots', *Auckland Star*, 1 November 1924.
74. 'The Governor-General/A Crowded Day', *Press*, 4 November 1924.
75. *Hawke's Bay Tribune*, 22 October 1924 and 22 May 1926.
76. 'Fern Leaf Produce', *Hawera Star*, 26 March 1925.
77. 'The Proper Brand', *Wairarapa Age*, 14 April 1925.
78. 'Empire Show Cards/Marketing Board's Idea/New Zealand Kiwi', *Otago Daily Times*, 7 August 1928.
79. 'Trade and Sport Sections', *New Zealand Herald*, 7 October 1932.
80. 'Fine Empire Building/British Architects' Headquarters', *Press*, 28 December 1934.
81. 'Finance and Commerce', *Press*, 14 January 1933.
82. 'Trade Prospects Brighter', *Manawatu Times*, 14 June 1939.
83. 'The Butter Market', *Press*, 24 February 1934.
84. 'National Flower and Bird', *Nelson Evening Mail*, 22 March 1939.
85. 'Nature and Man/Tui in the Lead', *Wanganui Chronicle*, 8 May 1939; 'News of the Day/Kowhai and Tui', *Auckland Star*, 10 April 1939.
86. 'The Exhibition/Figures Maintained', *Evening Post*, 18 April 1940.
87. 'Transport at Exhibition', *Press*, 4 September 1939.
88. 'Auctions', *Evening Post*, 7 May 1942; 'Relic Under Hammer', *Auckland Star*, 20 May 1942.
89. 'Casual Comments/Friends and Enemies', *Press*, 19 November 1927.
90. 'Air Language/Officer Not a Pilot is a Kiwi', *Southland Times*, 8 July 1925.
91. 'Idolised Kiwi/Not for Lindbergh', *Auckland Star*, 23 February 1928.
92. 'The Tasman Flyers', *Evening Post*, 24 September 1928; 'Four Kiwis Will Fly Back to Australia', *Sun* (Auckland), 26 September 1928'; 'Week-End Postponement/Blenheim Disappointed', *Auckland Star*, 1October 1928.
93. 'Tasman Air Mail', *Evening Post*, 1 March 1934.
94. 'College Mascots', *Evening Star*, 19 March 1929; *Dominion*, 5 April 1929.
95. 'The New Penny Stamp', *Fielding Star*, 22 November 1926.
96. 'News of the Day/Criticism of Stamps', *Evening Post*, 18 March 1932.
97. 'New Stamp Issue', *Dominion*, 19 August 1933.
98. 'New Stamp Issue', *Dominion*, 25 August 1933.
99. 'News of the Day/New Penny Stamp', *Evening Post*, 30 June 1938.
100. 'The New Penny Stamp/Disgusted' (letter to the editor), *Otago Daily Times*, 7 July 1938.
101. 'The Exchange Rate/Its Mechanism and Its Function', *Auckland Star*, 2 February 1933.
102. 'In the Public Mind/Exchange Rate', *Auckland Star*, 8 February 1933.
103. 'Exchange Mystery/A Problem to Solve', *Waikato Times*, 23 December 1933.
104. 'The New Zealand Pound', *New Zealand Herald*, 21 August 1934.
105. 'Newly Minted/New Zealand Sixpences', *Northern Advocate*, 22 January 1934.
106. 'Warlike Shilling/Experts Criticise New Zealand Coins', *Dominion*, 30 April 1934.
107. 'Motueka/Rugby Sub-Union', *Nelson Evening Mail*, 20 April 1935.
108. 'Mr Holyoake in Sport', *Press*, 13 August 1957; 'What the Candidates Are Saying', *Press*, 16 November 1957.
109. 'Farewell Dinner/Mr Holyoake Honoured', *Ashburton Guardian*, 18 July 1946.
110. 'Mr Nash Speaks in Christchurch', *Press*, 19 November 1960.
111. 'News of the Day/Lord Rutherford's Arms', *Evening Post*, 29 April 1932.
112. 'Toothache Free/Children of Today', *Auckland Star*, 30 May 1938.
113. 'Our Mother Tongue/Random Notes and Little Problems', *New Zealand Herald*, 18 February 1939.
114. 'Plant Acclimatisation/Activities in Auckland/Propagation of Exotics', *New Zealand Herald*, 20 September 1921.
115. *Auckland Star*, 24 November 1921.
116. 'Plant Acclimatisation' (editorial), *Press*, 24 January 1923.
117. 'The Chinese Gooseberry/Valuable Jam Fruit', *New Zealand Herald*, 21 June 1923.
118. *Manawatu Standard*, 18 January 1924.
119. 'Valuable New Fruit/The Chinese Gooseberry, Beauty and Utility', *New Zealand Herald*, 5 October 1925.
120. *Hawke's Bay Tribune*, 14 October 1927.
121. 'The Chinese Gooseberry/An Attractive Fruit', *New Zealand Herald*, 6 July 1928; 'Chinese Gooseberry/Cultivation Methods', *New Zealand Herald*, 13 July 1929; 'Profitable Crop/The Chinese Gooseberry', *New Zealand Herald*, 5 October 1935.
122. 'The Chinese Gooseberry', *Waikato Times*, 23 July 1938.
123. Roly Earp, *The Kiwifruit Adventure*, The Dunmore Press, Palmerston North, 1988, pp. 16–17.
124. David Yerex and Westbrook Haines, *The Kiwifruit Story*, Agricultural Publishing Associates Limited, Masterton, 1983, pp. 11–14; P.R. Sale, *Kiwifruit Culture*, V.R. Ward, Government Printer, Wellington, 1983–85, pp. 8–9.

9 Back to the Front: The kiwi during World War Two

1. H.W. Orsman, *The Dictionary of New Zealand English*, Oxford University Press, Auckland, 1997, p. 207.
2. 'Third Generation' (Letter to the Editor), 'Our National Bird', *New Zealand Herald*, 3 April 1944.
3. 'Spring Has Come to Mata', *Northern Advocate*, 17 September 1940.
4. 'Draping of Coffin/Ensign and Kiwi Mat', *Evening Post*, 30 March 1940.
5. 'Naval Warfare/Part Taken by New Zealand', *Ashburton Guardian*, 16 December 1939; 'Work of the Navy', *Press*, 16 December 1939; *Press*, 22 April 1963; 'Kiwi for Scrap', *Press*, 5 September 1963; *Press*, 10 February 1964.
6. 'Work at Sea/The Navy's Task', *Evening Post*, 27 April 1940.
7. 'Maori Honours/Squadron Commander/Chief's Insignia Given', *New Zealand Herald*, 19 March 1941.
8. 'Kiwi Mat for Patriotic Funds', *Northern Advocate*, 17 January 1941.
9. 'Army Dentists/Work at Trentham', *Otago Daily Times*, 5 March 1940.
10. 'New Zealanders in Greece/Journey and Early Preparations', *Press*, 21 April 1941.
11. New Kiwi Club/Opening in Cairo/Facilities for New Zealand Troops', *Auckland Star*, 13 August 1940; 'Kiwi Club/Opened in Egypt', *Auckland Star*, 6 September 1940.
12. *Northern Advocate*, 7 March 1941.
13. 'Kiwi Launched/Home-Made Yacht/To Race in Middle East', *Auckland Star*, 13 May 1942.
14. 'Nazi Bomphlets/Change in Desert/Message to N.Z. Men', *Gisborne Herald*, 26 August 1942; 'Kiwi on German Pamphlet', *Northern Advocate*, 5 December 1942.
15. 'Springbok and Kiwi', *Nelson Evening Mail*, 29 July 1941.
16. 'Middle East Rugby Supremacy', *Press*, 11 April 1944.
17. 'Kiwi Camera Club', *Auckland Star*, 18 December 1943.
18. 'Lively Show/Kiwi Concert Pary/Music, Mirth and Melody', *Timaru Herald*, 30 September 1943.
19. 'Army Entertainment/The Middle East', *Evening Post*, 7 June 1941.
20. '"On the Road" Again/Kiwi Concert Party', *Evening Post*, 27 September 1941; 'Kiwi Concert Party', *Kaikoura Star*, 20 October 1941; 'Egypt — to NZEF', *Auckland Star*, 31 December 1941.
21. *Waikato Times*, 3 May 1943; *Ashburton Guardian*, 17 May 1943.
22. 'Patriotic Fund Board/Itinerary of Kiwi Band Announced', *Evening Star*, 9 August 1943.
23. 'Kaitaia Boy in Pacific Kiwi Concert', *Northern Advocate*, 19 February 1943.
24. 'Pacific Forces/Welfare Provision', *Evening Post*, 10 April 1943.
25. 'Kiwis in Pacific/Concert Party at New Caledonia', *Grey River Argus*, 24 May 1943.
26. 'Own Newspaper/New Zealanders in Pacific', *Press*, 20 January 1943; Soldiers' Newspaper/Published in Pacific Area', *Auckland Star*, 24 March 1943.
27. 'Another Kiwi Club/For New Zealanders in New Caledonia', *Wairarapa Times*, 18 February 1944.
28. *Evening Star*, 29 April 1944; 'Artists in Uniform', *Otago Daily Times*, 3 May 1944.
29. 'Kiwi Courage/Individual Feats', *Gisborne Herald*, 19 April 1945.
30. 'Kiwi Picture for New Zealand Squadron', *Evening Post*, 22 October 1942.
31. *New Zealand Herald*, 15 January 1945.
32. 'Sporting/Wellington Fields/For Spring Meeting', *Evening Post*, 6 October 1942.
33. 'Social Security in New Zealand', *Press*, 27 April 1944.
34. 'Strong Call for National Council to Meet Crisis', *Northern Advocate*, 21 May 1940.
35. 'New Zealand Air Force Badge', *Wanganui Chronicle*, 23 October 1940.
36. *Hokitika Guardian*, 23 March 1931.
37. 'Post-War Production/Preparing for Change-Over/Manufacturers' Campaign', *Otago Daily Times*, 15 January 1943.
38. *Manawatu Standard*, 5 March 1940.
39. 'Kiwi at Moengawahine', *Northern Advocate*, 10 April 1940.
40. 'Wants Live Kiwi'. *Auckland Star*, 29 April 1940.
41. 'Tourist Sees Kiwi', *New Zealand Herald*, 3 July 1940.
42. 'Kiwi at Meeting/Egmont Park Novelty', *New Zealand Herald*, 8 August 1940; 'News in Brief', *Otago Daily Times*, 12 November 1940.
43. *Ashburton Guardian*, 2 August 1940.
44. *Pahiatua Herald*, 3 August 1940.
45. 'Forest Destruction/Role of Noxious Insects', *New Zealand Herald*, 15 July 1940.
46. 'Local and General/Survival of Kiwi', *New Zealand Herald*, 26 August 1940.
47. 'Rare Exhibits For Zoo/Kiwi Wanted From Dominion', *Press*, 24 September 1941; 'Gift of Kiwi/ "Unpleasant Possibility"', *Auckland Star*, 13 October 1941; 'Kiwi For Bronx Zoo?/Sad Life Predicted', *River Argus*, 17 October 1941.
48. 'Kiwis Killed by Dogs/Position at Arthur's Pass', 25 March 1942.
49. 'Kiwis Increasing', *Otago Daily Times*, 12 December 1945.
50. 'Bush Vermin Trapped', *Auckland Star*, 1 November 1945.
51. 'Kiwi Chick/First Born in Captivity', *Otago Daily Times*, 20 September 1945.
52. *Northern Advocate*, 20 September 1945.
53. 'Says First Kiwi to Be Hatched in Captivity Was At Kawakawa', *Northern Advocate*, 24 September 1945.
54. 'Active Kiwi Chick/Insatiable Appetite for Worms', *Nelson Evening Mail*, 4 October 1945.
55. 'Second Kiwi Chick', *Ashburton Guardian*, 10 October 1945.
56. 'Male Kiwi Is Still Looking After Family', *Northern Advocate*, 12 November 1945.
57. 'Local and General/Kiwi Chick Dead', *Ashburton Guardian*, 1 February 1946.
58. 'Kiwi House/Hostel for Our Troops', *New Zealand Herald*, 1 June 1942; 'Popular Place/Kiwi House in London', *Evening Post*, 12 December 1942; 'Kiwi House/Doors Now Closed', *Ashburton Guardian*, 4 December 1945.
59. 'Opens New N.Z. Service Club in London', *Northern Advocate*, 22 December 1944.
60. 'Kiwi Invasion/Soldiers from Italy', *Auckland Star*, 15 October 1945.
61. 'VJ Celebrations', *Evening Post*, 20 August 1945.
62. 'Work for Returned Men', *Bay of Plenty Times*, 22 November 1945.
63. 'Homes After War/Promising Scheme/Young Kiwi Architects'. *Auckland Star*, 1 November 1944.
64. *Auckland Star*, 3 November 1944.
65. 'The Kiwis', *Timaru Herald*, 7 December 1944.
66. 'The Kiwis', *Ashburton Guardian*, 28 November 1945.
67. 'Kiwi Street Day', *Press*, 25 January 1945.
68. 'The Kiwi Drive/Name of New Street at Highfield', *Timaru Herald*, 18 September 1945.
69. *Waikato Times,* 17 March 1945.

10 Aftermath: the post-World War 2 kiwi

1. 'General News/"Kiwis" or "Diggers"', *Wanganui Chronicle*, 23 April 1946.
2. 'Anzac Service/Tribute to Fallen', *Opotiki News*, 26 April 1946.
3. 'News of the Day/Kiwi Predominance', *Gisborne Herald*, 5 April 1947.
4. 'Waihi Beach RSA', *Waihi Daily Telegraph*, 14 May 1947; 'The R.S.A./Annual General Meeting', *Te Awamutu Courier*, 9 April 1948.
5. 'Digger Spirit Shared by Kiwi Groups in RSA', *Gisborne Herald*, 3 July 1950.
6. 'Wanted to Rent', *Gisborne Herald*, 9 August 1946.
7. 'Kiwi Is NZ's Most Interesting Bird', *Northern Advocate*, 16 June 1949.
8. Wooden Legged Kiwi', *Press*, 29 December 1948; 'Kiwi with Wooden Leg', *Ashburton Guardian*, 21 September 1948.
9. 'Zoo Kiwi May Be Fitted with Leg Like Soldier', *Grey River Argus*, 25 August 1949; 'Worms as Currency', *Te Awamutu Courier*, 26 August 1949; 'One-Legged Kiwi Dies', *Press*, 17 December 1949.
10. 'No Kiwi's Egg', *Northern Advocate*, 5 July 1946.
11. 'Kiwi Export Ban Critic', *Gisborne Herald*, 2 August 1947.
12. 'No Kiwi for Mr Churchill/Minister is Adamant', *Ashburton Guardian*, 5 September 1946.
13. 'Present for Princess Elizabeth', *Press*, 3 July 1947.
14. 'Royal Dinghy to Be Named 'Kiwi'. *Northern Advocate*, 19 October 1948, 'Dinghy Races in England', *Press*, 6 December 1952; 'Yachting/NZ Wedding Gift to Duke', *Press*, 1 June 1953.

15. 'Kiwi Team Meets King', *Greymouth Evening Star*, 7 March 1946.
16. *Evening Star*, 4 April 1946.
17. 'Kiwi Concert Party/Stubborn Success in Melbourne', *Ashburton Guardian*, 17 July 1947; 'Record Houses/Kiwi Concert Party in Australia', *Te Awamutu Courier*, 31 October 1947.
18. 'Kiwi Concert Party/Success in Melbourne', *Press*, 2 April 1948.
19. 'Kiwi Concert Party/Unprecedented Run at Melbourne', *Ashburton Guardian*, 30 June 1948.
20. 'Kiwi Concert Party Ends Record Run in Melbourne', *Northern Advocate*, 5 January 1949.
21. *Otago Daily Times*, 6 January 1949.
22. 'New Zealand Ahead of Australia Along Road to Totalitarianism Socialism', *Otago Daily Times*, 4 May 1949.
23. 'Kiwi Entertainers/Finest Ambassadors', *Gisborne Herald*, 27 September 1949.
24. *Gisborne Herald*, 9 August 1947.
25. 'Local and General/Shield Given to RNZAF', *Ashburton Guardian*, 1 October 1949.
26. *Waikato Independent*, 23 January 1946.
27. 'El Alamein — Landmark in N.Z. History', *Bay of Plenty Beacon*, 24 October 1947.
28. 'With the Sappers/New Zealanders in Greece', *Otago Daily Times*, 11 December 1946.
29. 'New Books/"Kiwis in Tour in Egypt and Italy"', *Evening Star*, 6 July 1946.
30. *Auckland Star*, 24 August 1899.
31. 'Random Notes', *Western Star*, 27 May 1927.

11 Mid-century: the 1950s kiwi
1. 'Kiwi Sign in Korea/Lasting Memory to K Force', *Press*, 11 September 1953; 'Kiwi Altered to Kangaroo Australian Troops Blamed', *Press*, 17 March 1954; 'Kiwi Gunners in Korea/White Kiwi Marks Camp Site', *Press*, 25 November 1954; teara.govt.nz/en/photograph/34528/kiwi-hill-headquarters-of-16th-field-regiment-1953.
2. 'N.Z. Tank Crew in Korea', *Press*, 22 July 1952.
3. *Greymouth Evening Star*, 15 December 1950.
4. 'N.Z. Delegation to Greece', *Press*, 17 April 1952.
5. 'Many Native Birds Live in Urewera', *Bay of Plenty Beacon*, 13 January 1950.
6. 'No Danger of Kiwi Dying Out', *Greymouth Evening Star*, 24 July 1950.
7. '"Queer, Eccentric Bird"', *Press*, 28 October 1955.
8. 'One-Legged Kiwi Eats Steak Instead of Worms', *Press*, 22 March 1955.
9. '"Kiwi" Dies', *Opotiki News*, 28 November 1950.
10. 'Kiwi for Christchurch Zoo', *Press*, 10 January 1956; 'Kiwi Arrives By Air/Private Zoo Addition', *Press*, 9 March 1957.
11. 'Kiwi Lays Egg', *Press*, 29 September 1960; *Press*, 5 November 1960.
12. 'A Kiwi on Television', *Press*, 10 October 1952.
13. 'Kiwi Misses Flight', *Press*, 5 August 1953; 'Kiwi For London Zoo', *Press*, 18 September 1953.
14. 'Peter, the Kiwi in London/Meeting the Appetite for Worms', *Press*, 9 October 1953.
15. 'Zoo Kiwi "Settling Down"', *Press*, 30 September 1953; 'Ngapuhi Meets the All Blacks', *Press*, 11 November 1953.
16. 'Kiwi in London Not Well', *Press*, 13 July 1955; 'Kiwi Dies in London Zoo', *Press*, 13 August 1955.
17. 'Kiwi Will Fly North Pole', *Press*, 3 October 1958; 'General News/Kiwi Unable to Fly', *Press*, 9 October 1958.
18. 'Kiwi Arrives in London/Press Reception at Zoo', *Press*, 16 October 1958; 'Feather Busby', *Press*, 28 October 1958; Dear Diet for Kiwi/£1 A Day at London Zoo', *Press*, 17 March 1959; 'Kiwi Probably Died Of Old Age', *Press*, 24 November 1961.
19. 'Inkstand for Queen Mother', *Press*, 6 February 1958.
20. 'Wedding Gift from N.Z./Design Criticised by Artist', *Press*, 11 May 1960; 'Controversy About N.Z. Royal Wedding Gift', *Press*, 13 May 1960.
21. 'First Kiwi for U.S.', *Press*, 13 November 1954.
22. 'Battalion Mascot', *Press*, 27 November 1957.
23. 'Underestimated Power', *Otago Daily Times*, 23 February 1950; 'Kiwi Concert Party Coming Home', *Ashburton Guardian*, 11 May 1950; 'Kiwi Concert Party Plans a Wider Tour', *Wanganui Chronicle*, 12 May 1950.
24. 'Kiwi Review Company/Members' Civilian Roles', *Press*, 17 February 1954.
25. 'Special Dance Evolved/"Kiwi Polonaise" for Royal Visit', *Press*, 19 December 1953.
26. '"Pressure Group" Danger for Nurses', *Press*, 3 October 1957; Letter to editor, *Press*, 4 October 1957; 'New Zealand Made', *Press*, 23 February 1959'; 'All Blacks Showing New Determination', *Press*, 16 July 1960; *Press*, 8 March 1960.
27. 'Call of "Come on Kiwi" Heard at Wimbledon', *Press*, 3 November 1956.
28. 'Opening by Duke', *Press*, 21 July 1958.
29. '"Tourists' Baggage Sticker", *Press*, 12 October 1951.
30. 'New Tanker to Be Launched', *Press*, 6 July 1959.
31. 'Kiwi Lost Chord Club Formed in Auckland', *Press*, 14 November 1956.
32. 'Inauspicious name? Kiwi Rocket Project', *Press*, 12 October 1960.
33. 'Decimal Coinage Favoured', *Press*, 15 October 1959.
34. 'N.Z. Athletes' Uniforms/Criticism by Rowing Official', *Press*, 4 November 1958.
35. 'World Ploughing Meeting', *Press*, 20 September 1960.
36. 'Nautical Record', *Press*, 18 June 1958.
37. 'Work in the Garden/Further Notes on Fruit by Dr. J.S. Yeates, Massey Agricultural College', *Putaruru Press*, 3 Auckland 1950.
38. 'Chinese Gooseberry Exports a Record', *Press*, 28 August 1969; David Yerex & Westbrook Haines, *The Kiwifruit Story*, Agricultural Publishing Associates Limited, Masterton, 1983, pp. 25–26.
39. 'Chinese Gooseberry/Export Problem', *Press*, 31 March 1959.
40. 'New Export for New Zealand/Chinese Gooseberries for Britain', *Press*, 20 July 1959.
41. 'General News/Vine Saved', *Press*, 16 November 1959.
42. nzhistory.govt.nz/the-chinese-gooseberry-becomes-the-kiwifruit
43. 'Kiwi fruit', *Press*, 24 October 1975.
44. 'General News/Chinese-American', *Press*, 9 October 1967.
45. 'American Seeking "Kiwi Fruit" Plants', *Press*, 28 August 1969; 'Chinese Gooseberry Exports a Record', *Press*, 28 August 1969.
46. 'Royal slice of fruit', *Press*, 28 June 1975.
47. *Press*, 24 September 1959.
48. 'Elizabeth', 'Punga Pie Is a Truly New Zealand Fish', *Press*, 26 July 1961.
49. *Press*, 24 November 1970, 1 February 1972 & 11 October 1975.
50. 'Chinese Gooseberries Make Steaks Tender', *Press*, 27 September 1961.
51. David Yerex & Westbrook Haines, *The Kiwifruit Story*, Agricultural Publishing Associates Limited, Masterton, 1983, p. 36.
52. Yerex & Haines, p. 38.
53. '"Kiwi bear", the newest meat for Asian tables?', *Press*, 4 September 1987.
54. Richard Wolfe, *Kiwi: More Than A Bird*, Random Century New Zealand Ltd, Auckland, 1991, pp. 45–48.
55. 'Eketahuna's big bird moved to its new perch', www.nzherald.co.nz/hawkes-bay-today/news/eketahunas-big-bird-moved-to-its-new-perch/KALI3QWL4X6GZGM5EQAZ6ASUVA/
56. 'Large fibreglass "Claude the Kiwi"', canterburystories.nz/collections/archives/star/prints/1988/ccl-cs-2250

12 Cultural matters: kiwi to the fore
1. Bob Riley, *Kiwi Ingenuity: A Book of New Zealand Ideas and Inventions*, AIT Press, 1995, pp. 1–2.
2. Riley, p. 11.
3. *Daily Telegraph*, 8 June 1885.
4. 'Games', *Otago Daily Times*, 27 January 1864.
5. *Akaroa Mail and Banks Peninsula Advertiser*, 22 March 1878.
6. *Press*, 25 May 1887.
7. 'Random Reminder/Agony Column', *Press*, 10 April 1965.
8. *Press*, 25 August 1972.
9. Jon Bridges and David Downs, *No. 8 Re-wired: 202 New Zealand Inventions that Changed the World*, Penguin Group (NZ), Auckland, 2014, p. 8.
10. Various authors, introduction by The Hon. Barry Jones, MP, *Made in Australia: A sourcebook of all things Australian*, William Heinemann Australia, Richmond, Victoria, 1986, pp. 8, 40, 203.
11. 'Blimp's Woodville Cup', *Taranaki Daily News*, 21 February 1929.
12. Stephen Barnett and Richard Wolfe, *New Zealand! New Zealand! In Praise of Kiwiana*, Hodder and Stoughton Ltd, Auckland, 1989.
13. 'New Emblem for N.Z./Romney Breeder Suggestion', *Press*, 5 January 1962.

14. 'Mr Kirk Wants Kiwi on Flag', *Press*, 27 July 1962.
15. www.nzstory.govt.na/stories/the-Kiwi-burger-that-contains-no-kiwi; H.W. Orsman (ed.), *The Dictionary of New Zealand English*, Oxford University Press, Auckland, 1997, p. 415.
16. 'Barrier "Tottering"', *Press*, 9 June 1967.
17. 'Kiwi Bungalow Out', *Press*, 22 July 1967.
18. 'Pacific Travel Exciting Despite Limited Funds', *Press*, 27 May 1967.
19. 'First Lottery Expected to Be Sold Out Today', *Press*, 5 December 1961.
20. 'Kiwi "Too Small"/Golden Moa Soon', *Press*, 9 May 1962.
21. 'Four £1 Lotteries A Year', *Press*, 7 April 1964.
22. 'Success of Lottery', *Press*, 18 September 1965.
23. 'Golden Kiwi Condemned/Effect on Life Of Community', *Press*, 20 September 1962.
24. 'N.Z. Gambling, Drinking Habits Criticised', *Press*, 31 October 1963.
25. 'Church's Attitude on Lotteries Explained', *Press*, 26 November 1965.
26. 'Golden Kiwi Money', *Press*, 18 December 1963.
27. 'State Lotteries', *Press*, 5 December 1963.
28. 'Golden Kiwi Is Losing Its Gilt', *Press*, 11 April 1967.
29. 'The Ranfurly Shield', *Press*, 1 October 1970.
30. 'Kiwi soon extinct', *Press*, 17 July 1989.
31. 'Suggested N.Z. Hallmark', *Press*, 6 July 1965.
32. 'Kiwi Symbol/Criticism and Praise', *Press*, 23 September 1965; canterburystories.nz/collections/archives/star/prints/1965-1969/ccl-cs-1843
33. 'The Kiwi Symbol/Response Good', *Press*, 20 October 1965.
34. 'Symbolic Kiwi/N.Z. Promotion Value', *Press*, 13 October 1966; 'Kiwi Symbol', *Press*, 20 February 1968.
35. 'Kiwi Best Symbol for Asian Trade', *Press*, 9 June 1966; 'Kiwi Symbol Seen Throughout World', *Press*, 19 August 1967.
36. 'Thought Fern was Feather', *Press*, 25 November 1964.
37. 'Evolution of A Species', *Press*, 28 March 1970.
38. 'Kiwis for Japan', *Press*, 23 June 1970; 'Ailing Kiwi', *Press*, 10 July 1970.
39. *Press*, 17 February 1970.
40. 'Roundel to be changed', *Press*, 15 September 1970.
41. nzhistory.govt.nz/first-official-tv-broadcast
42. 'New Zealand's Future/"No One Will Keep Kiwi As Pet"', *Press*, 27 October 1961.
43. 'Export of Kiwi/Speaker Rules Out Question', *Press*, 3 November 1961.
44. 'Edinburgh Kiwi Prefers Sleep to Meeting Public', *Press*, 13 July 1964.
45. 'Kiwi to Rest', *Press*, 2 December 1967; 'Stuffed Kiwi', *Press*, 18 December 1967.
46. 'Kiwis for Princess', *Press*, 25 October 1961.
47. 'Royal Tour/All Maori Tribes Welcome Queen', *Press*, 23 March 1970.
48. 'Screams Greet Beatles at Airport, Hotel', *Press*, 22 June 1964.
49. 'Kiwi for Pope', *Press*, 22 June 1965.
50. 'The Coin Polls', *Press*, 12 April 1966.
51. 'Counterfeit Florin', *Press*, 22 September 1966.
52. teara.govt.nz/mi/cartoon/25627/telecom-kiwi-share; www.beehive.govt.nz/release/government-announces-updated-kiwi-share-obligation; www.beehive.govt.nz/release/kiwi-share-being-reviewed-meet-changing-times
53. www.kiwibank.co.nz/about-us/who-we-are/our-history/
54. www.msd.govt.nz/about-msd-and-our-work/publications-resources/journals-and-magazines/social-policy-journal/spj36/36-kiwisaver-a-model-scheme.html; www.ird.govt.nz/about-us/tax-statistics/kiwisaver/joining/member-demographics/number-and-age-of-kiwisaver-members
55. Thomas Coughlan, 'KiwiBuild reaches first target — two years late 15,000 homes behind schedule', 1 July 2021, www.stuff.co.nz/national/politics/300347258/kiwibuild-reaches-first-target--two-years-late-15000-homes-behind-schedule
56. www.kiwi.com
57. Lincoln Tan, 'End of the shine in the UK for shoe polish brand that made Kiwi world famous', *New Zealand Herald*, 2 January 2023.

13 The high-flying kiwi(fruit)

1. David Yerex and Westbrook Haines, *The Kiwifruit Story*, Agricultural Publishing Associates Limited, Masterton, 1983. pp.81–82.
2. Roly Earp, *The Kiwifruit Adventure*, Dunmore Press, Palmerston North, 1988, pp. 18, 55.
3. www.zespri.com/en-AU/blogdetail/history-of-zespri-sungold-kiwifruit
4. Earp, pp. 85, 95–101.
5. Earp, pp. 129–60.
6. Earp, pp. 113–15.
7. Yerex, pp. 89–90, 93.
8. Giant kiwifruit for Te Puke, *New Zealand Herald*, 1 December 2015, www.nzherald.co.nz/nz/giant-kiwifruit-for-te-puke/PICW75HHYTYV6WVQA3UXMKVRCU/
9. 'New attraction: Te Puke's kiwifruit slices now in place', *Bay of Plenty Times*, 2 Mar, 2020, www.nzherald.co.nz/bay-of-plenty-times/news/new-attraction-te-pukes-kiwifruit-slices-now-in-place/IN4GUFRCHW23DHK7VSDQXKA3OU/
10. Earp, pp. 207–208.
11. www.zespri.com/en-NZ/zespri-history.
12. www.sciencelearn.org.nz/resources/2638-kiwifruit-learning-to-live-with-psa.
13. Andrea Fox, 'Zespri boss focused on growth to lift gloom', *New Zealand Herald*, 14 August 2023; Andrea Fox, 'Offshore base of Zespri chief queries', *New Zealand Herald*, 16 August 2023.
14. nzhistory.govt.nz/the-chinese-gooseberry-becomes-the-kiwifruit.
15. Andrea Fox, 'Zespri boss focused on growth to lift gloom', *New Zealand Herald*, 14 August 2023.
16. 'Report on Zespri's export dominance for growers' eyes only', *New Zealand Herald*, 11 November 2023.
17. Andrea Fox, 'Great leap in kiwifruit to China "Big task"', *New Zealand Herald*, 6 December 2023.
18. www.kiwifruitbreeding.com/our-story.
19. John Ross, 'An inventor's dream — Kiwi fruit to London by flying saucer', *Press*, 9 May 1978.

14 In survival mode: conserving the kiwi

1. R.G.F., 'New Zealand Fauna/Some Curious Features/Danger of Extinction', *Wanganui Chronicle*, 4 October 1924.
2. Rex J. Dixon, 'New Zealand's Tuatara and Mystical Moa', *Otago Daily Times*, 4 January 1938.
3. E.L. Kehoe, 'Opossums and Kiwis/Bush Tragedies in Outback Westland', *Press*, 1 September 1951.
4. Jamie Morton,'3 Oct 2016, 'The battle for our bird: 100,000 kiwi by 2030'; www.nzherald.co.nz/nz/the-battle-for-our-bird-100000-kiwi-by- 2030/TZKRXJG6YMB6GCGKKKOVKCWLW4/
5. www.bnzheritage.co.nz/archives/story/kiwi-and-the-bank-of-new-zealand; www.bnzheritage.co.nz/archives/story/our-brand-and-logo-journey
6. www.bnzheritage.co.nz/archives/story/kiwi-and-the-bank-of-new-zealand
7. 'Kiwi brings home bacon', 8 May 2005, www.nzherald.co.nz/nz/kiwi-brings-home-bacon/ZBVSTHAWTLJDLV2DJPGRBZUIGE/
8. www.backyardkiwi.org.nz/useful-information/faqs
9. www.doc.govt.nz/nature/native-animals/birds/birds-a-z/kiwi/facts/
10. www.sciencelearn.org.nz/resources/1388-kaitiaki-of-the-kiwi
11. www.landcareresearch.co.nz/discover-our-research/biodiversity-biosecurity/ecosystem-resilience/species-and-ecosystem-conservation/kiwi-rescue/
12. www.islandconservation.org/protecting-the-kiwi-maoriculture-and-nz-ecosystem/
13. www.rotoruanz.com/things-to-do/family-fun/the-national-kiwi-hatchery-aotearoa
14. savethekiwi.nz/about-us/what-we-do/
15. www.capitalkiwi.co.nz
16. Jamie Morton, 3 October 2016, 'The battle for our bird: 100,000 kiwi by 2030'; www.nzherald.co.nz/nz/the-battle-for-our-bird-100000-kiwi-by-2030/TZKRXJG6YMB6GCGKKKOVKCWLW4/
17. www.birdoftheyear.org.nz/; www.forestandbird.org.nz/resources/bird-year-becomes-bird-century-celebrate-100-years-forest-bird
18. 'Dog owners implicated in kiwi deaths', *New Zealand Herald*, 9 August 2023.
19. 'New 'Robo-Kiwi' protecting kiwi from uncontrolled dogs', 15 August 2023, www.scionresearch.com/about-us/news-and-events/news/2023-news-and-media-releases/new-robo-kiwi-protecting-kiwi-from-uncontrolled-dogs
20. 'Store pulls kiwi dog toy from shelves', *New Zealand Herald*, 16 December 2023.

Bibliography

Books

Barnett, Stephen and Richard Wolfe, *New Zealand! New Zealand! In Praise of Kiwiana*, Hodder and Stoughton: Auckland, 1989.

Best, Elsdon, *Forest Lore of the Maori*, E.C. Keating, Government Printer: Wellington, 1977.

Bridges, Jon and David Downs, *No. 8 Re-wired: 202 New Zealand Inventions that Changed the World*, Penguin Group (NZ): Auckland, 2014.

Dalley, Bronwyn and Gavin McLean (eds.), *Frontier of Dreams: The Story of New Zealand*, Hachette Livre:, Auckland, 2005.

Earp, Roly, *The Kiwifruit Adventure*, Dunmore Press: Palmerston North, 1988.

Glover, Denis, 'Zealandia' in A.H. McLintock (ed.), *An Encyclopaedia of New Zealand*, E.R. Owen, Government Printer: Wellington, 1966.

Hiroa, Te Rangi (Sir Peter Buck), *The Coming of the Maori*, Maori Purposes Fund Board: Wellington, 1958.

Keith, Hamish (text) and William Main (picture research), *New Zealand Yesterdays: A Look at Our Recent Past*, Readers' Digest Services Pty Limited: NSW, 2020.

King, Carolyn M. (ed.), *The Handbook of New Zealand Mammals*, Oxford University Press: Auckland, 1990.

Lee, Michael, *Navigators & Naturalists: French Exploration of New Zealand and the South Seas (1769–1824)*, David Bateman: Auckland, 2018.

Lewis, Jeremy, *Penguin Special: The Life and Times of Allen Lane*, Viking, Penguin Books: London, 2005.

McLintock, A.H., (ed.), *An Encyclopaedia of New Zealand*, R.E. Owen, Government Printer: Wellington, 1966.

Nicholas, L.L., *Narrative of Voyage to New Zealand* (originally published as *Narrative of a Voyage to New Zealand*), James Black and Son: London, 1817.

Orsman, H.W., (ed.), *The Dictionary of New Zealand English*, Oxford University Press: Auckland, 1997.

Pendergrast, Mick, *Te Aho Tapu: The Sacred Thread*, Reed Methuen Publishers: Auckland, 1987.

Polack, J.S., *New Zealand: Being a Narrative of Travels and Adventures During a Residence in that Country Between the Years 1831 and 1837*, originally published by Richard Bentley: London, 1838, Kiwi Publishers: Christchurch, 2000.

Reed, A.W., illlustrations by Roger Hart, *Maori Legends*, A.H. & A.W. Reed: Wellington, 1972.

Reischek, Andreas, *Yesterdays in Maoriland*, originally published as *Yesterdays in Maoriland: New Zealand in the 'Eighties*, Jonathan Cape: London, 1930, facsimile edition published by Wilson & Horton: Auckland, 1970.

Riley, Bob, *Kiwi Ingenuity: A Book of New Zealand Ideas and Inventions*, AIT Press, 1995.

Sale, P.R., *Kiwifruit Culture*, V.R. Ward, Government Printer: Wellington, 1983–85.

Various authors, introduction by the Hon. Barry Jones MP, *Made in Australia: A sourcebook of all things Australian*, William Heinemann Australia: Richmond, Victoria, 1986.

Ward, John, Secretary to the New-Zealand Company, *Information Relative to New-Zealand Compiled for the Use of Colonists*, John W. Parker: West Strand, London, 1840.

Wolfe, Richard, *Kiwi: More Than a Bird*, Random Century New Zealand: Auckland, 1991.

Yate, William, *An Account of New Zealand and of the Church Missionary Society's Mission in the Northern Island*, 1835, facsimile edition by A.H. & A.W. Reed: Wellington, 1970.

Yerex, David and Westbrook Haines, *The Kiwifruit Story*, Agricultural Publishing Associates: Masterton, 1983.

Electronic resources

Coughlan, Thomas, 'KiwiBuild reaches first target — two years late 15,000 homes behind schedule', 1 July 2021, www.stuff.co.nz/national/politics/300347258/kiwibuild-reaches-first-target--two-years-late-15000-homes-behind-schedule

Morton, Jamie, 3 October 2016, 'The battle for our bird: 100,000 kiwi by 2030', www.nzherald.co.nz/nz/the-battle-for-our-bird-100000-kiwi-by-2030/TZKRXJG6YMB6GCGKKKOVKCWLW4/

Phillips, Jock, 'Kiwi – Kiwi and people: early history', Te Ara, the Encyclopedia of New Zealand, http://www.TeAra.govt.nz/en/kiwi/page-4 (accessed 17 July 2023)

Robertson, Craig, 'Gondwana, How it got its name', March 2008, www.thestudy.net.au/projects/gondwana-name.html

Tan, Lincoln, *New Zealand Herald*, 2 January 2023; 'End of the shine in the UK for shoe polish brand that made Kiwi world famous', www.nzherald.co.nz/nz/end-of-the-shine-in-the-uk-for-shoe-polish-brand-that-made-kiwi-world-famous/

canterburystories.nz/collections/archives/star/prints/1965-1969/ccl-cs-1843

canterburystories.nz/collections/archives/star/prints/1988/ccl-cs-2250

collections.tepapa.govt.nz/topic/1326

environment.govt.nz/publications/the-state-of-new-zealands-environment-1997/chapter-eight-the-state-of-our-land/pressures-on-the-land/

librarycompany.org/2021/03/04/Elizabeth-nodder-and-the-naturalists-miscellany/#/4-6

nzbirdsonline.org.nz/species/huia

nzetc.victoria.ac.nz/tm/scholarly/tei-SmiMaor-t1-body-d53.html

nzhistory.govt.nz/the-chinese-gooseberry-becomes-the-kiwifruit

polynesia.com/blog/maori-legend-how-the-kiwi-bird-lost-his-wings

projectcrimson.org.nz/

savethekiwi.nz/about-kiwi/threats-to-kiwi/loss-of-habitat/

savethekiwi.nz/about-us/what-we-do/predator-control/

southseas.nla.gov.au/journals/banks/17700117.html

teara.govt.nz/en/object/37131/trading-bank-banknotes-bank-of-new-zealand-note

teara.govt.nz/en/photograph/34528/kiwi-hill-headquarters-of-16th-field-regiment-1953.

teara.govt.nz/mi/auckland-places/page-1914. Banks's Journal, 17 January 1770.

teara.govt.nz/mi/cartoon/25627/telecom-kiwi-share;

www.aucklandartgallery.com/explore-art-and-ideas/artwork/5907/te-rangi-o-te-moa

www.aucklandmuseum.com/discover/stories/blog/2015/did-the-kiwi-ever-fly

www.backyardkiwi.org.nz/useful-information/faqs

www.bbcearth.com/news/who-really-discovered-new-zealand

www.beehive.govt.nz/release/government-announces-updated-kiwi-share-obligation;

www.beehive.govt.nz/release/kiwi-share-being-reviewed-meet-changing-times

www.biodiversitylibrary.org/item/296719#page/234/mode/1up]

www.bnzheritage.co.nz/archives/story/kiwi-and-the-bank-of-new-zealand

www.bnzheritage.co.nz/archives/story/our-brand-and-logo-journey

www.britannica.com/animal/kakapo

www.canterbury.ac.nz/news/2021/unfolding-the-mystery-of-the-first-kiwi-specimen.html

www.capitalkiwi.co.nz

www.doc.govt.nz/nature/conservation-status/threatened-birds

www.doc.govt.nz/nature/native-animals/birds/birds-a-z/kiwi/facts/

www.doc.govt.nz/nature/pests-and-threats/animal-pests/possums/

www.ird.govt.nz/about-us/tax-statistics/kiwisaver/joining/member-demographics/number-and-age-of-kiwisaver-members
www.kiwi/com/en/
www.kiwibank.co.nz/about-us/who-we-are/our-history/
www.kiwifruitbreeding.com/our-story.
www.kiwivapour.com/en
www.msd.govt.nz/about-msd-and-our-work/publications-resources/journals-and-magazines/social-policy-journal/spj36/36-kiwisaver-a-model-scheme.html;
www.newzealandantiqueprints.co.nz/gallery/birds/shaw.html
www.nzherald.co.nz/bay-of-plenty-times/news/new-attraction-te-pukes-kiwifruit-slices-now-in-place/IN4GUFRCHW23DHK7VSDQXKA3OU/
www.nzherald.co.nz/hawkes-bay-today/news/eketahunas-big-bird-moved-to-its-new-perch/KALI3QWL4X6GZGM5EQAZ6ASUVA/
www.nzherald.co.nz/nz/giant-kiwifruit-for-te-puke/PICW75HHYTYV6WVQA3UXMKVRCU/
www.nzherald.co.nz/nz/kiwi-brings-home-bacon/ZBVSTHAWTLJDLV2DJPGRBZUIGE/
www.nzstory.govt.na/stories/the-Kiwi-burger-that-contains-no-kiwi
www.rotoruanz.com/things-to-do/family-fun/the-national-kiwi-hatchery-aotearoa
www.scionresearch.com/about-us/news-and-events/news/2023-news-and-media-releases/new-robo-kiwi-protecting-kiwi-from-uncontrolled-dogs
www.zespri.com/en-AU/blogdetail/history-of-zespri-sungold-kiwifruit
www.zespri.com/en-NZ/zespri-history

Other sources

Owen, Richard, 1st lecture, 30 April 1839, 'Introduction to the Course'. Notes made by Wm. W. Cooper later revised and corrected by Owen, Collection of Royal College of Surgeons, 42C.27.

Owen, Richard, 10th lecture, 29 May 1838, 'Digestive System of Birds'. Notes made by Wm. W. Cooper later revised and corrected by Owen, Collection of Royal College of Surgeons, 42C.26.

Owen, Richard, 'Exhibition of a Bone of an Unknown Struthious Bird from New Zealand', *Proceedings of the Zoological Society of London*, 7:169–71, 1840.

Proceedings of the Zoological Society of London, 1839, 7:63–65.

Tasmanian Journal of Natural Science, vol. 2, 1846, no. 6, pp. 239–40, reprinted from *Athenaeum*, no. 850, p. 138.

The Annals and Magazine of Natural, vol. 1, Second Series, 1850, pp. 147–52.

Walsh, Rev P., 'On the Disappearance of the New Zealand Bush', *Transactions and Proceedings of the Royal Society of New Zealand*, Vol. 29, 1896.

Newspapers

Akaroa Mail and Banks Peninsular Advertiser
Ashburton Guardian
Auckland Star
Bay of Plenty Beacon
Colonist
Daily Southern Cross
Daily Telegraph
Ellesmere Guardian
Evening Post
Fielding Star
Franklin Times
Free Lance
Gisborne Times
Globe
Grey River Argus
Greymouth Evening Star
Hauraki Plains Gazette
Hawera Star
Hawera & Normanby Star
Hawke's Bay Herald
Hawke's Bay Tribune
Hokitika Guardian
Horowhenua Chronicle
Lyttelton Times
Manawatu Standard
Manawatu Times
Marlborough Express
Mataura Ensign
Nelson Examiner and New Zealand Chronicle
New Zealand Advertiser and Bay of Islands Gazette
New Zealand Gazette and Wellington Spectator
New Zealand Herald and Auckland Gazette
New Zealand Spectator and Cook's Strait Guardian
New Zealand Mail
New Zealand Times
New Zealander
North Canterbury Gazette
Northern Advocate
NZ Truth
Observer
Ohinemuri Gazette
Opotiki News
Otago Daily Times
Otago Witness
Pahiatua Herald
Press
Putaruru Press
Rangitikei Advocate and Manawatu Argus
Stratford Evening Post
Taranaki Daily News
Taranaki Herald
Te Awamutu Courier
Temuka Leader
Thames Advertiser
Thames Star
Timaru Herald
Waikato Independent
Waikato Times
Waipa Post
Wairarapa Age
Wairarapa Daily Times
Wairarapa Times
Wairarapa Times-Age
Wairoa Bell
Wanganui Chronicle
Wanganui Herald
Wellington Independent
Western Star
Woodville Examiner

Index

1st Battalion New Zealand Regiment 149
1st New Zealand Expeditionary Force (NZEF) 135
2nd NZEF 121–23, 131, 135, 138, 140–41
16th Field Regiment 145–46

A
Abberley, Aldwyn 141
Acarie-Baron, Jacques Reyne Isidore 31
acclimatisation societies 96
Achilles (cruiser) 120
Air New Zealand 176
AKTV-2 172
Alamein Club, Cairo 123
Albert Street, Auckland 61
Alexandria, Egypt 83
All Blacks 73, 78, 99–100, 105, 148
'All Golds' 78
Allen, James 69
Allison, Alexander 69, 156
Anderton, Jim (Deputy Prime Minister) 175
Angas, George French 40–41
Animals Protection Act 1908 79
Arawa (tribe) 103
Armstrong-Jones, Antony 149
Arthur's Pass National Park 129
Auckland Acclimatisation Society 116
Auckland City Council 76, 106, 149
Auckland Game Fowl Club 104
Auckland Institute 47
Auckland Mechanics' Institute 36
Auckland Museum Tamaki Paenga Hira 20, 40, 43, 85, 129, 158
Auckland RSA 84
Auckland Society of Arts 149
Auckland Town Hall 87, 120
Auckland University College 71
Auckland Weekly News 73, 79, 85
Auckland Zoo 97, 104, 137, 147–49, 173

B
badges, kiwi 82
Bank of New Zealand 53, 56–57, 189
Banks, Joseph 20
Barclay, Captain Thomas 27
Batten, Jean 20, 103
Bay of Islands 193
Bay of Plenty 181
Beacon Hill, Salisbury Plain 90
Beatles 174
Belgian Fund 84
Bellamy, David 11
Bennett, George 32
Berlin Airlift 140, 145
Best, Elsdon 17, 19, 25
birds, flightless 13
    protection of 96
Birdwood, General 87
Bledisloe, Lord and Lady 103
Blenheim Palace 138
Blenkarne, Sergeant Major Percy 90
BNZ Kiwi Recovery Trust 190
    Operation Nest Egg 190
    Save the Kiwi Trust 190
'bomphlets' 122

Boy Scouts Association 154
Bracken, Thomas 64
Bridge Pa 162
Brisbane 176
British Association, London 40, 42
British Empire and Commonwealth Games 1958 150
British Empire Games 1930 100
British Kiwi (ship) 151–52
British Museum 27, 70
British Museum (Natural History) 39, 90, 148
British Ornithologists' Club 37
Brno, Czech Republic 177
Bronx Zoo 129
Brunner, Thomas 25
Buckingham House 138
Burns, Robbie 138
'Busby' (kiwi) 148
Buzzy Bee 164

C
Cairo 122
Canterbury Chamber of Commerce 171
Canterbury Clothing Company 100
Canterbury Museum 38, 42, 83–84
Canterbury Progress League 169
Canterbury University 29, 38, 42, 193
Capital Kiwi Project 192
Captain Cook Bicentenary 174
Carlton Gore Road, Auckland 60
cats 42, 53, 129, 190
Centennial Exhibition 1939–1940 103, 107–108
chamois 39
Charles, Prince 155
Cheeseman, Thomas 43
Chinese gooseberry 7, 69, 116–17, 132, 154–56, 179, 184
Christchurch 149
Church Missionary Society 32
Churchill, Winston 138, 171
coat of arms 76
    New Zealand 75–76
Coburg Street, Auckland 60
Cold War 145
College of Arms, London 75
colloquialisms 150
Colonial Museum, Wellington 42–43
Combined Irish Societies of New Zealand 174
Concise Oxford Dictionary 114
Cook, Captain James 17, 20, 25, 51–52, 71, 113, 174
Cornwall, Duke and Duchess of 70
Court of Appeal 88
Covent Garden 185
Covid-19 176, 183
Crown Lynn Potteries 151
Crozet, Julien 17
Cunningham, Allan 34
currency, alternative names 107, 152

D
de Bougainville, Louis Antoine 29
decimal currency 57, 174
deer 95, 129, 191
Defence Act 1909 81
deforestation 47–48

'degeneration' (of kiwi) 73
Denmark 106
Dental Corps 121
d'Entrecasteaux, Antoine Bruni 29
Department of Conservation 190–92
de Pietri, Vanessa 29
Derby, 14th Earl of 29
de Surville, Jean-François 29
Devonport, Auckland 120
Devonshire Regiment 91
Dickinson, Sergeant Major J. 145
Dieffenbach, Ernst 36
Digger 8, 119, 135
Diggers (Concert Party) 139
dinosaur 11
Dogger Bank, Battle of 104
dogs 24–25, 30, 42–43, 47, 51, 70, 94, 96–97, 105, 129, 193, 195
Dominion Breweries 187
Dominion Day 75
Dominion Museum 97, 110, 147, 149, 170
Drummond, James 25, 73, 94
du Fresne, Marion 29
Durham Lane, Auckland 89
d'Urville, Dumont 29
Dusky Sound 71

E
Earp, Roly 179–80
Eastern Airlines 176
Edinburgh, Duke of 138, 174
Edinburgh Zoo 171–72
Edmonds baking powder 164
Edward VII, King 75
Egmont, Mount 128, 137
Egmont National Park Board 129
Eketahuna 158
El Alamein, Battle of 140
Elizabeth, Princess and Queen 138, 155, 174
Elizabeth, Queen Mother 149
Ellerslie Racecourse 167
Eltham 96
Empire Marketing Board 106
emu 30
Endeavour (ship) 20
Enzedder 8
Evans, W. 29
Expo '70 170
Eyre, Lieutenant-Governor Edward John 37

F
Falla, Sir Robert 94, 105, 137, 147
Featherston 84
Federated Farmers of New Zealand 113, 162
Feilding 116
Fenton, Thomas 157
Ferguson, Lady Alice 101
Fernland 62
Fernlander 8
Fernleaf Club, London 130
ferret 52–53
Fiordland 137
'Flagstaff Hill', South Korea 145
Fleming, Jubal 58
Flemington, Canterbury 71
florin 174

Forbes, Hon. C. W. 103
Forest and Bird Protection Society of New Zealand 129, 190, 192
Forty Mile Bush, Taranaki 47
Fox, William (Prime Minister) 25
Fraser, Mary 69
Fraser, Peter (Prime Minister) 146

G
George V, King 70, 87, 110
George VI, King 111
Gisborne 103, 136, 147
  RSA 135
Glasgow 138
'God's Own Country' 64–65
Godzone 65
Golden Kiwi 167–68
'Golden Moa' 167
Gondwana(land) 10, 12–13
'Goodnight Kiwi' 172
Gotz, Hon. L 167
Gould, John 22, 35, 40
Gowing, Rev. E.A. 167
Graf Spee (cruiser) 120
'Great Fleet' 15
Greenmeadows, Hawke's Bay 105, 130, 137
Grey, George 37
Grey District 129

H
Haast, Julius von 25, 42
Hagley Park 65
Haines, Westbrook 156, 181
Halsey, Sir Lionel 103
Hamilton 176
Hanna, Pat 139
Hawkins, Lieutenant J. 145
Hayward, Rudall 20
Hayward kiwifruit 180
harakeke (flax) 19
Hawke's Bay Acclimatisation Society 105
Hawke's Bay Game Park 130
Heaphy, Charles 25
Helm, A.S. 141
Helwan, Cairo 122
Henry, Richard 71
Hine-o-te-Rangi 103
Hochstetter, Ferdinand von 35, 40, 42
Holland, Sidney (Prime Minister) 139
Holyoake, Sir Keith 94, 113, 170, 172
Hori Kingi Te Anaua 21
Howard Morrison Quartet 172
Howes, Edith 73
huia 9, 50, 68–72, 108, 112, 114, 137
Hunterian Museum, London 32–33

I
Imperial Institute, London 87
'Industries Week' 70
ingenuity, Australian 163
Insurance Australia Group (IAG) 56
Internal Affairs, Department of 105, 147, 167
Islington, Lord (Governor-General) 79

J
Jellicoe, Lord 104–105
Johnson, S.C. 177
Jones, Hon. F. 127
Josef, Emperor Franz 39
Jutland, Battle of 104

K
kahu kiwi 20–21, 70, 79, 101, 120–21, 147, 174
kahu huruhuru 20
kahu kurī 19–21
Kaiapoi Woollen Mills 65
Kaiti, Gisborne 103
Kapiti Island 71
Karangahape Road, Auckland 86
Kawakawa 104, 130
Kay Force 145
Kempthorne, Prosser & Co. 58, 61, 67–68, 88–89, 109
King Country 42
Kingsford Smith, Charles 109
kiore 18, 50
Kipling, Rudyard 48
Kippenberger, Sir Howard 137
Kirk, Norman (Prime Minister) 164
Kirkaldie & Stains, Wellington 84
Kitchener, Lord 81–83
kiwi (bird) albino 96
  eggs 18, 25, 34, 37, 39, 43, 51–53, 87, 104–105, 130, 138, 147, 190–92
  endangered 94, 188–89 195
  evolution 72–73
  export of specimens 37, 39, 43, 79, 138, 147–49
  feathers 101
  hunting of by Māori 17, 19, 25
  legend of 18
  population 70, 189–90, 192
  protection of 69, 96
  rarity of 96
  senses 94
  species of 13, 17
  straying 97
  taste of 19, 24, 48
  value of in bush 95
Kiwi (horses) 59, 127
Kiwi ingenuity 8
Kiwi, magazine 71
Kiwi (minesweeper) 120
Kiwi polish 58, 80, 82, 87
Kiwi products 61, 69, 89, 98, 126
Kiwi rabbit trap 61
Kiwi (ships) 54–55
Kiwi (troopship magazine) 85
Kiwi-A3 (rocket) 151
Kiwi (newspaper) 126
Kiwi Bacon Co. 67, 98, 109, 146, 157–58, 190
'kiwi bear' 157
Kiwi Blues 132
Kiwi Boys, The 87
Kiwi businesses 98–99, 126, 131, 136
Kiwi Bowling Club, London 74
Kiwi Camera Club, Cairo 123
'Kiwi Canal', Cairo 122
Kiwi Club, Helwan, Cairo 122
Kiwi Club, London 85
Kiwi Club, Noumea 126
Kiwi Concert Party (Middle East) 123, 131, 139, 149
Kiwi Concert Party (Pacific) 125
Kiwi Defence Rifle Club 81
Kiwi (dinghy) 138
Kiwi, Dr M.L. 114
Kiwi (French comic)
Kiwi Gallery, Dunedin 126
'Kiwi Hill', South Korea 145
Kiwi House, London 130
Kiwi ingenuity 161–62
Kiwi International Airlines 176
Kiwi International Hotel, Auckland 158

Kiwi lager 187
Kiwi League 84
Kiwi Lost Chord Club 151
Kiwi magazine (2nd NZEF) 147
'Kiwi Magic' 187
Kiwi, *nom de plume* 166–67
kiwi, on currency 112
kiwi, on postage stamps 110–11
Kiwi Polish Co (NZ) Ltd 89
Kiwi Polish Co. (London) 91
Kiwi Polish Company Pty Ltd 87–88
'Kiwi Polonaise' 150
'Kiwi Pride' 187
Kiwi products 126–127
Kiwi Quartette 87
Kiwi Rifle Club 82
'Kiwi Share' 174–75
Kiwi Soldier Concert Party 87
Kiwi sports clubs 100
Kiwi streets etc 131
'Kiwi Train' 108
Kiwi Tamaki 22
Kiwi Travel International Airlines 176
Kiwiana 163–64
Kiwiana exhibition 158
Kiwiana (horse) 163
Kiwibank 175
Kiwi.com 176
kiwifruit 7, 116–17, 132, 154–56, 179–84
'kiwifruit aristocracy' 181
Kiwifruit Breeding Centre 184
Kiwifruit Export Promotion Committee 180
Kiwifruit Marketing Licensing Authority 180, 182
Kiwifruit Queen 182
KiwiBuild 175–76
Kiwiburger 166
Kiwiland 62, 142
Kiwis, The (theatrical party) 86
KiwiSaver 175
Knox, F.J. 36, 42
Kohukohu 141
Korean War 145
kōtuku 8, 50
Kumara (ship) 39
Kupe 15
kurī 17

L
L'Astrolabe (ship) 29
La Coquille (ship) 29–30
Lambton Quay, Wellington 75
Lane Walker Rudkin 100
La Pérouse 29
Lake Waikaremoana Hapu Restoration Trust 191
Laurasia 10
Lee, Michael 30
Leffelaar, Cees 169
Lesson, René 29–30
'levity disc' 185
Lilford, Lord 105
Limpey, Michelle 195
Lindbergh, Charles 109
Liverpool Museum 29
Lloyd, Trevor 66, 68, 73–74, 85, 187
Logan, Dr 32
London Zoo 86, 104–105, 138
Lotto 168
Low, Sergeant Major V. T. 90
'Lucky Kiwi' art union 131
Lupton, 'Snow' 59
Luxton, Lynne 150

M

Maadi, Egypt 122-23
MacLoughlin, Jim 117
Malayan Emergency 149
Mangahouanga Valley 11
Manuaki Whenua/Landcare Research 191
Maoriland 62, 141-42
Maorilander 7
Margaret, Princess 149, 174
Marsden, Samuel 30
Massey, William (Prime Minister) 101
Master Builders' Federation 166
Maungakiekie 22
McDonald's 166
McGregor, James 69
McIntyre, Duncan 180
McLennan, John 191
Meek, Annie Elizabeth 87
Melbourne 139
Melbourne Cup 59
Melonette 154
Meola Road, Auckland 61
Methodist Church 168
miha 8
Milford, Auckland 174
Ministry of Business, Innovation & Employment 191
Ministry of Transport 170
Ministry of Works 136
Mirror polish 88
Mitchell, Leonard C. 108
Mitre 10 195
moa 25-25, 33-35, 38, 47, 70, 74, 111-12, 195
Moa baking powder 61
Moa (minesweeper) 120
'Moa's Ark' 11
Molesworth St, Wellington 97
mongoose 51
Moorhouse, Dr B.M. 83
Motuara Island 52
Motueka Rugby Union 113
Mountbatten, Lord 104
Museum of New Zealand Te Papa Tongarewa 20, 42
Muturangi 15

N

Nash, Walter (Prime Minister) 113, 152
National Kiwi Hatchery Aotearoa 190, 192-93
National League of New Zealand 81
National Patriotic Fund 125-26
Natural History Museum, London 82-83
Natural History Museum, Vienna 42
Nelson Park, Hastings 173
Neon, Claude 157
New Caledonia 125
New North Road, Auckland 158
New Plymouth 129
New Zealand, HMS (battle cruiser) 103-104
New Zealand Company 24, 36, 45
New Zealand Co-operative Pig Marketing Association 157
New Zealand Drug Company 61
New Zealand Forestry League 95
New Zealand Fruitgrowers' Federation 154
New Zealand Insurance Company 56, 189
New Zealand International Exhibition 1906-07 65, 72
New Zealand Kiwifruit Marketing Board 182-83
New Zealand Kiwis 78
'New Zealand Made' 169
New Zealand Manufacturers' Federation 127-28, 169
New Zealand Native Bird Protection Society 110
New Zealand Post Office Department 68
New Zealand Rugby Union 78
New Zealand Survey Battery 122
Newark, New Jersey 176
Newmarket, Auckland 104
Ngāi Tahu Claims Settlement Act 1998 191
Ngāpuhi (kiwi) 148
Ngāruawahia 103
Ngati Hine Rua (kiwi) 191
Ngati Hine Tahi (kiwi) 191
Nicholas, John Liddiard 25
Nikau bacon 157
No. 8 wire 161
Northern Wairoa RSA 135
Nugget polish 88
Numismatic Society of New Zealand 112

O

O'Brien, Brian 151
Oliver, John 193
Oliver, W.R.B. 110
Onehunga 101
Opotiki 116, 135, 137
Orana Wildlife Park 158
Orbell, Geoffrey 137
Orpington rooster 128
Osaka 170
ostrich 28, 33-35, 37, 101, 105, 107, 127, 148
Otago Museum 43
Ottawa 106
Owen, Richard 26, 32, 34, 36
Oxford Dictionary of New Zealand English 166

P

Palmerston North 75
Pangaea 10
Paparoa Range 95
Parry, Captain 120
patents 161-62
Patterson, Colonel G.W.S. 83
patupaiarehe 74
Pearl Harbour 125
Pearse, Richard 162
Perrott, Mrs G. 87
pigs 51, 191
Plunket 164
Polack, Joel 19, 23-25
Pomare, Sir Maui 104
possum 50-51, 95-96, 129, 137, 147, 157
Ponsonby Swimming Club 79
Post Office 174
PostShops 175
Poynton, J.W. 116
Presbyterian Church 168
Prince of Wales 87
Protection of Animals Act 1880 50
Providence (ship) 27, 40
Psa (kiwifruit bacterial canker disease) 183
Puhaka Mt Bruce National Wildlife Centre 158
Puketukutuku Peninsula 191

Punga Pie 155
pūteketeke 193

Q

Qantas 176
Quarterly Review 37
Queen Charlotte Sound 20, 52

R

rabbit 52, 95-96, 162
Ramsay, William 87-88
Ranfurly, Lord 39
rat 49-50
Rayner, Sapper C.F. 132
Reed, John E. 127
Regent's Park, London 148
Reischek, Andreas 42, 95
Remuera Road, Auckland 97
Rendells, Auckland 86
Reserve Bank of New Zealand 57, 113
Resolution Island 71
Riley, Bob 161
Rimutaka Forest Park 192
River Plate, Battle of 120
Roberts, Lord 82-83
Robo-Kiwi 193
Romney Marsh Sheep Breeders' Association 164
Rongotai 107
Roslyn Mills, Dunedin 100
Rothschild, Lord 37, 39
Rotorua 96, 101, 103, 190
Rough River (Otututu River) 94
Royal College of Surgeons, London 32-34
Royal Empire Society of New Zealand 138
Royal Horticultural Society 69
Royal Institute of British Architects 107
Royal New Zealand Air Force 127, 140, 170, 172
Royal New Zealand Navy 120, 138
Ruatāhuna 25
Ruatoki 103
Ruatoria 101
Ruawai 135
Rudkin, Alfred and Sarah 100
rugby league 78
Rugby Park, Rotorua 174
Rudolf, Crown Prince 39
Rule, Dr John 34
Rutherford, Ernest 114, 162
Rutland Hotel, London 130

S

Salisbury Plain 90
sanctuary, Resolution Island 71
San Diego Zoo 149
Savage, Michael Joseph (Prime Minister) 120, 146
'Save the Kiwi' campaign 195
Savidan, Billy 100
Scion (New Zealand Forest Research Institute Ltd) 193
Sclater, Dr 40
Seddon, Richard John (Prime Minister) 20, 62-65
Servicemen's Re-establishment League 137
Seventy Mile Bush 47
Sharland & Co. 61
Shaw, George 27, 30-31
sheep 57-58, 107, 164, 166
Shortland Street, Auckland 172
silver fern 5, 99-100, 149, 152

Simpson, Prof. H.J. 173
SkyPicker.com 177
Sling Camp, Salisbury Plain 90, 145
Smith, G. 33
Smith, S. Percy 15
Smith-Stanley, Edward George Geoffrey 29
Smithsonian Conservation Biology Institute 191
Solomon Islands 120
Southampton 138
Southern Cross 5, 76, 86, 108, 128, 170, 189
Southern Cross (aircraft) 109
State Advances Corporation 136
Stead, Edgar F. 95
stoat 52–53, 95, 129, 191
Stone, Captain 121
Strange, P. 35
Strutt, William 47
Supreme Court, Wellington 88
Sutherland, Temple 151

T
Taiwhiao, King 57, 113
takahē 53, 137
Tāne (Tāne-mahuta) 15, 18, 97, 189
Tāne-hokahoka 18
Tattersalls Sweeps 167
Taylor, Rev. Richard 19, 25
Te Awamutu RSA 135
Te Puea Herangi, Princess 103
Te Puke 117, 154, 179, 181–82, 184
Te Urewera National Park 191
Telecom 174
Territorial Force 81
Te Waeke-a-Muturangi 16
Thomson, Dr A.S. 25
Tikitiki 101

Tongariro National Park 147
Tourist and Publicity Department 151
Treaty of Waitangi 8, 164, 191
Trentham Camp 121
Tring, England 37
tuatara 10–11, 39, 112, 114
tūī 8–9, 17–19, 25, 29, 56, 62, 65, 72, 95, 98, 104, 107, 152, 192
Tui (minesweeper) 120
Turbott, E.G. 129
Turkington, James 149
Turner, Jack 154
Turners & Growers 154

U
Union Steam Ship Co. 79, 117
United States Pacific Fleet 121
University of Auckland 72, 109–110
Upham, Captain C.H. 147
Uren, Martyn 127
Urewera 147

V
Vienna 39, 42

W
Waikaremoana, Lake 101, 191
Waitākere Ranges, Auckland 157
Walker, J.D. 166
Wall, Arnold 114
Wallace, Alfred R. 72
Walsh, Rev. P. 47
Wanganui/Whanganui 94, 101, 105, 156
weasel 52–53, 95, 129
Webster, William 141
'Well Made New Zealand' 128
Wellington Acclimatisation Society 129

Wellington Airport 174
Wellington coat of arms 76
Wellington Mechanics' Institute 36
Wellington Zoo 148
Whakatane 192
Wheeler, Chas. M. 141
Wiffen, Joan 11
'Wiki' (kiwi) 172
Williams, William 35
'Willie Kiwi' 85
Wimbledon 150
Wilmshurst, Janet M. 15
Wilson, Ewan 176
Wilson, G. 104, 130
World's Fair, St Louis, 1904 71
Wright, Hayward 180

Y
Yate, William 30, 32
Yerex, David 156, 181
Young, Valerie 150
'Young Kiwis' 106

Z
Zealandia 10, 12, 57, 75–76, 108
Zespri International Limited 183–84
kiwifruit varieties 183–84
Zoological Gardens, London 39
Zoological Society of London 37, 86